This Virtual Life

*Escapism and Simulation
in Our Media World*

Andrew Evans

First published in Great Britain by Fusion Press, a division of Satin Publications Ltd.

Fusion Press
101 Southwark Street
London SE1 0JH
UK
e-mail: info@visionpaperbacks.co.uk
website: www.visionpaperbacks.com

Publisher: Sheena Dewan
Cover design © 2001 Justine Hounam
Typeset by FiSH Books, London
Printed and bound in the UK by Biddles Ltd.

ISBN: 1-901250-59-8

The publisher thanks Routledge for permission to reproduce the artwork on pages 11 and 12. They were originally published in *Odd Perceptions* by Richard Gregory. Introduction to *Peer Gynt* by Henrik Ibsen © James McFarlane 1989; text © Christopher Fry and Johan Fillinger 1970, reproduced by permission of Oxford University Press. *Peter Pan* by J. M. Barrie reproduced by permission of HarperCollins Publishers Ltd. 'The Secret Life of Walter Mitty' from the book *My World – And Welcome To It* © 1942 by James Thurber. Copyright © renewed 1971 by Helen Thurber and Rosemary A. Thurber. Reprinted by arrangement with Rosemary A. Thurber and The Barbara Hogenson Agency. All rights reserved. *Billy Liar* by Keith Waterhouse reproduced by permission of Michael Joseph. *Catch-22* by Joseph Heller (copyright © Joseph Heller 1955) reproduced by permission of A M Heath & Co. Ltd.

For my son, Adam

Contents

Contents

Foreword

Escapism is a fascinating subject. As a magician, when I think about escapism the first person that comes into my head is Houdini. He was a man who brought escapism to the masses, and even years after his death there were still those who held seances to try and communicate with him, and indeed those who believed that somehow he would come back from the dead. Such was the power of the escapist fantasies he created. To me, Houdini has a special meaning – the son of a rabbi, my theory is that he was a symbol for escaping the historical repression of the Jews.

On a different level, magic has always been my form of escapism, and I have survived many experiences in life with, quite literally, a pack of cards. In stand-up comedy I can escape from my numerous fears by taking on the character of 'Mister Fearless'.

In the first half of the 20th century, before the widespread popularity of cinema and TV, magic reached a golden age where people flocked to theatres like Maskelyne's to witness all manner of illusions – sawing women in half, levitations and a variety of unbelievable feats. In fact, the posters of the time promised audiences the 'unbelievable'.

Escapism means different things to different people. For Schopenhauer art was not only *the* form of escapism but the key to mankind's salvation. As we head into the 21st century, however, escapism has come to take on many new and often dangerous meanings. It is, in fact, a profound and largely unaddressed subject, which has become too important to ignore.

In this book, my friend Andy Evans opens the door to reality by allowing us to see the many and various ways we choose to escape: how, why and what from. In so doing, he enlightens us and forces our awareness of an area of human culture that seems to simultaneously threaten and benefit our existence. Television is a highly brainwashing medium, but as a Saturday night entertainment at least it beats witch burning!

The fact that Andy can explain, categorise and question such a vast topic in a writing style that someone like me can understand and enjoy is a massive bonus.

Jerry Sadowitz

Introduction

Roget's *Thesaurus* starts, like the Bible, with existence. In this first section are reality, actuality, fact and truth. The second entry in this noble book is 'Nonexistence'. Right on the heels of reality come the unreal, the virtual and the imaginary.

Man's whole evolution seems to have been an exploration of these two concepts. On the one hand man has developed his ability to reason, giving us science, logic and technology. On the other hand he has developed his imagination, giving us creativity, invention and the arts. His greatest development, however, may be the unique ability to simulate, as sociobiologist Richard Dawkins puts it: 'The evolution of the capacity to simulate seems to have culminated in subjective consciousness. Why this should have happened is, to me, the most profound mystery facing modern biology. Perhaps consciousness arises when the brain's simulation of the world becomes so complete that it must include a model of itself.'[1] At the dawn of human culture primitive man took time off from the hunt to make cave paintings on the walls of his rudimentary home. These showed 'a model of himself' hunting his quarry. Life was a tough, day-to-day struggle requiring constant vigilance. Something motivated early man to stop and contemplate his existence. Maybe a desire for magical powers of hunting, maybe an urge for graphic representation, maybe some form of escapism. Centuries later it is hard for us to say for sure.

In the year 2001 we find an evolution of this primitive scene. By this time man's hunting activities have atrophied to a couple of keystrokes on the computer to order a packaged meal, while his 'simulated' hunting, to pay for that meal, is a pleasant eight hours a day in a heated office. The cave painting, however, has taken over the culture – it has become action movies, computer games, rented videos, a computer screen to discuss hunting technology with distant colleagues; in short, the whole phenomenon of the modern mass media.

This quantum shift in importance from satisfying real needs to indulging in escapist activities has been made possible by man's cleverness and capacity for survival, and above all by man's imagination and his capacity for simulation. Man has developed abstract thought, language for describing abstract concepts, and images for showing abstract ideas. Imagination has given man the creative freedom to explore abstract worlds, while his cleverness has provided the technology to explore these worlds – whether real worlds, as in space exploration, or imaginary worlds, as in computer virtual reality simulations.

One theme that becomes evident is man's innate dissatisfaction with existence and his constant hunger for change. He escapes from the countryside to the city, and then goes on adventure holidays in the wild. He escapes from hard physical activities to modern creature comforts and then joins a health club to lift weights. Nothing seems to satisfy him in his paradoxical search for variety and novelty. What is often sought is a middle way, a middle culture between old reality and advanced civilization. Farmers' children migrate to the city and fill their houses with plants – city folk migrate to the country and fill their homes with computers. What we end up with is neither nature nor culture but gigantic theme parks.

Here we stand in the year 2001 – the year of Arthur C. Clarke's *Space Odyssey* – with one foot in the real and the other in our 'brave new simulated world', already caught up in huge cultural upheavals that have changed our day-to-day activities and our perception of the world we live in. This book is an exploration of this new shifted reality. It begins its journey with what we consider to be reality and how we register it in our conscious mind – the world of perception and thinking, with its attendant illusions and paradoxes. It then continues by asking if what we get from our media and what politicians tell us about our world is the truth or something else – a version of life distorted by spin, consumerism and vested interests.

The middle part of the book explores a popular idea – escapism – which has to date been very sketchily researched and written about, despite its importance in a world increasingly flooded by escapist entertainment and activities. It has been a challenge and a pleasure to research and document this phenomenon, and the more one is conscious of it the more obvious its presence is felt in everything.

Our journey through our quasi-real, quasi-simulated culture finishes with the cutting age of technology – robots, expert systems, artificial intelligence, computer games, computer graphics, avatars, virtual reality and the expanding Internet, soon to be the backbone of our whole converging entertainment industry. Such is the speed of change that hardly an issue of any popular science magazine seems to appear on the shelves without some article on new technology, and there are huge developments waiting in the next few decades.

This exploration of our mass media-dominated society throws up some key questions:

- Will the future be utopia or dystopia – a dream leisure society or a technological madhouse?
- Can humans cope with so much artificiality in their lives, or will they become aggressive, maladjusted, simulation sick and unable to communicate with each other in the real world?
- Will the increasing power of the mass media unify human society, or simply homogenise it so that essential differences are smoothed over and essential truths are dumbed down?
- Will we still believe that truth matters?
- Will we be able to dominate our new technology or will it dominate us?
- Will our lives continue to be flooded by ritualised escapist entertainment activities sold to us by huge multinationals to assuage our supposed dissatisfaction with life, or will we increasingly return to nature for a more real view of our world?

Some of these questions can only be answered in the future – a world we can only guess at, but one that many writers and theorists, from science fiction to the psychologists, sociologists and technology experts of today, have helped us to formulate. Many of these have been referred to in the text and their contributions to our present world view are gratefully acknowledged.

We live in exciting times, where the speed of change appears to be accelerating. Already many older people are being left behind in the Internet revolution, and to fully understand the world we currently live in requires a deliberate attempt at keeping up. For many people, new technology means little more than increasingly mass-produced entertainment products. For those that want to look behind this brightly coloured but often shallow façade, there are much more compelling undercurrents of transformation. It is these that this book seeks above all to address.

Special thanks for support and inspiration go to my whole family, and additionally to Luis Gambolini, John Taylor, Bill Mulholland, Martin Lloyd-Elliott, Ian Baker, Chris Found, Jill Sack, Jerry Sadowitz, Martin Ditcham, Will Heath, Mike Jay, Jeff Young, Patrick Allan and Caroline Jory.

PART I

This Virtual Life

ONE

Perception and Representation

The word 'virtual' is an interesting one, and one that is steadily acquiring more and more importance in our culture. It is used to describe something that is not exactly real, but real in effect – 'such for practical purposes though not in name or according to strict definition' as the *Oxford English Reference Dictionary* puts it. *Chambers Dictionary* defines it very nicely: 'in effect, though not in fact; not such in fact but capable of being considered as such for some purposes'.

Much of our contemporary culture gives the effect of being real without being so in fact – wood-effect furnishings, synthetic wool carpets, TV soaps, Hollywood movies... The surprising thing is that we largely accept all kinds of artefacts as willingly as we accept the real thing. We retain the ability to distinguish them apart, and in the case of forgeries we have elaborate methods of doing so, but we live – more or less happily – in a world that includes both the virtual and the real.

Any discussion of the reality or otherwise of the world we live in has to include our primary window onto that world – the window of our senses, which should give us all the information we need to survive and flourish. The fact that we do so and mostly live to a ripe old age, dying more from disease than accidents, shows that information from the senses is sufficient for us to construct a good (though not necessarily perfect) working model of our environment in which to exist. The way we 'see' this world is through perception.

Perception

> No animal can survive unless it perceives its environment as it really is.
>
> Yi-Fu Tuan

There is an old philosophical argument about whether the environment actually exists at all if it is not being perceived in any way. The argument and its counter-argument were wittily put in the following two verses about whether a tree 'existed' in the college quadrangle or not:

> There was once a man who said God
> Must think it exceedingly odd
> If he finds that this tree
> Continues to be
> When there's no one about in the Quad.
>
> (Ronald Knox 1888–1957)

> Dear Sir, Your astonishment's odd
> I am always about in the Quad.
> And that's why the tree
> Will continue to be
> Since observed by Yours Faithfully, God.
>
> (Anon)

Whichever path we take, there is something out there that we can see, and we do so through the complexities of perception. Perception is the sensory process enabling knowledge of the external world to be obtained. It can be broken down into 'sensation' – the sensory stimulus itself, giving us colour, shape, etc, and the 'cognition' of it – how we mentally organise and classify it, for instance 'a red bus'. Since no perception can take place without thought, perception is typically used in the wider sense of describing the entire sequence of events from acquiring the sensory stimulus to interpreting it, and incorporating the following key features:

Attention. To perceive something we have to focus our attention on it so that it stands out from competing stimuli.
Constancy. We see objects – a chair, a plate – from many different angles, yet we recognise them as familiar because we retain a sense of constancy for their shape.

Motivation. What we perceive is changed by our motivation – for example, a few days before Christmas, items in shops may all look like potential presents.

Organisation. Perception needs to be organised into coherent wholes or 'gestalts' – for instance, a house consists of walls, roof, garage, porch, conservatory and so on.

Set. What is perceived is strongly affected by one's cognitive and emotional stance, or attitude, towards a set of stimuli.

Learning. Some perception is innate and some is learned as part of the process of recognition.

Distortion and hallucination. Perceptions can be distorted by strong emotional feelings, and we may hallucinate under the influence of sleep deprivation, drugs, psychosis or extreme fear. Such misperceptions show that part of the perception process is clearly inside the head rather than in the environment.

Illusion. What we believe we perceive may be different from what is really there, for a variety of reasons, including mistakes of perception, deliberate deception and various body states. Examples are mirages, conjuring tricks and perspective illusions.

Further to seeing is the process of recognition. We may see a shape that looks something like a book but turns out to be a videotape. We may see a shape like a bush that turns out to be a soldier in camouflage. This has been referred to as seeing 'things' and seeing 'facts', though we might say that 'facts' are simply correct perceptions. The process of recognition is a skill we gradually learn as children, as we start to make sense of the world around us and organise it into patterns and categories of experience, so we can recognise familiar objects at once without having to think. These familiar shapes also have a constancy – we can see them from many different angles, near to or far off, and still recognise what they are. We know this recognition of whole objects, or gestalts, is learned throughout childhood because when sight is restored to blind adults they take at least a month to recognise 'whole' objects such as tables and chairs as differentiated from their backgrounds.

One thing that helps us retain constancy of size in a three-dimensional world is our stereoscopic vision. If you want to find out how this works, try the following test. Hold up your left hand, palm away from you, in a flat shape with the fingers shut, about 15 centimetres (6 inches) away from your face. Then hold out your right hand, palm away from you, as far as it will comfortably go, again in a flat shape with the fingers shut, and with the thumb appearing to just touch the thumb of your left hand. Now, with both eyes open, the hands appear the same size. If you close the left eye, however, the right hand suddenly appears to be much smaller.

We can get the information we need from our environment by either direct or indirect perception. A great deal of what we perceive is a representation of something – TV, film, popular songs. This also applies to technology and measurement – we know we have an empty petrol tank when the meter reads empty, not when we see inside the tank itself.

We also have a threshold for conscious perception, what we call a 'limen', and below this any information is known as 'subliminal'. This applies to information too faint to pick up and also information too fast to recognise consciously, such as a brief frame of advertising embedded in a sequence of frames in a film. Since this may be picked up by the brain without our having processed it consciously, there are laws to prohibit its use. Such below-threshold images may influence behaviour just as conscious perception does, though we may be less aware of it. Considerable scientific debate has surrounded the ethics of this phenomenon and also its validity and how reliable its effects are. One view is that of American psychologist J. V. McConnell: 'All things considered, secret attempts to manipulate people's minds have yielded results as subliminal as the stimuli used.'

Our human perception does not give us a complete picture of our environment – there are a lot of things we cannot see or hear simply in terms of the wavelengths we pick up. Our knowledge of the world has been extended by inventions such as radio telescopes, X-rays and ultrasound. Neither do we have the sensory acuity of many animals – the bat's radar or the whale's ability to pick up signals underwater. Recent perception theory at its most extreme would suggest that human perceptions are no more than accounts, descriptions, or indeed hypotheses of the object world.

Our perception of the world may not be true 'in fact', but it is good enough 'in effect' for us to have survived well in evolutionary terms. There remain, though, some fascinating instances where our perception can be apparently tricked. There are sound scientific reasons why railway lines appear to meet in the distance and a stick appears to bend in water, but both phenomena can be initially perplexing, as can our colour perception – is a brown table seen through red glasses still a brown table?

Tricks of perception

With rare exceptions, humans proceed on the assumption that 'seeing is believing' – they trust their senses and their perception. But at the sensory end the eye can be tricked by various *trompe-l'œil* images, as at the cognitive end our ability to recognise, remember and describe objects depends on what we believe they are, or how we name them.

There are several sensory illusions, the most famous being the Muller–Lyer illusion (shown below).

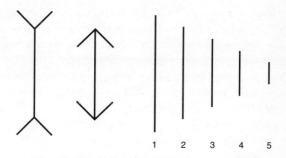

Figure 1.1 The Muller–Lyer illusion

If asked to judge the length of the lines between the arrowheads, the first image of the arrowheads pointing out appears to be approximately length number 2, while the second image with the arrowheads pointing in appears to be approximately length number 3. In fact they are both the same length.

All our senses can suffer illusions, but since we use our vision the most, we are more familiar with visual illusions. Professor Richard Gregory, Professor of Psychology at Bristol University, says in his book *Odd Perceptions*:

> The fact that there are illusions of the senses is a fundamental embarrassment for philosophers who wish to hold that knowledge is securely based on perception. Although this is the empiricist tradition it is easy to show empirically that perception is not reliable. It is very easy to fool the senses and to disturb perception

11

systematically, so that all observers agree on what they see – or hear or whatever – though all are wrong. And misperceptions may be disastrous in real-life situations such as driving a car.[1]

This may be over-stating the case – perception is generally reliable but not infallible, and philosophers would not contend that it is. And while it is quite possible to fool the senses, they generally serve us well. But the exceptions remain.

Self-generated deceptions

Psychologist Hermann von Helmholtz (1821–94) believed that perception was linked to cognitive processing. He further stated that perceptions may be 'conclusions' of unconscious inferences – that they may be the result of internal computations. Some of these computations can fool us by providing information that is not there. One optical illusion shows this very nicely – that of Kanizsa's triangle (shown below).

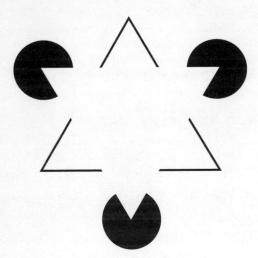

Figure 1.2 Kanizsa's triangle

In this illusion we see two triangles, neither of which is actually drawn. The second 'white' triangle is seen as if superimposed upon the triangle behind it, which in turn is constructed from only three corners. The brain has inferred and constructed two triangles from the information already present. We saw, in this case, what we 'expected' to see, using the basis of sensory perception and filling in the rest cognitively. Again, this kind of illusion could in theory be dangerous. If we only see 'probable' perceptions we could be blind to the unlikely. But the unlikely does in fact occur.

This principle lies behind some clever military deceptions. An elaborate strategy was used to persuade the Germans in the Second World War that the British would invade via Pas de Calais (which the Germans considered the rational choice) and not Normandy – a strategy that succeeded in getting a large proportion of the German force to defend the 'hoax' landing point. The trick used was to reinforce the enemy's primary expectation of what was 'probable' by false reports, the principle being that we are more likely to accept evidence that confirms our initial or strongest belief than that which necessitates our abandoning it.

Our perception of reality

We appear to see our environment in good visual detail. How much detail do we need to have in our environment for it to have the appearance of reality? The Federal Aviation Administration, the standard setter for virtual reality flight simulators to be used in pilot training in the USA, has gone so far as to specify a required realism in terms of 3-D resolution of a minimum of 1,000 surfaces or 4,000 points for a daylight simulator (1991 figures), which doesn't come near the infinite patterns of nature. Rendering techniques in computer graphics are becoming increasingly refined towards the goal of 'photo realism', yet the eye can still distinguish them from the real thing. So maybe our vision is quite sophisticated? Not if we consider the totality of what there is in front of our eyes – humans may actually 'see' a lot less of reality than we think.

One error humans can be prone to is change blindness. As conditions change in our field of view we may focus on one or two elements and fail to see changes in the remainder of the picture. This was startlingly proved by psychologists Simons and Levin[2] when they instructed an interviewer to stop a succession of people in the grounds of a college campus. Soon after the interviewer engaged with the subject, two people carrying a large door would pass in between them, after which the 'interviewer' would continue the conversation. The interviewer had in fact been switched – the original interviewer walking off behind the door, leaving another in his place. Fully 50 per cent of the people taking part failed to recognise the switch. This trick, together with a lot more research evidence, confirms how little of what we see is 'processed' by the brain. The change in the door passing in front of our field of view superseded the change of the interviewer coming up, so our focus switches to that which is more immediate, letting go of the recent past.

We can also be blind to changes in our visual field that occur during eye movement, when we are actively 'tracking' something else, as computer-generated experiments confirm. A lot of what we see depends on where we focus – a complex process both unconscious and conscious. We are able to 'see' all that is in front of us, but we actually take in surprisingly little. Our brains simply do not have enough storage facility to deal with everything in front of us, so what we do is store a basic visual scene in our short-term memory – the lighting, layout of objects, foreground and background, then give focused attention to that which changes, 'sampling' and updating it periodically as elements change.

This process explains why experienced chess players can play several games of chess simultaneously – they know the usual repertoire of openings, expected moves, strategies and end game theory. What they concentrate on is the departures from the expected. We largely assume what has not been drawn to our attention remains predictably the same, an assumption that can be proved wrong, as in the case of the door experiment above.

The same capacity for deception is found even when the picture is static rather than moving, as shown by several other experiments where viewers failed to see subtle changes in the background of static scenes presented to them like a slide show, with small gaps between each presentation. As well as 'change blindness' we also suffer from 'inattentional blindness' – we don't see things we are not paying attention to, things that are not in the forefront of our vision. This is of crucial importance in road accidents, where estimates of driver error – failure to properly see and react to crucial elements – may be as much as 50 per cent of all fatal accidents.

Some of the error may be caused by faulty beliefs and expectations, according to Stephen Kosslyn of Harvard University. 'Seeing', he believes, is mostly an illusion, and relies as much on memory and imagination as on basic visual perception. Rather than actually seeing what is in front of us, we mix what we see with memories of what we have just seen and imagination of what we expect to see. Some of the same parts of the brain are activated during imagination and actual seeing.

This whole human process is analogous with the way we now encode information digitally, say in the recording of a piece of music on a CD. Samples of the music are taken at regular intervals and from those samples the full sound wave is recreated, using logical predictions and 'error correction' to fill in the missing parts. Additionally, parts of the music that we don't need to hear, because they are below the threshold of hearing or otherwise dispensable, are left out as the musical information is 'compressed' to take up less memory, as with MP3 or MiniDisc. An MP3 track is a pretty accurate facsimile of a musical performance nevertheless, just as our complex perception processing of our surroundings gives us a total effect analogous to actually seeing what is before us.

Much of this perception processing is unconscious, and is going on all the time outside our consciousness. We are, effectively, slaves to this automatic process, which diverts our attention constantly from one thing to another – very little of what we see is under our conscious control. Neither do we make a full inventory of what we see unless we have to – we do not consciously take in the colour of a person's shoes, their haircut, their clothes and so forth, which is why we can be fooled by deliberate tricks and why bystander evidence is so sketchy and unreliable, particularly when we fill in what we don't really see with what we 'expect' to have seen. We rarely, in fact, make a distinction between what we have actually seen and what we 'think' we have seen – the two processes go hand in hand.

Conscious and unconscious thought

We have so far talked about conscious and unconscious perception, which leads us on to ask: how much of thought itself is conscious? 'A lot less than we think', is the view of neuroscientists Peter Halligan and David Oakley.[3] This observation is not new – Helmholtz described perceptions as 'conclusions of unconscious inferences', an unpopular notion at the time because it threatened the need for consciousness as the process behind moral decisions, duty and blame. Resistance came both from the church and the law. The intellectual resistance that met Freud's theories of the unconscious was similarly based, and made more acute by his emphasis on sex and instinctive drives as a central part of its workings.

Halligan and Oakley resist Freud's terminology and opt for calling consciousness Level 1, and the unconscious Level 2. In a rather neat modern way they call transferring information to consciousness 'outing' it. In typical organisational parlance, they describe the control of the process as lying in the CES (Central Executive System). Their argument is that thoughts originate in Level 2, and that the vast majority of mental processes are, in fact, also carried out in Level 2 before they even reach Level 1, including what we might think of as most of our decision-making functions – altering our seating posture, getting up, making a coffee, picking up a book; the list is almost endless.

Sometimes Level 2 feeds the 'result' of a process to consciousness, such as the answer to the question 'What is two plus two?', where the word 'four' seems to simply emerge into our conscious state as if popping into our head. Often the CES seamlessly goes from one process to another, as when we are turning pages in a book, looking at pictures, changing the book over to the other hand. In all this, very few 'decisions' are actually made in Level 1. Halligan and Oakley even argue that most of our talk is from Level 2 – that most of the time we don't actually know what we are going to say until we have said it. Experiments with hypnosis suggest that while Level 1 is hypnotised, eg to induce temporary blindness, Level 2 continues to function and can see and respond to cues. The hypnotised 'conscious' self believes that there is no sight. This model suggests that Level 2 activity can continue quite independently of conscious belief.

Consciousness, it seems, is just the visible tip of the submerged iceberg – the last part of a complex inner process, occurring far too late to change the bulk of the processing that has already taken place. It may not even be a new or different way of thinking, but more a selection of material that pre-exists in Level 2. The idea that consciousness is simply the experience of 'being me now', the conviction that 'I think this' or 'I do that' is unsettling in many ways. What about our conscious control over behaviour? What about our free will?

Psychologists such as Nicholas Humphries of the London School of Economics suggest that this may be more of a myth than we would like to admit. Our conscious self may serve more of a purpose in relating to others, to give continuity and enable us to appear credible and constant. But even this believable façade can break down when we are asked awkward questions. Rather than consciously analysing the evidence (if necessary saying that we do not have enough reliable information) we tend in practice to search through Level 2 material for something plausible to say that appears to fit the context. We are subjectively aware of this search process as we fumble and tend to hum and ha. We are also subjectively aware of times when the answer just 'dawns on us'.

This fundamentally challenges the idea of a 'conscious intention' to talk or act. Research has suggested that indeed, preparations of an intent to act can be seen in brain activity before it becomes conscious to the person involved. Psychologist Peter Derks has even discovered brain activity that detects incongruity before we laugh at jokes, suggesting that even humour can be processed in Level 2. It seems likely that in many different ways the conscious part of thinking waits for the brain to make its own mind up, then outputs the result. The conscious thought can often occur at a different point from the action. We are more likely to have the thought 'I must get up', cogitate on it for a short period, and then find that the action of getting up appears to occur automatically.

Creatives would certainly agree that the bulk of inspiration occurs internally – even in sleep – and then just seems to 'pop out' when the muse is congenial. Besides such 'public' output, information is also outed to Level 1 in the form of private memories, internal images and feelings – our internal 'virtual reality'. The sophisticated instrument in our brain is therefore not conscious thought, but the CES, which regulates all the myriads of decisions to be made about prioritising perceptual data. It is the CES that is also responsible for initiating bodily movement, channelling information from one state to another and monitoring brain activity.

The CES appears to have an important role in switching from external awareness to internal awareness – from directed activity to non-directed activity, where there is no imperative to act. This includes all our daydreams, worries and idle wish-fulfilment fantasies of riches, beauty, fame or success. The CES would by implication have a fundamentally important role in escapism – evading more consciously prioritised activities by procrastinating, indulging in more pleasurable activity or fantasising, for example evading conscious dieting by just dreaming of being thin or worrying about being overweight.

Halligan and Oakley's model suggests that if it is Level 2 and the CES that are responsible for the large part of our thought processing, then our 'self' or unique identity may be more defined by our unconscious than our conscious. They realise that this contradicts centuries of culture, and expect a hard time trying to convince traditional thinkers, yet they appear firm in their views, and their evidence contains much that appears convincing.

Illusion, magic and the paranormal

> Any sufficiently advanced technology is indistinguishable from magic.
>
> Arthur C. Clarke

> It doesn't seem to me far-fetched to call Leonardo a magician. Indeed, a much later figure, Isaac Newton, has been called a magician, the last one.
>
> Yi-Fu Tuan

How do we deal with those things in our environment for which there appears to be no reasonable conscious explanation, or those things for which our existing knowledge has not prepared us?

For centuries the inexplicable was given the term 'magic'. Sometimes what we have labelled magic turns out in time to be science, just as alchemy was the forerunner of chemistry. Sometimes it remains in the realm of the paranormal. How do we separate one from the other? Richard Gregory sums up the dilemma:

> Discoveries of undoubted lasting importance have been made from magical practices. The trouble here, though, is that once accepted by science they are no longer seen as magic. A clear example is the origin of the magnetic compass in China in the 3rd century BC with the diviner's board. The diviners discovered that the pivoted lodestone always pointed south, so they had a magical device that worked. By the 10th or 11th century it became a magnetic needle floating on water – a practical mariner's compass. When it became reliable it no longer looked like magic, even though magnetic attraction itself remained mysterious.
>
> Marconi's transmission of the letter M across the Atlantic in 1901 was truly amazing as it was known that radio waves travel in straight lines like visible light, and so could not possibly go far beyond the horizon. This was before the discovery several years later of an unsuspected reflecting layer of ionised gas in the upper atmosphere, which bends these long waves – though not light – round the earth. And much in science is just as mysterious. So how are we to separate science from magic?
>
> Science makes discoveries because it looks carefully at surprising phenomena, so 'abnormal' or surprising cannot be equated with

'paranormal'. Paranormal is somehow incompatible with and rejected by science – ESP is rejected not only as incompatible with present science but with any conceivable future science. This, however, is strictly impossible to justify. Some kind of emergence of 'mind' from brain function may be safe science, but this may look dangerously spooky when it comes to consciousness. I greatly doubt whether there are disembodied intelligent forces or any other paranormal phenomena to bother about. But just to be sure, I wish I had infallible crystal balls.[4]

Magic and 'paranormal' phenomena have survived from the beginning of time, and magicians would claim that this is because the magician provides people with something they need and want – images, ideas, symbols and dreams. But stage magic does something else – tricks. Our response to tricks is partly to try to see through them, partly to abandon ourselves to their fascination. It is a little like Freud's dream world in which the 'censor' blinds us to the real reasons behind what is going on and sends us on wild goose chases full of incongruity and strange switches. We try to see how the magician does the trick so we can try to protect ourselves from being conned, but we do not try too hard, and allow ourselves to be both humiliated and entertained. The reaction of children – and indeed adults – may fall into two types: those who see the tricks as a challenge to their observation, and those who prefer to abandon themselves to make-believe just as they like to believe in Santa's Grotto. Such reactions are not dependent on age or sex so much as on personality type, though audiences can vary in different countries and cultures.

The façade of magic – sometimes combined with comedy – hides the considerable skill and ingenuity behind it. Magic, illusions and escapology as practised by magicians are fundamentally based on trickery. Close-up magic, more specifically, is based on a small number of 'plots', many invented by the great Austrian 19th-century parlour magician J. N. Hofzinser. The most obvious plot is 'make the card disappear and reappear', a version of the small child's battle with object permanence, but there are many others. The magician is powerful because he can con, fool and cause deception, but without causing harm. He allows us to escape from 'reality' into a harmless world one remove away, where implication, metaphor and tricks replace harsh facts, and we don't even lose the £10 note that the magician later produces from the orange.

Magic has retained its perennial links with the occult not only because the trickery is kept secret, but also because it is hard for magicians to achieve large-scale fame. Close up – the essence of magic – can only be seen by a small number of people, hence the very use of the term 'close up'. Larger tricks – the size of a stage – require larger props, and then become illusions done by illusionists such as David Copperfield. Some of these larger-scale illusions, like making a jet plane disappear, have attracted widespread fame, as have popular stunts like those of Houdini.

The psychology of deception

Conjuring as a study of deception intrigued many important figures in modern psychology. In 1896, Jastrow began working in his laboratory with famous magicians of the period, Leon Herrmann and Harry Kellar, to see what distinguished the skilled magician from the norm. The main finding was prestidigitation, or rapidity of hand movement – magicians are enormously skilled operators.[5] The deception is easily invoked in the audience because of the fallibility of human perception. Even early audience research showed that observers invented events that did not actually occur, omitted important events that did occur and recalled others in an incorrect order.[6] And as we know from 'change blindness', when we focus on one element, others may change without our seeing them.

Conjuring is perhaps the ultimate deception because it deceives even people who know that they are being deceived, and so is referred to as 'expert deceit' – a sanctioned form of deceit in which the majority of observers actually want to be fooled. One interesting fact, though, is that magicians are generally men. Do men have a 'Peter Pan' side to them that never grows up, or are they more fond of tricks and trickery, and continue to play tricks into adulthood? Men have traditionally been a more willing audience for magic and trickery than women; magician Jerry Sadowitz thinks this is partly because women are more sensitive to being 'tricked', and show more dislike for being hoodwinked.

The magician as escapist

Magic can also be seen as an 'escape from reality', or from the natural physical laws that bind us. The magician – seemingly in control of the audience – may be the real escapist, as Jerry Sadowitz recounts:

Magic for me had a definite purpose – it was my escape from a poor reality. I was frequently in hospital and there were difficulties at home and at school. Card tricks were my initial escape. To me, the magician is more involved in escape than the audience. The audience goes back to reality; the magician lives in a kind of arrested development, where he has never really grown up. You only have to go to any magic convention to see magicians behaving entirely like children. They often start at the age of eight and sometimes progress little from that point emotionally and in their ability to deal with the world. They don't go on to learn adult coping mechanisms – instead they inhabit a world of escapism, continuing to play games on other adults instead of growing up and joining them.

Sadowitz is both magician and comedian, but three famous modern stage 'magicians' – Houdini, Tommy Cooper and Uri Geller – were not strictly speaking magicians at all. Houdini was an escapologist, Cooper a comedian and Geller a self-declared psychic. The paranormal is, by definition, a strange and spooky world. So how 'real' is the 'unreal'?

Parapsychology and the paranormal

The faking of psychic ability is an area that has been studied continuously by psychologists, the difference between this and magic tricks and illusions being that the deceiver denies the deception. This is a potentially more dangerous pursuit, since mental trickery ('miracles', 'healing', etc) has in the past been associated with the personal shamanistic power of cult leaders, such as the 'Reverend' Jim Jones who in the seventies instigated the mass suicide of most of his followers.

Psychologists who have addressed this area of the paranormal generally exhibit two responses – scepticism and a kind of intrigued fascination. Some, like Blackmore and Hart-Davis, have written 'do it yourself' manuals for experimenters giving clear instructions on how to carry out experiments at home.[7] Their book *Test Your Psychic Powers* covers the key areas of parapsychology – telepathy, crystals, dreams and lucid dreaming, dowsing, premonitions, precognition, psychokinesis, Ouija, planchette, palmistry and astrology.

Mainstream psychologists such as Andrew M. Colman, however, dismiss most of this as anecdotal, contrived or unproven:

Most subjects become more interesting the more one learns about them, but the paranormal seems to be a striking exception. Paranormal phenomena dissolve under scrutiny, the scientific evidence turns out to be either methodologically flawed... or merely fraudulent... and nothing of significance is left to explain. Why bother carrying out more experiments into these obviously non-existent phenomena? Numerous empirical studies have shown, for example, that astrology is humbug – the Gauquelin effects are irrelevant to conventional astrology, may be interpretable as merely the effects of being born at different times of the year, and may in any event be artefacts – but the studies were pointless anyway because the theory is self-evidently ridiculous. The qualities of the constellations (ram, bull, twins, etc that would look quite different from another angle) are beside the point because the precession of the earth's axis has caused all of them to slip out of place since astrology was devised. At the Spring equinox the sun is supposed to be in Aries, but is nowadays actually in Pisces.[8]

Richard Gregory is another who remains sceptical:

The claims of mediums and psychics do not stand up well, for their reported observations or claims almost always fail to be repeated in controlled experiments. It seems the better the experiments are designed and carried out the less they provide evidence for paranormal phenomena such as telepathy, clairvoyance, telekinesis or spoon bending. What usually emerges is statistical artefacts, conjuring, or more or less conscious fraud.[9]

Psychologist Susan Blackmore defends continuing to do experiments, but joins the scepticism by agreeing that when properly conducted, experiments into phenomena like dowsing do not stand up to scientific scrutiny in terms of objectivity and eliminating human participation. Professor of Parapsychology at Edinburgh University, Robert L. Morris, also defends studying such phenomena because of 'the consensually accepted finding that many people have experiences or observe events which they cannot explain conventionally'. Such study discovers 'self-deception, innocent cognitive mistakes as well as strategies of deception and exploitation by clever frauds', but leaves the door open to 'genuinely new means of environmental interaction still to be uncovered'.[10]

Deliberate fraud has certainly been documented in psychological studies, for instance when American magician James Randi sent two young magicians in 1978 to be assessed for paranormal powers at the McDonnell Parapsychology Laboratory in the USA. They used conjuring techniques to fake 'psychic' feats such as metal bending and ESP, and these were apparently not picked up by the assessing staff. The revelation of the hoax contributed to the closure of the laboratory.[11] Later studies by psychologists have helped identify common hoaxes and ways of avoiding them, such as not permitting special circumstances demanded by the supposed psychics like total darkness, and joining hands round a table to prevent wandering arms touching any part of the manipulation.

Representation in the arts and the media

We continue our exploration of our 'virtual world' by looking at the representation of reality through the arts and the media – films, TV soaps, art, fiction and all those things that give us the 'effect' of real life rather than the experience of actually participating in it. Representation of reality is as old as the earliest cave paintings showing animals and the hunt. This is representation as 'resemblance', and also pictorial resemblance using our main sense, that of sight. Visual representation then gained in sophistication with the passing centuries until it reached the heights of the great painters, photographers and artists of the last millennium. As Magritte pointed out in his painting of a pipe with the words 'Ceci n'est pas une pipe', representation is not reality, but is recognisable as portraying reality – the reality is virtual. The medium in the case of Magritte is art, which is a time-shifted medium – it can be experienced and re-experienced at will, for as long as it remains intact.

Aural representation of reality started with events, real and made up, which formed the stories and epics of early peoples. Strict resemblance is not necessary for representation. Words, for example, do not resemble the things they represent any more than a clock resembles time. So representation also depends on the interpretation we put on it. With the printed word, language became the medium of books, enabling writers to represent the whole richness of human experience and evoke strong imaginative reactions in readers. Events real and imaginary were staged in theatre performances. This was not time shifted, like books, but a real-time event. Like musical performances, once performed it was lost to the ages, until time shifting of the theatre, music and all live events became possible with the advent of recording media.

How did our evolution get as far as art and language? Through the use of imagination.

Imagination may lay claim to be the highest form of intellectual activity, since it takes us further than knowledge. There is a symbiotic link between imagination and knowledge since one feeds the other, but it is imagination that has more scope. It challenges us to answer questions like 'Why does a stick bend in water?' It invents hypotheses to explain phenomena and gives us innovation and creativity. Imagination is essential to the process of explaining anything, since if we only repeated what is known already, then the growth of 'knowledge' would be impossible – it would simply not have the means to develop.

Any discovery by definition goes beyond what is known, beyond induction, and the only way to do this is through the use of imagination. Imagination can draw us towards important conclusions about our world, as with a scientist like Einstein, who set out to solve problems and construct new hypotheses. Imagination can be used to disprove the false, as in the case of King Canute, who might lay more claim to be the 'father of British Empiricism' than Locke, when, with all his royal authority, he proved that not even a king could change the laws of physics and stop the waves. Or imagination can explore the abstract world, as in the music of Mozart, which needs no conclusion to justify its beauty or abstract truths. His artistic answers were products of personal questions that were real for him alone. Imagination for him was exempt from truth and falsity.

Yi-Fu Tuan sees man's escapist tendencies as underlying this shift from the actual to the virtual:

> A human being is an animal who is congenitally indisposed to accept reality as it is. Humans not only submit and adapt, as all animals do; they transform in accordance with a preconceived plan. That is, before transforming, they do something extraordinary, namely 'see' what is not there. Seeing what is not there lies at the foundation of all human culture.[12]

Once our ancestors could, through imagination, 'see' what was not literally in front of them, the next step in evolution was to fix this image with some name so that it could be described to others. Thus we had the beginnings of language. The image of a mammoth could be communicated between cavemen by a sound denoting 'mammoth'. Just as the image is not the animal, so the sound is neither the image nor the animal, but it conjures up the idea of both, as Shakespeare wrote:

Think, when we talk of horses, that you see them
Printing their proud hoofs ' th' receiving earth;
For 'tis your thoughts that now must deck our kings,
Carry them here and there, jumping o'er times,
Turning th' accomplishment of many years
Into an hour-glass.

(Introduction to Henry V)

Through language man can not only examine the past but also think about the future. Through language we can even further refine thought itself, since we can use language for describing instances where there is no natural correspondence between a word and a thing. We have a word called 'simultaneity' but we cannot see such a thing in our mind. It cannot be 'perceived' in any way. The very looseness of language allows for expansion, for example in the use of metaphor – dog, dogged, dog-like. Abstract thought is possible because of non-representational language, which gives us the ability to think in the absence of something.

Imagination goes beyond imaging in so many ways, particularly in art. When we read a novel, for instance, we see in our mind's eye the characters, background and events. But a novel is not crude imaging – it constructs things. It is not about truth or falsity – we accept that the characters are fictional, but we 'see' them as if they were real – 'in effect, though not in fact', as *Chambers Dictionary* puts it. The same absence of truth and falsity applies to other representations – a photo, or what you see in a mirror. This is the 'true' use of our human imagination – the rich fund of thoughts we have, for example, when looking at a photo from the past, for instance a picture of ourselves as a child. This is so much more than mere 'imaging' or resemblance. It is not even a 'willing suspension of disbelief' – we make no conscious attempt to suspend our belief, we simply accept things as quasi-real. Not entirely real, but real in effect.

When we make a videotape of a TV film, the process is quite natural to us. We don't say to ourselves, 'I am storing on a thin film of plastic several hundred metres long a representation of actors representing events that might or might not have happened in the way they were described.' It is the same with riding a bicycle, something we have become so accustomed to doing that it feels 'natural'. It is often joked that if we had to analyse how we ride a bike we would never be able to do it. Once a whole activity, or gestalt, is familiar we have no wish to complicate our brains by deconstructing it – our brains need to get on with other things. Humans are wonderfully adaptive. If we were to reconstruct our token 'cave man ancestor' and place him in our living room as we were archiving our TV entertainment he would be utterly bewildered. Our children hardly even realise the progress we have made as they innocently learn to use sophisticated technology.

The effect of the medium

Imagination has now taken us as far as lifelike moving pictures, captured for use in our homes by electronic technology. The rapid progress we made in media science in the last century brought us eventually to examine the whole function and significance of the 'medium' itself, and the popularisation of the idea that the medium itself could profoundly influence its content, or as McLuhan and Fiore put it in their 1967 book, 'the medium is the massage':

> The medium, or process, of our time – electronic technology – is reshaping and restructuring patterns of social interdependence and every aspect of our personal life. It is forcing us to reconsider and re-evaluate practically every thought, every action and every institution formerly taken for granted. Everything is changing, you, your family, your neighbourhood, your education, your job, your government, your relation to 'the others'. And they're changing dramatically. Societies have always been shaped more by the nature of the media by which men communicate than by the content of the communication.[13]

One telling example the book gives of film and television changing society is these words of President Sukarno:

> The motion picture industry has provided a window on the world, and the colonised nations have looked through that window and have seen the things of which they have been deprived. It is perhaps not generally realised that a refrigerator can be a revolutionary symbol to a people who have no refrigerators. A motor car owned by a worker in one country can be a symbol of revolt to a people deprived of even the necessities of life… Hollywood helped to build up the sense of deprivation of man's birthright, and that sense of deprivation has played a large part in the national revolutions of postwar Asia.

Perhaps the most omnipresent social effect of the popularisation of film and television is the phenomena of celebrity and fame, the creation of an entirely new type of hero.

The false world of fame

Just as the content of stories, songs, films and theatre and the sounds of music appear 'real' to us in the sense that we willingly accept them as representations, so the protagonists of the whole media world appear to us as real heroes. As all writers about fame have noticed, the media-created fame of the last hundred years is a qualitatively different phenomenon from fame in its original usage, as the renown that comes from exceptional achievement in the real worlds of battles, science, politics and commerce.

It is clear to all who have spent any time considering the phenomenon of fame that it is something which has changed considerably throughout the ages. This process of change has reflected changes in society. In times of constant war the famous were either heroes who saved their peoples, or spiritual leaders who offered salvation of the soul. In times of discovery the famous were explorers and inventers. In the media age the famous are simply those who are most familiar to the worldwide media audience. We have gone from being famous for deeds good or bad to being famous simply for being well known. The cynic would claim that what was considered the 'moral' emptiness of fame in previous ages now applies even to the emptiness of its definition: 'The celebrity is a person who is well-known for his well-knownness' (Boorstin, 1962).[14]

What is remarkable about the whole 20th century is the substitution of fantasy for reality. The real heroes of history are played by the actors of the movie industry. Media reality substitutes for actual reality, as hours of the day are spent in the virtual reality of TV. Fiction substitutes for fact, or interrelates with it in 'infotainment'. Our present day versions of celebrity are media ones – at least two thirds of those we consider famous are the actors, musicians, presenters and entertainers of the media world. Even if in cultural terms our highest awards are the Nobel Prizes, the well-known ones are the Oscars, Grammies and Golden Globes. Most of the Nobel Prize-winners could walk unnoticed into any restaurant in the world. Few of the Oscar–winners could do so without dark glasses and a suitable disguise.[15]

The media's choice of celebrities can be seen in the obituaries they feature at the end of each year. If we look at the 1998 obituaries in the *Sunday Express* and *The Sunday Times*, for instance, we see that about two thirds are people from the entertainment world (70 per cent in the *Express*, 62 per cent in *The Times*, including 10 per cent musicians in the *Express* and 16 per cent in *The Times*). The rest is made up of sportspeople (10 per cent in both) and politicians (6 per cent in the *Express*, 16 per cent in *The Times*) and then a smattering of discoverers, inventors and miscellaneous others who had at one time or another featured in the news. Here, the only difference between the 'serious' broadsheet newspaper and the tabloid is that in the former a small number of media celebrities are replaced with politicians – the sport content stays the same. Much the same trend can be seen with *Cosmopolitan*'s list of 'Men We Love', where 80 per cent are from the entertainment world (including 18 per cent musicians), 10 per cent are sportsmen and 7 per cent are politicians (omitting people from the fashion world as particular to the *Cosmo* readership).

So, at the end of the 20th century, when we talk of 'fame' we are talking about a heavy bias towards the celebrities of the media world – the Hollywood stars, the national TV celebrities, the big musical acts. We then have the sportspeople – our contemporary 'strongest and fastest' – down at 10 per cent. But the politicians, who have traditionally been the heroes of history, barely match the sportspeople in fame. It is worth pointing out that in today's world there are almost no monarchs with any power. Politicians in democratic countries are frequently changed every five years (or less in countries like Italy), so the chance of their doing enough in their lives to be truly famous is far less likely than it was in the past. And despite their modest achievements, politicians generally lack the charisma that keeps media stars like Marilyn Monroe or Elvis Presley alive in the hearts of the people.

The phenomenon of fame is likely to further change with the convergence of media on the Internet. On the one hand, huge investment in new technology is likely to favour the big stars – for instance, Sony Entertainment's new online streamed music video channel will feature Sade, Bob Dylan, Michael Jackson, Oasis and Fatboy Slim as well as the usual suspects. On the other hand, the proliferation of content and content providers on the Net will allow access to all kinds of independent material, including the most up-to-date mixes favoured by DJs. Thinking further ahead, home-based music studios, such as produced Fatboy Slim's original hits, will become home-based video studios as digital video cameras and the associated hardware come down in price and as more and more Net users become content providers themselves.

Celebrities and media shows as 'social currency'

One other reason for the survival of the bigger stars and those currently on screen is the observation by media analysts like Douglas Rushkoff that as more and more of the younger generation spend more and more time watching the same media content, whether broadcast or online, they will use this content as the subject of their conversations since it will be the most obvious area of mutual interest and convergence, replacing what was previously a greater variety of conversation around subjects and topics more directly related to 'reality' – the actual world.

> We think of a medium as the thing that delivers content. But the delivered content is a medium in itself. Content is just a medium for interaction between people. The many forms of content we collect and experience online, I'd argue, are really just forms of ammunition – something to have when the conversation goes quiet at work the next day. An excuse to start a discussion with that attractive person in the next cubicle: 'Hey! Did you see that streaming video clip at streamingvideoclips.com?' Social currency is like a good joke. When a bunch of friends sit around and tell jokes, what are they really doing? Entertaining one another? Sure, for a start. But they are also using content – mostly unoriginal content that they've heard elsewhere – in order to lubricate a social occasion. And what are most of us doing when we listen to a joke? Trying to memorise it so that we can bring it somewhere else. The joke itself is social currency. 'Invite Harry. He tells good jokes. He's the life of the party.' Think of this the next time you curse that onslaught of e-mail jokes cluttering up your inbox. The senders think they've given you a gift, but all they really want is an excuse to interact with you. If the joke is good enough, this means the currency is valuable enough to earn them a response. That's why the most successful TV shows, Web sites and music recordings are

generally the ones that offer the most valuable forms of social currency to their fans. Sometimes, like with mainstream media, the value is its universality. In the US right now, the quiz show is enjoying tremendous ratings because it gives its viewers something to talk about with one another the next day. It's a form of mass spectacle. And, not coincidentally, what is the object of the game? To demonstrate one's facility with a variety of forms of social currency! Contestants who can answer a long stream of questions about everything from sports and movies to science and history, are rewarded with a million dollars. They are social currency champions.[16]

TWO

Reality, Deception and Spin

To a philosopher, reality is a concept that requires careful definition and use. We can say, for instance, that a car is real – we can see it and touch it, even drive in it. But a headache is also real in as much as it actually occurs, and we are in no doubt about it when it does occur. Then again, a painting is 'real' if it is not a fake. What do these three things have in common, what 'core essence' is there to this abstract noun 'reality'? A car, a headache and a painting that is not a fake have nothing obvious in common. Not only that, but a deception is also in a sense real – a fake Rembrandt is still a painting. Philosophers warn us continually to beware of how we use abstract nouns purporting to describe the world we live in – abstract nouns are not the truth about entities. The word 'truth' requires similar care. The 'whole truth', though a phrase used legally, is a very mysterious phrase. Is it 'everything that could be known'? Strictly speaking, there are truths but not truth, real things but not reality.

In common usage we use the word 'reality' loosely, without much care for definition. And increasingly we use it as the opposite of 'virtuality', since we need some way of distinguishing between the two. Despite the increasing use of 'actuality' as an opposite, we appear comfortable with the term 'reality'. One expanded aspect of the term's usage is the opinions, knowledge and attitudes shared by humans, something often referred to as our 'social reality'. Social reality is a psychological term for a kind of reality dependent upon or defined by the consensus of a group. As Arthur S. Reber suggests in *The Penguin Dictionary of Psychology*: 'The term is applicable to anything from very small groups to a whole society. Thus, the social reality shared by a small band of fanatics who are awaiting the end of the world on a mountaintop is as 'real' as the nearly universal belief in the value of education.'[1]

How does our media world reflect our search for social reality? One aspect of television quite distinct from fiction and fantasy is its documentation of real people, and increasingly, real people are taking the roles previously played by actors. Instead of soaps we have docu-soaps. In a post-Freudian world where airing and sharing problems is commonplace, we have 'reality TV'. To make it more interesting we have 'ambush TV'. And as we turn surveillance cameras onto game show hopefuls we have 'surveillance TV'.

Reality TV

Why does the television audience want more of this 'reality TV'? It may be that as we tire of too much fantasy we return to real figures doing real things, much as we do when we turn from daydreams to real things. What we do, in fact, is switch from one to the other – the general TV audience appears to be the same for fantasy and reality. When we tire of one we can turn to the other. We don't even have to register the difference as we switch channels. Roman Polanski described the secret of his art as the ability to move seamlessly from reality into fantasy, and this seems to be what we all do to some extent. Sometimes – as in the film *Titanic* – we move seamlessly from computer reconstructions to actual people, and judging by the success of the film we are happy to do so. Sometimes the real and the escapist are combined, as when ordinary people are converted into millionaires, given blind dates or flown to Ibiza and other exotic places to live in villas and go clubbing.

As the camera changes roles from surveillance instrument to film instrument, TV programmes are increasingly borrowing both actual footage and conceptual ideas from surveillance TV. Home videos, police chase videos and surveillance videos have all become popular viewing, along with a new type of programme putting a number of people together in a location like an island or a house and filming their actions on a 24-hour basis. One very successful pioneer programme of this kind is *Big Brother*, originally a Dutch invention, which has had multiple spin-offs. Many other variations will follow, such as *The Big Diet* – a German show where people are locked up in a house and forced to diet – and *MIR*, where 10 people are locked up in a house, trained as astronauts, and the winner gets to go up into space.

But how 'real' are such programmes? We have, on the face of it, constant observation of actual people in shows like the aptly titled *Big Brother*. Contestants on the UK *Big Brother*, however, strongly criticised the programme for not being real. Contestant Melanie Hill emphasised the manipulation of the characters that occurred in the editing process, and thinks the contestants were exploited. She says, 'I feel angry with the programme makers because we had no idea what they were going to do with all the footage and what they did was manipulate it into our little stereotypes and unfortunately these stereotypes aren't real, they're just caricatures, which is a shame.'

Contestant Nick Bateman took the opposite view, that the programme was never a 'real kind of social experiment' in the first place, and criticised the public itself for thinking that a simple 'game show' was deeper than it was supposed to be: 'I think that one of the problems with the whole show, the public thought it was real. They lost sight that it was a game show.' One simple fact supports this game show analogy – the device built into the programme for raising finance. Because of the public selection procedure involved in choosing which competitors were to be eliminated, the telephone calls more than paid for the making of the whole programme, just as it is the telephone calls that pay for the prizes on *Who Wants to be a Millionaire?*

A new twist to *Big Brother* was *Celebrity Big Brother*, transmitted in the UK for a week in aid of the charity Comic Relief. The result was a great deal of confusion for the participants as to whether they were being celebrities or being themselves. Boxer Chris Eubank chose to retain his celebrity image, striding about in his impeccable wardrobe, carved walking stick in hand, while comedian Jack Dee, actress Clare Sweeney and musician Keith Duffy behaved largely as their real selves. One factor in this might be that comedians and musicians (though not all actors) are traditionally 'natural' in the flesh. The greatest confusion was in the TV presenters: despite the obvious fact that the show was a charity event, Anthea Turner deliberated over whether she should be wearing make-up or not and Vanessa Feltz swung emotionally between worrying that she might be 'humiliated' in front of her viewers and pouring her heart out as her real self. Both looked agonisingly vulnerable as they awaited news of who was to be evicted. Clearly 'reality' is something that needs to be in the heads of the participants as well as in the context they are seen in, and fame is a phenomenon that can easily split the 'self' and go on to reveal significant cracks in the ego. The public voted for naturalism – Chris, Vanessa and Anthea were the first to go.

Ambush TV

Philosopher Sir Isaiah Berlin wryly remarked in 1981, with hindsight on human history, and some degree of foresight: 'When a man speaks of the need for realism one may be sure that this is always the prelude to some bloody deed.'[2]

Scott Amedure and Jonathan Schmitz came to grief following an episode of *The Jenny Jones Show* in America, where Amedure revealed a crush on Schmitz. Three days after the programme Schmitz exacted his revenge on Amedure, and was sentenced for second-degree murder. Blame was levelled at the TV show, and in a civil case headed by attorney Geoffrey Fieger, $25 million was judged in compensation against Warner Bros (Warner are currently appealing and vow to fight until the judgment is overturned). Even though guests are briefed in advance of all possibilities for their onstage surprises, the defence in the trial claimed that *The Jenny Jones Show* ambushed Jonathan Schmitz with an outcome that he never anticipated, and was not (due to a history of mental problems) emotionally prepared for.

In the Florida town of Sarasota another incident took place. Nancy Campbell Panitz appeared on *The Jerry Springer Show* and was humiliated publicly. Ralf Panitz, her ex-husband who also appeared on the show, watched it later when it was broadcast, and the same day allegedly bludgeoned Nancy to death. He has been charged with second-degree murder.

Geoffrey Fieger lays the blame with the programme. He told BBC's *Panorama*, 'That show took a known, already volatile relationship and exploited it and re-enacted and re-created and created more hurt and more fear and more embarrassment.' The view of the Springer show was that they could not be responsible for individual reactions, because 'People have to be responsible for their own behaviours, and if someone chooses to go on television, that's their responsibility' (Jerry Springer speaking on *Panorama*).

So has 'reality TV' gone too far? The ambush factor continues unabated – if it is 'good television' then ratings would be enough to determine content. What has changed is the emergence of 'aftercare'. Jamie Huysman is one prominent US psychologist and entrepreneur who offers an aftercare option called Aftercare™. Guests get help at a treatment centre as part of a package deal. He claims that TV is exploitative and as such his services are necessary. 'If I were an attorney measuring risk and future liability I would put the screening process at the front door. It would be facilitated by a professional who knew the needs of entertainment but, first and foremost, an advocate for the guests' needs.' Coincidentally, he and his mother, a clinical psychologist who uses the epithet 'Dr Mom', also have their own talk show called *Family Affairs*, guaranteeing that 'On our new show *Family Affairs*, all our producers are trained in both health and entertainment'.

Jeanne Albronda Heaton, an Ohio University psychologist and co-author of *Tuning In Trouble*, a 1995 book about reality talk shows, volunteers the opinion that these shows promote the idea, appealing but infantile, that one's problems are always someone else's fault, and that such shows can become 'a kind of parade of pathology with nobody minding the shop and nobody responsible for the outcome'.[3] Heaton points out, as others have, that busy producers seem to be primarily concerned with ratings rather than ethics, thus reinforcing the case for some kind of aftercare to make sure guests do not leave TV studios harbouring grudges.

It is worth also pointing out that the degree of 'reality' present in at least one of these programmes has been compromised by admissions that some researchers have used actors in place of genuine members of the public. And even if the participants are real, the confrontations, swearing, mutual recriminations and physicality expected of them on shows like Jerry Springer's is so formulaic that the pattern in which situations unfold is highly predictable. This is, in other words, a very narrow window on 'reality'. It is not the pure 'surveillance' of Andy Warhol's groundbreaking camera observations. *Big Brother* is a game show where players are eliminated, and daytime TV shows deliberately feature inadequate people in emotional conflict. There is generally some kind of 'hook' for other reality programmes like car chases or comical accidents caught on camera. And of course, programmes are edited – we don't watch TV in our sleep so 24-hour surveillance in real time is a physical impossibility.

Psychologists are routinely used to give reality TV a cachet of depth and gravitas. In fact, they are often ignored, and their opinions are frequently only some of many taken into account, the needs of entertainment being more pressing than 'safety first' judgements of psychological vulnerability. There are, however, many examples of good practice. *The Big Trip*, a BBC adventure programme sending groups of young volunteers on filmed trips, used an extensive selection procedure with standard psychometric tests and specially devised questionnaires and activities supervised by media psychologists (Martin Lloyd-Elliott and Andrew Evans, 1994), and the production team worked closely with the psychologists on the selection criteria.

'Escapist' realism

If we take our surveillance camera to exotic locations, we end up with another increasingly popular type of programme – the 'escapist' version of reality TV. The desert island scenario has been used for several 'social experiments' since the groundbreaking Defoe novel *Robinson Crusoe*. Films like *Castaway* (the 1987 version starring Oliver Reed and Amanda Donohoe) paved the way, and now the genre has become a game show. In 2000 American TV company CBS televised a programme called *Survivor*, in which 16 individuals were placed on a deserted island in the South Pacific. The formula mimics *Big Brother*, where contestants form their own society and vote off one member each week. As Nick asked on the British version of *Big Brother* – is this a game show or a social experiment? The appeal of *Survivor* is, presumably, escapism from the over-cultivated city world to a primitive culture closer to survival needs. The questions were the same as the ones posed in the film *Castaway* – how to find food, what happens if you don't find enough food, how people can accommodate to others they can't escape from, how far you let go of modesty on a beach in the sun, and what you do with any sexual attractions that ensue. Less a social experiment and more a media-fest, two months in paradise for the chance to win a million dollars hardly appears too taxing. Worse still is the 'fabulously tacky' (www.salon.com) *Temptation Island*, where four couples – each with some strains in their relationship – are sent to a Caribbean island. The men and the women are separated and left for two weeks in the seductive company of a dozen members of the opposite sex, unsurprisingly good looking. Social experiments, anybody?

At present the BBC, as public service television, is not interested in such examples of 'reality TV' as *Big Brother*. It did, though, have *Castaway 2000*, which it described as a 'sociological experiment', replete with its resident psychologist. Since it was a year-long 'experiment' it was less fast moving and sensational than *Big Brother* or *Survivor*. Ex-castaway Ron, however, echoed the same complaints as the members of *Big Brother* – manipulation of the characters through editing. The BBC denied this and claimed that his portrait was characteristic of how he is. He responded that 'it felt like being psychologically beaten up'. Since editing down 24 hours a day of footage obviously requires selection, and selection will prioritise the most exciting viewing, complaints of bias are very easy to understand – what is 'characteristic' of a person?

The pressure to chase ratings makes for dilemmas in the production process. TV is mass entertainment, and a means of getting people to watch commercials, so there is constant pressure to satisfy the needs of the audience. How does television make reality more interesting? It manipulates it, it dramatises it and increasingly it 'adrenalises' it. Anything that adrenalises people will cause more arousal, and therefore in theory more attention. But Stuart Fischoff, Professor of Media Psychology at California State University, is one of many who fear that as people tire of the current formats 'they are going to have to escalate the ante – escalate it to the two basics – sex and violence – so we are going to see more shows that will put people in greater jeopardy'.[4]

Public access TV

Another form of 'authentic' television is public access TV, which has built up a following in the USA. Basically individuals with cameras making their own shows, it is an anarchic mix of talk, chat, cooking, acting out, exhibitionism, self-promotion and provocation of bystanders in public places. In this world of cheap technology, anybody can be a TV station and so the ability to broadcast from a 'nonconstructed space' is available to the normally disenfranchised – the poor, minority groups and those with alternative beliefs. Results are even more raw than so-called surveillance programmes made by the regular TV companies, and while there is undoubtedly a shock value and an authentic feel, there is also a tendency for the various exhibitionists turning cameras on themselves night and day to become seriously boring after a short period of viewing. Nonconstructed space it may be, but nonconstructed programming needs to be brilliant to be more than ephemeral fun.

Truth, lies and deception

Television offers us much that is interesting and educational in its documentary broadcasting, and its treatment of the real world can be considerably more serious than the ironically titled 'reality TV' shows. Its current affairs and news broadcasts purport to give us the truth about the world we live in. But how can we tell true from untrue? How do we know the 'truth' about the world we live in? Much thought has been devoted by philosophers and scientists to this subject. Verification, however, is not a 'monolithic concept'. It embraces many fields, including:

- scientific verification, experimental results, reliable methodology, replicable studies;
- historical verification – research, archaeological finds, dating;
- psychology and studies involving data – probability, degrees of confidence (not conclusive as such);
- philosophy – debate but not necessarily verification, since deductive reasoning only works in logic and maths.

Verification and the search for methods of proof have a long and distinguished history, and until recently traditional logic was routinely taught to generations of high school students in Scandinavia, Germany and other European countries. Some version of truth as an imperative was taught to generations of journalists at one time.

But truth can be as difficult to achieve in theory as it is in practice. Modern thought now embraces quasi-truth and paradoxical truth, as with chaos theory, probability, fuzzy logic and the world of subatomic particles. And in our spiritual culture verifiable facts co-exist with faith as we grapple with the uncomfortable dilemma of whether to have faith in a comforting God or whether to abide by a belief in godlessness that offers no succour beyond the grave.

Does the establishment provide us with the truth?

We should believe academics, should we not? An academic place of study is in theory an environment where the conditions are right for the advancement of knowledge. Selflessness and altruism can exist in academics just as it can at times in politicians (for instance, Atlee's post-war government, which implemented the National Health Service). But academics are also subject to economic realities and incentives, and with performance-related pay universities have changed a lot. It's 'publish or perish' and so quantity may influence quality. Add to that political leanings on management staff and at worst you can get job cuts, departments starved of funds if they don't serve 'useful' political ends, and 'directives' such as vocational teaching and particular selection criteria imposed on academics by non-academics.

Science is based on verification, so is science exempt from spin and massage? It may depend who is picking up the bill for the work. A section of the scientific community bankrolled by the tobacco industry claimed for years that there were no harmful effects from smoking. Recent statements by scientists about BSE have been clearly 'sanitised' by political spin.

To some extent there is an opposite trend in medicine towards telling the truth – doctors tell the truth more about cancer, for instance. Partly this is because of the development of the NHS, which gave everybody access to treatment. Partly, due to advances in medicine, it is because cancer is a treatable disease that needs to be diagnosed early. Partly there is a different social attitude since the end of the fifties – more openness, more counselling and a belief that harbouring secrets does one less good than facing up to the truth. Partly the spread and consequences of litigation in the medical arena force doctors to accurately document their steps and procedures so they can justify themselves later if need be.

Where is the truth in law? Every time a person is rightfully convicted in a criminal trial after giving evidence, a lawyer will have assisted a guilty person to promote his or her untrue case. Professionally, a lawyer cannot actively promote anything he or she knows to be untrue. What happens in practice is that lawyers 'suspend disbelief' in the case of clients who may be lying. Once they take on the case they generally proceed, since everyone has a right to be represented.

But the law is not primarily about truth and untruth – it is about proving someone guilty 'beyond reasonable doubt' in the case of a criminal trial, and 51 per cent likelihood in a civil trial. Witnesses may be 'truthful but mistaken' – they may simply not realise they are in error. Neither can you assume that a person who lies is guilty. The goal is not to reconstruct the truth of what happened, but to be 'satisfied' that the evidence points one way or the other. The case itself may include many cases of untruth or partial truths. Working out the truth may, indeed, be an impossible task. But such details are not essential for the decision-making process itself – whether the charge is dismissed or upheld.

European countries such as France have an inquisitorial system, which has a 90 per cent record of 'putting criminals away', as opposed to the 50 per cent record of British courts. But whether the defendants are truly guilty or just judged to be guilty is another story.

How do we find the truth?

> People never lie so much as after the hunt, during a war or before an election.
>
> Otto von Bismarck

The search for truth can be complicated by persuasion and vested interests, and this can be particularly true in instances like wars and foreign policy. To maintain views contrary to the bulk of the population – not eating beef, for instance – would imply some degree of courage and independence, since this would put us in a position of being in disagreement with media spin and those influenced by it. Finding the truth amidst media spin would additionally require some skill in reasoning, an ability to see vested interests at work and some knowledge of where to look for such vested interests. We could throw in, for good measure, a useful familiarity with Machiavelli's *The Prince* and a working knowledge of the unconscious and how it shows up in body language. Even so, the back room conversations that take place in parliament, multinational organisations like NATO and the broadcasting companies would be opaque to us.

We are often ill-informed about risk and probability. The likelihood of winning the British National Lottery is five times less likely than being struck by lightning. Yet the Lottery is played by millions. Do players not know, or do they not care? Often we act with little heed to risk. People smoke cigarettes even though the risk of serious illness as a consequence is around 50 per cent. We seem to be particularly bad at judging hypothetical risks and trying to avert them. Many people don't pay attention to global warming, even if it might destroy the earth's ecosystem. Is it because they personally won't be about to see it or because they just shrug it off and think 'that's life'?

We don't even pay much attention to telling the truth at all times – recent figures in the UK show that two thirds of people have lied at work. Is lying more generally acceptable these days? Certainly it is in the media, PR and advertising worlds. PR guru Max Clifford justifies lying to defend his clients, and states he is happy to do so since otherwise the media could destroy them through intrusive investigative journalism. He adds that not only does he make things up, but so does the rest of the press: 'When I give interviews, 70 per cent is Max Clifford and 30 per cent is purely made up by journalists and editors to suit the story.' But lies, he states, are as old as history. People have always lied and always will. We may simply be more aware of lies because the media relays the words people speak to a previously unprecedented extent.

The psychology of lying

Psychologists investigating deception have looked at a number of different phenomena such as conjurers, psychic fraud, lying, confidence games and con artists and military deception. There has to date been no satisfactory unified theory of deception because the phenomena are quite disparate, though individual areas have been well researched.[5] Likewise, lying has also been investigated in different forms, such as in interpersonal relationships and the development of lying in children.[6]

The science of lie detection has a long history, and psychologists have researched how it is possible to pick up cues to lying in verbal behaviour, body language and other behaviour. In 13 of 16 studies of detection, judges' accuracy was above chance levels.[7] This also applied when recordings of lying were judged by video alone, sound alone or transcript alone. Deception in con artists has been studied by researchers who interviewed and even joined groups of them, and has uncovered elaborate disguises and strategies both to con the 'mark' and stop him or her from going to the police. Recent research has even investigated the possibility of deception in animals – hard to prove in the case of the firefly, more plausible in the case of primates like baboons but still hard to distinguish from learned behaviour.[8]

Lying and deception is as old as human nature. Some untruths are innocent and come from the conscious brain simply being unsure of what to provide under stress, when others are seeking information from us. Eyewitness reports vary considerably, partly due to errors in perception, but partly due to errors in what we describe as conscious thought. Not only do we experience tip-of-the-tongue phenomena, we also feel ourselves to be guided by hunches – something easily seen on the programme *Who Wants to be a Millionaire?*, as contestants agonise over whether their hunches are worth large sums of money or not. Our Level 1 consciousness, in Halligan and Oakley's model (see Chapter 1), may simply output whatever 'hunch-like' Level 2 material appears to be the best fit, without a correct analysis of how precise or risk-free this output is. The same kind of process may be behind lying – we search for a publicly acceptable 'output' from Level 2 information.

White lies – for many people sensitive to the reactions of others – can be considered to make life tolerable. Also, many people are economical with the truth, or simply don't discuss certain things. 'Tell the truth' is also not the same as 'do not lie', just as 'I see what I eat' is not the same as 'I eat what I see'.

Are we still taught not to tell untruths, and to value truth? One of the greatest forces advocating the truth was religion – despite the obvious problem that if you honestly declared you were an unbeliever you got your head chopped off. The Bible and the example of St Augustine promoted telling the truth, however painful, as in the commandment

'Thou shalt not bear false witness'. The Bible is in many ways a good recipe for social behaviour, the problem being that much of it is difficult or even impossible to carry out in practice – poverty, no sex outside marriage, loving one's enemies. Nevertheless, the decline in Christian teaching has surely taken some of the brakes off the imperative to tell the truth.

Spin in politics

> The truth, cleverly told, is the biggest lie of all.
> Thomas Hardy, *The Return of the Native*

Spin is different from white lies in that there is no sensitivity to others' feelings – on the contrary, the purpose is to persuade others in a direction that suits the persuader. Spin is a studied and deliberate distortion of reality, where meaning is turned around. The term originated in America in the early 20th century and comes from the spin given to the ball in baseball to control and turn its trajectory, so as to fool the person who receives it.

Experts in spin, 'spin doctors', appeared in British politics under Margaret Thatcher, changing her voice, hair and TV image. They started to proliferate in the Labour Party as it desperately sought to overturn four lost general elections in a row, and are now widely employed by political parties, government departments and businesses to present information in ways favourable to the presenter and so as to cause the least embarrassment or negative consequences. Spin is a powerful political tool that can be used to reinforce political 'escapism' from reality, or blind populations to what is actually happening (eg during wars when losses are sustained, or other cases 'in the national interest'). Routinely through commercial advertising, spin distorts truth and encourages us to spend more money than we have on products we may not really need. This commercial version of spin is justified as 'stimulation of demand'.

Our tolerance for lies in general and our familiarity with advertising gives us a certain basic tolerance of spin. In addition, our familiarity with slogans in advertising prepares us for the 'sound bite' – a segment of a political speech carefully contrived to be taken out and used in the media. An example of the use of a sound bite is the much-mocked statement by Tony Blair on signing the Northern Ireland Peace Agreement: 'Now is not the time for sound bites. I feel the hand of history on my shoulder.' Not surprisingly, sound bites have found their way onto the comedy circuit, like Clinton's avowal that he did not have sex with Monica Lewinsky and the idea that it 'depends what you mean by sex'. Sound bites, of course, are nothing new and those provided by generations of theatre critics have decorated the fronts of theatres for many years ('will run and run', 'probably the best murder thriller in a vicarage setting currently running in the West End', 'we laughed until we stopped', etc).

Spin is 'encoded' by sophisticated methods like 'plausible deniability', 'prebuttal' and 'wiggle room'. As yet there is no obvious way of 'decoding' spin, except with robust cynicism, such as that expressed by Russians with their characteristic black humour. Since Russia has two main newspapers, *Pravda* (The Truth) and *Izvestia* (The News), the saying goes that 'There's no truth in The News and there's no news in The Truth'. In theory it would probably be possible to devise sophisticated methods of decoding spin, analogous to the way code breakers were used in the Second World War. In practice, decoding spin is left to journalists covering events and increasingly to media psychologists. Psychologists – and in particular those skilled in interpreting body language – are contacted when journalists are floundering or in the dark and asked to pad out stories with plausible explanations and analysis of motivation and behaviour, a practice paralleled by the decoding of criminals' minds by Cracker-type forensic psychologists. As for the general public, there is a new attitude growing in some quarters of 'dispute the text' – a backlash like that against surveillance, which preaches that we are all our own filters of information and that we have to learn to use that filter efficiently to avoid the ever-increasing information traps that gullibility can lead us into.

A. Alvarez is one farsighted media critic who could see the effects of spin in the media as far back as 1963, writing in *The Listener* that 'Mass democracy, mass morality and the mass media thrive independently of the individual, who joins them at the cost of at least a partial perversion of instinct and insights'. We surely need some protection from spin as it proliferates in a world increasingly characterised by persuasion and distortion of all kinds – advertising, political, media, lies and hype. Even photographs used in newspapers and magazines, once considered things that never lied, can now be electronically retouched, so there is no guarantee that they represent reality. Truth is not just cheapened and devalued, it is mixed with spin, propaganda and entertainment in ways that can subtly blind us to reality.

Information plus entertainment gives us 'infotainment', something increasingly part of our celebrity-dominated media culture. As Donna Leigh-Kile points out, 'Stars inhabit a surreal world where fact, fiction and fantasy collide. We see them posing "at home" in houses that have been borrowed for the photo shoot. We read their fabricated life stories. Some of it may be fact, some of it may not. But ultimately in this world of infotainment it is not important. What matters is to be true to the image.'[9]

Publicist Max Clifford, creator of the headline 'Freddie Starr Ate My Hamster', defends 'infotainment' on the grounds that the public wish to be entertained as much as they wish to know the truth.

> In the sixties most of my experience was with pop and rock stars and you could get away with murder. I could say, for instance, 'The Beatles sold 50,000 albums this week' when they sold five. No one would check. I had no misgivings about making up stories because it gave the press something bigger and better to generate. What's the truth anyway? Trying to draw the line between reality and fiction is impossible. We're not dealing in reality. It's virtual reality. It's infotainment – information as entertainment.[10]

He puts the case simply: 'My work is to create false images. I have a public relations company: I lie every day of my life' (on BBC TV).

Big corporations are increasingly using spin, to the point where public relations may occupy a space on the management table somewhere beneath acquisitions and mergers and somewhere above operations or health and safety. Public utilities have inevitable accidents, but saving face and one's franchise is crucial to business. How to handle information about disasters and shortcomings is big business, with the threat of big lawsuits if they get it 'wrong'. Running operations is day-to-day stuff. It's not what you do, it's how you are seen to be doing it, in a world where cameras are on everything. The bottom line is profits, ratings, audiences or votes. The 'citizen' has become the 'consumer'. The 'passenger' on the train has become 'the client'. We're all punters now.

Spin in government

When our enemies indulged in spin – particularly if they were of a communist persuasion – it used to be called propaganda. But in wartime, propaganda is a universal phenomenon. The British government lied in the First World War about Belgians being used by the Germans as human shields. It lied about the date of D-Day (for obvious reasons). It lied about certain facts in the Falklands war. Such lies are considered justifiable in terms of national security. Larger bodies like NATO are equally prone to distortion of information, as seen during the progress of the war in Yugoslavia, where 'the international community' became a nebulous entity invoked to support NATO, and where a strategic operation to stabilise the Balkan corridor became, according to NATO publicity, 'the first humanitarian war in history'.

Spin in electioneering is so widespread and exaggerated it goes beyond lies and verges on pure nonsense, a recent example being George W. Bush's 'Our nation is chosen by God and commissioned by history to be a model to the world of justice and inclusion, and diversity without division' (campaigning in Washington, 28 August 2000). No doubt he was referring, amongst other things, to the 'inclusion' of the first black or female President, the 'lack of division' over the Florida recount fiasco, and the 'justice' of the Supreme Court consequently dividing on party lines to reach their decision. Spin in legal cases is starting to run electioneering close for pure silliness, a good example being the statement of Tory politician Jonathan Aitken: 'If it falls to me to start a fight to cut out the cancer of bent and twisted journalism in our country with the simple sword of truth and the trusty shield of British fair play, so be it.' (These being the words of a man who subsequently spent 18 months in prison for perjury and perverting justice.)

We expect simplistic 'goodies and baddies' propaganda in wartime and electioneering, but should we expect it in peacetime? The function of political parties is partly to administrate, but equally to act as advocates, so we are back with the division between advocacy and truth. Politicians as advocates are thus the equivalent of lawyers, and increasingly they are lawyers. Their advocacy of a particular party line may well cause them to joke 'Has anyone got questions for my answers?' And if we are to count the large numbers of spin doctors reported to be buzzing about the corridors of power under Tony Blair's Labour government, then clearly we should expect a commensurate amount of spin or propaganda, whichever we choose to call it.

Additionally we should expect some degree of secrecy – for a start, 'sensitive national information' can be suppressed by the government in the press and media through D notices. And then what about information on health issues? The truth about the health risks of smoking was camouflaged for many years. Several years went by before we were told the truth about health issues like AIDS and BSE. How much is still hidden from us, for instance in the risks of using depleted uranium in present-day conflicts, a story unfolding as this book is being written? The British government that repeatedly said 'beef is safe' was aware of some degree of risk. The same evasive response was then seen in a number of European countries, and in EU directives themselves.

We are increasingly – in post-BSE Britain – getting cynical about any statement from the government that anything is 'safe'. Public mistrust of such assurances may last decades, suggest experts in risk perception like Dr Ian Langford of the University of East Anglia. Consumers have become suspicious of any new food technology, and at least some of them possess an understanding of potential risk that is clearly more sophisticated than the infantile level of explanation they are being offered. 'The approach to communication of risk was shaped by a consuming fear of provoking an irrational public scare,' wrote the BSE report, sounding the old bell that being 'economic with the truth' is justified 'to stop panic'. A less than infantile public reads this as 'to stop government embarrassment' and steadfastly refuses to see the justification for withholding essential information on public safety.

Nor does the public appreciate the massaging of the degree of risk expected from certain courses of action, such as eating beef. Once we get into 'justifiable risk', 'acceptable degree of risk', 'minimising risk' and other forms of massage, we are on a slippery road to justifying 'certain numbers' of accidents or deaths. This is not in any sense an absolute interpretation of the term 'carries no risks', and the public is justified in expecting adequate information in clear terms, for instance on ambulance response times or the admission of emergency cases to hospital. Politicians are accountable to the people and their utterances should be equally accountable. The public may consider that private misdemeanours in politicians like sexual encounters are not a hanging matter, but matters of public safety are (sometimes literally in the case of farmed salmon) another kettle of fish.

One problem spotlighted by the recent BSE inquiry is the chain of information, which includes scientists, civil servants and various government departments. Information can be changed, massaged or withheld anywhere along this chain, and in the BSE episode clearly was. The government often claims that the briefing papers it receives from the civil service have to be censored – that papers cannot be given willy-nilly to the press. It has also periodically claimed that the press is not responsible enough to act properly on such information as it gets. This was given as a reason for the secrecy over BSE – that the press had sensationalised issues like salmonella in eggs in 1988 and listeria in cheese in 1989. Nevertheless, the duty of the government is to provide 'essential knowledge' and ultimately 'the buck stops with the president'. It is not entitled to deny access to information that the public needs to make informed choices. What is deplorable is covering up issues like BSE so as not to adversely affect the Tory party, and not to adversely affect farming interests, when the true risk was to the human population of Britain.

As to the argument that populations need to be protected from 'panic', this is surely overstated and used in an expedient way as a justification of secrecy. The British public was in a state of great fear over the Cuban missile crisis, but it did not panic. On the contrary, it organised itself into groups like CND and went on well-run marches. A further argument is that the public simply does not have a realistic understanding of 'risk'. This argument is more sustainable – smoking carries a risk of around 50 per cent of causing serious health problems, yet people still smoke. However, they carry on smoking despite government health warnings, so that is no reason for the public not to be informed. Is it safe to use trains, or cars, or aeroplanes? At least statistics for deaths from these causes are known and so can be factored in when people use them. So why, then, is there no health warning on beef? There are health warnings on nuts, even down to trace quantities, though the percentage of the population with life-threatening reactions to nuts is small. There is a risk and people are warned of it. Could it be that we don't have much of a nut industry in this country?

In many ways spin seems to have backfired on the government, just as crying wolf backfired in the old parable. Newsreader Peter Hobday, author of a book on 'managing the message' in politics, nevertheless advocates the fundamental principle of telling the truth in the first place:

> I think everyone should operate on the basis of knowing that if they do anything wrong or illegal, or are simply withholding uncomfortable facts, sooner or later they will be found out. If you start to lie, as President Clinton discovered, sooner or later, no amount of 'wiggle room' as his advisers called it, will stop the truth from emerging. Silence is no longer an option. Being 'economical with the truth' is even less of an option. As President Lincoln once observed, 'You can fool some of the people all of the time and all of the people some of the time, but you can't fool all of the people all of the time.'[11]

Politicians should by now be aware of the risks of trying to be 'cleverer than the public', as a whole chain of them up to presidents like Nixon have been sacked for their manipulation of information. Neither are spin doctors themselves exempt – British guru of political spin Peter Mandelson went down with the sound bite: 'I have allowed the impression to be created of wrongdoing.' Unfortunately there appears to be a counterproductive symbiosis between public figures and the spin industry – the further they sink into the quicksand of ill-repute the more desperate they get to massage their image. It reminds us of the words of Ralph Waldo Emerson: 'The louder he talked of his honour, the faster we counted the spoons.'

Spin in the media

I read the newspaper avidly. It is my one form of continuous fiction.

Aneurin Bevan, 1897–1960

Media implies a channel for transmitting a facsimile of an event to a different place, usually for the benefit of people who can't be in the primary place of activity. The principle is as old as the original marathon runner and as new as the last Olympic Games. Only the nature of the medium of transmission has changed, from oral reporting to written reports to the media of today. Since the recipients cannot be at the actual event, they are vulnerable to spin in the telling since they have no first-hand means of verification. Spin in the telling applied to the whole oral tradition, and to its latest form, 'infotainment'.

The media has taken a hand in the history of the world since reports of the first battle fought, whatever that was. History is full of spin – how else could one explain phrases like 'The Indian Mutiny' – a nonsensical description of an action by the inhabitants of India inside their own country to assert their own nationalism.

Is the news reality?

Journalists in the newsrooms of our major TV channels clearly try to get factual details right in their stories, and the vast majority of actual details are as correct as they can be – names of people, dates of incidents, numbers involved. This does not mean, however, that everything we hear on the news is always correct. With print journalism and the tabloids we find a sliding slope from integrity into sensationalism. Because of this a Mori poll put journalists below even politicians in terms of those whom we trust. Peter Hobday states, 'Wherever I go these days the same questions about the media are put again and again. Top of the list is "Why does the media lie?".'[12] The closest thing to truth in the media may be televised or radioed direct speech, where at least people's actual words are heard. For a start, news is a representation of reality – as is history. It is passed through media like telegrams, TV, radio and the telephone. It is further translated into codes – Morse code, digital code. It arrives at the other end as only a fraction of the actual experience, and a doctored one at that.

Second, it is information about reality. For every intention journalists might have about being objective, media news is as subjective as any bystander testimony. It is subject to all kinds of distortion and spin, and like the passage of information through government it goes through several stages of editing where parts can be changed or deleted and the overall direction or impression altered. There may be technical mistakes – in the Balkan conflict the same footage was used to depict victims of violence whether they were Muslim or Slav, inside a perimeter fence or outside it. Information may be withheld for reasons of national security and programmes not screened. Information used on the news may come directly from the press offices of organisations like NATO without having been checked for accuracy or spin.

And in any case, the first interest of the media – broadcast or press – is to sell copies and make money. Human interest stories about displaced war victims can and frequently do replace accurate strategic analysis of a conflict. On top of this, the media is biased according to its ownership – Rupert Murdoch is against the European Union and this influences all his papers, and consequently influences readers, who are also voters. So how can journalists who work under such owners change jobs and go overnight from writing right-wing copy to writing left-wing copy? They do so because a job is a job and because in the media sales are king. Films and newspapers have the basic goal of increasing profits. It's a profit and loss world, governed by consumer choices and sales.

The Roman satirist Juvenal summed it up in the words *panem et circenses* ('bread and circuses'), which in modern terms would be 'fast food and spectator sports' – what the dumbed-down masses want and believe they need. As Edward A. Cowan reports:

Here in the Dallas-Ft. Worth Metroplex last week, the firing of a local football coach was deemed by the media – all the major network stations and at least one independent station – so important as to pre-empt the 5.30 pm CST network national newscasts. And a couple of days later, the live coverage of the hiring of a replacement coach was also deemed so important as to interrupt the network newscasts during their reports on the upcoming New Hampshire primaries. We get what we want whether we want to get it or not.[13]

Dumbing down also carries the implication of escapism – reality is too much to take so it is made lighter and more palatable for the sake of the public. The public may be treated more like children than adults when politicians appear in the media, for instance in the use of language such as 'I would like to make it very, very clear that...', simple slogans like 'beef is safe' or grandiose claims like 'we have the best health service [education, legal system, safeguards against BSE, etc] in the world'. The whole process of vulgarisation and dumbing down is stimulated and continued by large corporations, many of whom also own mass media outlets, who have nothing in principle against nations full of simple-minded consumption slaves mainly interested in pulp, pop, porn, sports and trendy expensive objects – and ideally interested in the same things all over the globe. Most politicians have a tendency to want what the perceived majority want in order to get elected, so the dumbing down goes round and round.

The Internet

The Internet both helps and frustrates spin doctors. The Net is awash with spam and spin. But the Internet may also be one of the few ways in which completely independent views may be shared globally without censorship. It is a source of direct information, and individuals can write things in an uncensored way by using Internet cafés to disguise their identities. News reports from various countries can be compared so as to get some impression of where and how spin is applied. Reports from what were the non-aligned powers are informative – for instance, India was very useful in its coverage of the Balkan crisis. It is a strong irony that something like the Internet – a simulated world of virtual communication – can sometimes tell us more about reality than the flesh and blood politicians and journalists in our own government and newsrooms.

PART II

Escapism

THREE

What is Escapism?

We have seen that reality can be difficult to define, depends on our human perception of it, is often represented in other forms like art and film, and is subject to all sorts of distortions from lies and spin. But is living in reality actually the goal of the human being? We should expect that enough time be spent in reality to satisfy our basic needs. But what, then, do we do with the time left over? We are not obliged to spend large quantities of time hunting or grazing like most animals, neither are we obliged to remain in a state of constant vigilance against predators. We have time on our hands, time that we can spend – if we choose to – in activities only peripherally related to basic survival needs. And this is particularly true if our environment or 'perceived reality' is difficult, stressful or just plain boring.

Definitions of escapism

Escapism is a word that is part of common speech, yet it has no real underpinning in any of the major disciplines like philosophy or psychology. While there are innumerable books defining philosophic concepts like truth and reality, and while popular words like 'procrastination' are entering mainstream psychology, there still seems no place for the word 'escapism' in the annals of academic literature. Dictionary definitions vary in emphasis:

> *Concise Oxford Dictionary:* 'The tendency to seek, or practice of seeking, distraction or relief from reality.'

This underlines the difficulties in facing up to reality and the advantages offered by 'seeking' an escape from it – implying that the escapism is a process willingly initiated by an individual, not only for distraction but also for positive relief.

> *Random House Dictionary:* 'The avoidance of reality by absorption of the mind in entertainment or in an imaginative situation, activity, etc.'

This introduces 'entertainment' as a typical field for such escape, and emphasises the use of imagination.

> *Webster's Dictionary:* 'A temporary mental release from reality. A tendency to escape from reality, the responsibility and routine of real life, especially by unrealistic imaginative activity.'

Webster's introduces the episodic nature of such escapes, and implies that they finish up back in reality. It goes on to introduce a key concept in escapism – lack of responsibility. But while it may be a bad thing to escape from responsibility, it surely is quite understandable to want to escape from routine. In fact, as a job value, 'a predictable routine' is usually rated very low by most people, and lowest by a large margin in artists and creatives.[1] Dislike of routine is particularly felt by actors, musicians and singers who have to do long runs of a single theatre production, and who put in understudies to substitute for them so they can do more varied work. Artists rank the highest in 'imaginative activity' and rate variety as a high job value, so this is no surprise. A question raised by Webster's is: which imaginative activities are we to label 'unrealistic'? Should this include, for instance, the arts themselves?

In terms of a popular description of escapism, when asked 'what is escapism?', people in an Internet survey[2] typically responded with the fundamental idea that it is 'A mental and/or physical recreational activity or pastime which removes oneself from usual daily routines', as one respondent succinctly put it. Reality is often described as 'stressful', something needing relief from. Relief from it is considered 'temporary':

> Escapism is avoiding or shutting out reality, usually because it's too heavy to relate to without a break of some kind.

Escapism is resorting to fantasy or some pleasurable activity to avoid or blot out unpleasant reality or obligations.

Escapism is an activity that takes you away from your everyday life, from the mundane. It's connected to free choice, activities you are in control of, whereas in work you normally take orders and directions from others.

Clearly, in this life we need time out for entertainment – daydreams, dance, music, singing. Escapism is our 'cosmic coffee break' – coffee and tea being two of our basic symbols of escapism. Bad news? Let's first have a cup of tea. Tea and coffee in counselling? Let's first have a cup of tea, then talk about it.

People see escapism as a voluntary way of getting to the part of their brain that is most happy, pleased and relaxed, whether through activity or by not doing anything. The verb 'escape' implies going from somewhere we don't want to be to somewhere we do. It should be remembered that what we think we want on the ego-pleasing level is not always what we want or need on a higher spiritual level, so when we think that we are achieving escape it may be only an illusion of happiness, albeit one that serves a purpose at the time.

Equally relevant is the fact that what our consumer society persuades us to want – an elaborate commercial Christmas or a summer holiday in a crowded resort – may make us more dissatisfied and frustrated than the reality we were trying to escape from. There is an increasing symbiosis between escapism and a leisure and entertainment industry that is constantly dreaming up more varied and sophisticated consumer products and services. There are obvious economic reasons why multinationals want us to be escapists, since they package and sell the products we use. They stimulate our dissatisfaction with life through advertising, but rarely offer inner fulfilment as a 'product'. Ideally they want needs that have to be repetitively satisfied.

With a concept as ill-defined as escapism, there will clearly be knotty problems ahead in deciding on its scope, how the word is to be used and whether it is healthy or unhealthy. All the dictionary definitions above agree on one thing – the point of departure for escapism is 'reality', and a fair point of departure for our exploration of escapism can be an exploration of what it is we escape from.

What is this 'reality' we are escaping from?

Undoubtedly people escape from their own concepts of 'reality'. When questioned, they give the following definitions of 'unpleasant reality' or 'unhappy circumstances':

- A country that I cannot live in – eg East Germany (before reunification)
- Politics – frustration with parties, governments, local issues
- Work problems like pressure, bullying, long hours
- Unemployment and being made redundant
- School or university problems, study or course difficulties, exam pressures
- Financial difficulties, no money, inability to pay bills
- Problems at home such as family members, squabbles, fights
- Relationship problems – painful love affairs, pain of parting, living with an alcoholic
- Incompatibility with a partner ('I'm sick of your squeaky little voice in my head 24/7')
- Children – either the perpetual responsibility of looking after them or difficulties with them
- Interpersonal problems involving friends, colleagues, neighbours
- Life and its problems – illness, death of others
- Mundaneness and boredom, lack of stimulus, variety and change
- Solitude and loneliness
- The perception of not being in control of one's life, of losing one's grip
- Oppressive feelings of inadequacy and of doing nothing with one's life and precious time
- Failure – not achieving one's goals, frustration with thwarted plans, partner walking out
- Fear – of mugging, bullying, illness, natural disasters
- Worry – about children, loved ones, financial problems
- Pain – the afflictions of the body and the pain they cause
- Thoughts – drugs can stop analytical thinking and replace it with expressive fantasies.

We can see immediately from the above list that in some cases we escape from real-life problems – pain, caring for the sick, bullying, poverty, unpleasant arguments and fighting, social repression – and in other cases we escape from 'virtual stressors' or bad perceptions of reality: an impression of losing control, a pervasive feeling of failing to cope with life, feelings of boredom, of failure, worries, relationship dissatisfactions, even just 'thoughts'.

So we already see that for most people reality and perceptions of reality are equally valid points of departure. We might want to observe that if 'escapism' takes us into some form of 'non-reality' then perceptions of failure and boredom are 'real' enough for those that want to escape from them.

We already run into some paradoxes at this initial stage, however. First, a depressed person may escape from feelings of inadequacy by going comfort shopping and then binge eating – surely 'escapist' activities. But the point of departure for a depressed person is not a balanced perception of reality but a totally distorted one, where the sense of personal failure can be grossly exaggerated. Second, if we are to include in our definition of escapist activities those things that people commonly label and refer to as 'escapist' then we have to include all kinds of physical activities like drinking large amounts of alcohol, taking part in sports and pastimes, or going out dancing or clubbing, which are clearly 'real' in the sense that they are not imaginary. So it looks as if we need to extend our definition of reality to include perceptions of reality, and to extend our escapist activities to include real-life as well as imaginary ones.

Some people seek escape from boredom, others from stress – apparent opposites. Psychologists like Cary Cooper who specialise in stress make a distinction between over-stimulation and 'overwork stress', and under-stimulation and 'underwork stress'. Over-stimulation includes worry, stress, overwork and all those things that heat the system and tend towards the modern phenomenon of 'burnout'. Escapism here tends to be relaxing, the renewing of emotional, mental and physical forces. Maxwell Maltz, in his book *Cybernetics*, uses the word 'escapism' to mean 'time out', and includes sleep, holidays and quiet time alone as regenerative activities.[3] This is an increasingly familiar use of the word, partly because burnout is an increasingly familiar problem in overworked people, and such activities certainly assist in preventing burnout in those with unrelentingly stressed schedules. Much the same could be said for the current trend among the famous for time out in clinics offering rest and seclusion.

Over-stimulation is the bane of introverts who are 'vigilant' and more prone to overload, so they escape through reading, solitary walks and conversations with a small number of good friends. The converse, under-stimulation, includes boredom, tedium, monotony, loneliness, repetition, day-after-day drudgery and everything that inspires escapism of a colourful kind – variety, action, people, events. Under-stimulation is the bane of extraverts, who are 'stimulus hungry' by definition. So we can see that personality types are relevant both to perceptions of 'reality' and the type of escapism involved, something that will bring us on to consider the concept of 'the escapist'.

What are the popular escapist activities?

Having seen the range of things we escape from, the next step in our exploration of escapism is to look at what people generally consider to be 'escapist' activities.

Evasive activities

- Crying, sulking, walking out of arguments
- Pretending to others that nothing is bothering you
- Blocking, trying hard and consciously to suppress thoughts
- Leaving the outside world behind when returning home, as part of the need to unwind
- Superstition – not opening your post on Friday the 13th.

Active pursuits (Participant)

- Amateur dramatics, singing, dancing
- Diary writing, poetry, creative writing
- Tweaking the hi-fi system
- Re-creating the past – Civil War, cowboys, visiting old car rallies and air shows, collecting antiques
- Puzzles, crosswords and quizzes
- Playing cards
- Computer and video games
- Internet activities like newsgroups and chat rooms, particularly when donning other identities
- Sex, like SM activities, flirting, casual affairs outside marriage
- Cooking
- Shopping (mild)
- Gardening
- Fishing

- Sailing
- Exercise pursuits like hill walking
- Working out in a gym, lifting weights
- Travel, including cycling and driving for the pleasure of it
- Sport and games
- Adrenalin pursuits – bungee jumping, mountaineering, white water rafting, flying.

Passive (Non-participant)

- Daydreaming
- Zen, religion, meditation
- Listening to music
- Reading
- Films
- Television
- Being a fan – following sport or music and joining fan clubs
- Collecting, eg fine wines, CDs, dolls
- Light use of 'recreational drugs'
- Studying things like history, legends and mythology
- Following science fiction and fantasy
- Savouring fine perfumes.

More extreme

- Getting plastered, binge drinking, becoming an alcoholic
- Procrastination – constantly evading tackling the immediate or long-term problem
- Regular or excessive drug use, like smoking weed all day
- Sleeping for long periods, not getting out of bed in the morning
- Not answering the phone
- Leaving post unopened
- Passively watching 'trash' TV for hours and hours
- Binge eating
- Excessive or unrealistic gambling
- Manic house cleaning
- Compulsive shopping and collecting.

The first part of the list consists of 'evasion', pure and simple. When it comes to escapist activities, we can see at once that some are also essential activities – walking, cooking, sleeping. Others are purely recreational – reading, listening to music, going to the cinema. Some are 'halfway' activities like gardening, which mimics crop growing but is mainly done for participant and visual pleasure, or fishing where you throw the fish back. Likewise travelling for its own sake – 'driving for the fun of going somewhere', or exercise and working out with no end product except 'fitness'. Part of the pleasure in these cases may be the closeness to essential, primitive or rural activities.

Some activities are displacements of essential activities – enjoying fine wines and foods. Some are normal activities carried out excessively – binge drinking, gluttony. Writing fiction is escapism to an amateur but not to a professional. Many activities can be escapist as long as they provide an alternative to mundane activities. And while some activities are 'pointless', like watching boring TV programmes, others are in themselves interesting and constructive, like making models. The crucial thing is the context – the point at which such activities happen as an escape from some more pressing need.

Games figure in the above list also, but these will be considered later in the book because interactive games where there are winners and losers have an added dimension of simulating combat and a long evolutionary history as survival rituals. Some games are more like pastimes and lack a strong element of competition, and some, like solitaire, simply lack competitors. Such pastimes are also used as procrastination devices and so have a further escapist dimension.

When we look at the range of recreational activities that are popularly considered escapist, we can further note that most of them are 'leisure industries' promoted by heavy advertising. Such advertising emphasises the whole idea of 'getting away from it all', 'leaving your troubles behind', having a 'weekend break'. Even a food can be advertised in the same way: 'Have a break – have a Kit-Kat.' So while the dictionary definitions emphasise escape into an imaginative daydream state fuelled by romantic literature or films, this interpretation now seems to lag behind popular culture. Escapism needs to be extended to a wider range of activities – many physical – that give us a break from our daily routines. These activities are largely enjoyable, and people welcome a break, so this is a new definition that we might well call 'healthy escapism'.

When asked in an Internet survey whether they felt escapism was common in our society, many people responded that it is widespread: 'Everybody I know practises escapism,' said one. 'We are all escapists to some degree.' Others, while agreeing it was part of life, thought that it was not widespread because people were mostly consequent, practical beings. The consensus was that mild forms of escapism are probably universal, extreme forms less so. Our present society was generally considered less healthy than it used to be: 'Children don't read enough books, listen to enough decent music, play too many computer games – it's escapism on demand, not self-generated activity.'

This is a common criticism, not of escapism itself, but of the formalised escapist products provided for us. The trend towards spending many hours of each day with the various media forms – computers, games, TV, radio, video, DVD – was further considered to lead to social alienation and health problems like backache and obesity, though it was pointed out that people increasingly leading virtual lives might not have the time or inclination to wage large-scale wars in real life.

Escapism – though seen in all societies – was considered more typical of those where life is easier, especially when people can afford it. It was considered a sad paradox that societies that most needed healthy escapist activities could least afford them. In affluent societies it was considered more formalised – the soap opera, the football game. It was considered a fundamental part of industries like advertising, fashion, pop culture and magazines, which thrive on it. In its active forms it was considered a youth culture since it depends on age, health and stamina, and it was considered a child or teenage culture in the sense that children have fewer responsibilities to tie them down and ample money to spend.

But the more society itself is escapist, the more this shifts the ways we escape from it. Let us take, for instance, the example of a city dweller tied to a mobile phone, a banking job requiring eight hours a day looking at figures on a computer screen and then most evenings chilling out watching TV, with a film or two at weekends plus a few computer games. Almost the whole of his existence takes place in a virtual world, yet to him it is his 'reality'. He experiences a pressing need to work at a computer screen, get e-mails, phone people all day and receive calls, track the latest episodes of a couple of soaps and watch a film representing some violent outdoor action scene in LA. He considers this his real-life routine, his 'reality'. So what, then, is 'escapism' for this person? We could choose a few likely examples from our list above – fishing, gardening, lifting weights and hill walking. And joining a health club to lift weights could cost a week's salary or more.

But wait a minute – what is 'work' to an impoverished peasant in a contemporary Third World country? Fishing, gardening, lifting weights and hill walking. For that peasant, escapism would be taking time out to chat to friends on a mobile phone, watching TV instead of working in the fields, sending e-mails or playing games on a computer or hill walking to the local town to see a film. Too much of that and his subsistence farming would not even feed his children. So the actual application of the term 'escapism' depends heavily on the context of 'reality'. In an urban world ever more dominated by virtual media, escapism may take us back to a kind of halfway position between subsistence and culture, where subsistence is too rough but culture is too smooth, and the place escaped to is somewhere in between. This intermediate place is what geographers call the 'middle landscape'.

Halfway-house escapism – the middle landscape

The children of farmers yearn for the bright lights of the city – surely escapism from the rural imperative, in the same way as our ancestors built houses to escape from the threats of the natural environment. But by the time cities had bright lights, farmhouses had lights, radios and most of the technology found in the cities, and so had become little outposts of culture in a rural setting. Meanwhile, in direct contradiction, urban sophisticates migrate to the country, and will increasingly do so as teleworking becomes more common. On the human highway of progress the migration away from the countryside meets the migration straight back to it.

Both the escapists to and from nature have found this halfway state, this 'middle landscape'.

But while escape from nature is a primary urge, escape to nature is a secondary process in the sense that there has to be some form of more advanced culture to escape from. History documents the steady development of agriculture, industry, science, medicine and all the disciplines that have given us mastery and transcendence over the problems our race has encountered on earth and our need for knowledge of all things terrestrial and beyond. All this looks like a constructive drive towards a better life. Yet it is equally clear that many are unsatisfied with what Milan Kundera calls 'the unbearable lightness of being'. There is something in us, called by the French *nostalgie de la boue*, which yearns to sink to the bottom and seek the harshness of reality, to be, like Orwell, 'down and out in Paris and London', to survive close to nature on our wits, to be self-reliant, to be close to the elements.

Escape to nature is a very primitive idea – nearly as old as escape from nature. It is found in the epic of Gilgamesh as Enkidu regrets choosing civilization over his free life with the gazelles. It is part of stories like *The Jungle Book* and *The Call of the Wild*. What we often see in nature is a more acute sense of 'being there', a sense of the 'lucid' – a word used in dreaming when we realise we are dreaming within our dream. We want to feel the wind on our face, the rain on our body. We have some sort of yearning for the lucid, whether pleasant – the rays of the sun on a palm-fringed beach – or unpleasant, like the bitter cold of snow and ice. It may be a kind of authenticity – close to nature we realise we can't exercise control over moon, sun, weather and tides and consequently we feel a more realistic sense of our powerlessness in the grand scheme of things. When our culture becomes bland and predictable we seek the raw impact of the natural world. There is a cultural arrogance in treating the earth on a 'need to know' basis, and payback time comes when it reminds us of the power of its volcanoes, floods, hurricanes, earthquakes and freezes.

Escapism may be simply a product of the innate restlessness and desire for transformation that is typical of humankind, something that makes man move from whatever place he tires of to some other place – literally and metaphorically. Migrations and counter-migrations have followed one another across the face of history, some escaping social, political or economic conditions, some – as with the great famines – escaping the unpredictability of nature itself. The success of modern farming and industry has largely given us security and a sense of well-being, but there is still stress, envy and all the existential feelings that drive people to suicide. Seemingly we are never satisfied, or to put it another way, we do not trust our apparent increase in security.

This is seen particularly in immigrants from more suppressed regimes. Latin Americans in Norway, used to being regularly locked up by the police in their home countries, became not less but more distrustful when nothing happened and nobody arrested them. They began to suspect that the regime in Norway was worse – the threat was invisible, so they didn't even know where it was coming from. Sure enough, they managed to discover that there existed in Norway numerous *kaniner* ('rabbits') – secret agents that did not appear anywhere on ordinary census lists. Despite all the genuine help Norway gives to disadvantaged nations (it tops the foreign aid per capita list), the distrust remained. Soviet émigrés in Paris had similar problems – confused by the freedom to do anything and go anywhere, the more paranoid ended up not going out at all and getting friends to buy their shopping.

Maybe it is the extreme artificiality of our society of plenty that people distrust – the supermarkets with their mounds of food in convenient packages, banishing the slaughter of the abattoirs and the earth used to grow the vegetables to no more than a distant fiction. Maybe somewhere inside us we rebel against the unnatural, the way primitive peoples, when they first travelled in aeroplanes, sat on the runways when they arrived to wait for their souls to catch up with their bodies. Maybe it is the omnipresence of culture – hardly any habitable land seems untouched by the artefacts of modern living and the greed of developers, from city suburb to rainforest.

Farms, garden cities, national parks, are all examples of middle landscapes. The escalation in popularity of 'makeover' shows including sophisticated gardens testifies to the continued popularity of these halfway stages of culture. Such middle landscapes are unstable, because on the one hand they naturally tend to revert to wilderness and on the other they are subject to man's urge to cultivate, build and make over. A symbolic example of the middle landscape is the theme park:

> Leisure worlds are becoming increasingly artificial. While the natural world becomes increasingly polluted, resources are running out, ecological systems are disappearing, world capitalism seems to be grinding and stumbling to a halt and there is poverty and disease caused by Western greed, leisure pursuits increasingly appeal to individual selfishness and a fantasy geography. EPCOT in Disneyland with its reproductions of pyramids and exploding volcanoes and the reproductions of ancient Egypt in Las Vegas illustrate the differences between an increasingly fantasy-led tourism and the real experience of travelling the world.
>
> Why bother to travel out of your own yard and experience other cultures when you can have the plastic, sanitised version that exploits the cultural inheritance of developing nations without having to actually give them any money or communicate with them in any way? Similarly the Caribbean is becoming full of all-inclusive holiday complexes, usually owned by white people, enabling tourists to stay in the complex without ever mixing with black residents, who seldom benefit financially from them. In Miyazaki, Japan, there is a place called Ocean Dome. It is a domed environment containing a beach, artificial weather and waves. Outside hurricanes may rage, but inside the sun is always shining; there are no sharks or jellyfish; Japanese dancers simulate the Caribbean Carnival experience.[4]

Jean Baudrillard saw the post-industrial revolution as producing a mass migration from factory to fantasy. Disneyland he sees as a potent symbol for America itself:

> the perfect model of all the entangled orders of simulation... Disneyland is there to conceal the fact that it is the 'real' country, all of 'real' America which is Disneyland... Disneyland is *presented* as imaginary in order to make us believe that the rest is real, when in fact all of Los Angeles and the America surrounding it are no longer real, but of the order of hypertext and simulation.[5]

And if we look ahead, the fictionalisation of geography in simulated computer worlds represents a further withdrawal from the material world and its ecological and economic crises. 'Reality shudders and collapses and fragments into the vortex of many different alternative realities: some cybernetic, some designer, some residual, some an outmoded stock of the vanishing real.'[6]

Our hierarchy of needs

Mirroring our social evolution from nature to culture is our personal structure of needs, from basic survival to advanced concepts like aesthetics and self-actualisation. This evolution was formulated by Abraham Maslow into a 'hierarchy of needs'.

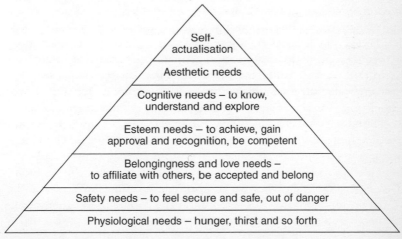

Figure 3.1 Abraham Maslow's 'hierarchy of needs'

The human race would not have survived if reality needs were not attended to adequately, and this pyramid of needs represents a hierarchy in which the most important factors in human life are at the bottom, rising towards those more optional things that make life rich and fulfilling rather than a simple case of survival. 'Lower functions' form the bottom foundation of Maslow's pyramid – basic physiological needs like food, drink and sleep. These needs correspond to the oldest parts of the human brain, the first in evolutionary terms. The levels of need proceed upwards to higher functions like 'self-actualisation' – the most recent in brain development, relating to several newer aspects of human culture like entertainment, creativity, the arts and self-expression. In terms of escapism we need to look at the top part of the pyramid – escaping from basic physical needs like food and drink is not possible for more than a very short time.

Maslow's idea is that the more basic needs will predominate – once we have eaten we can think about constructing a place of safety. Once in a place of safety we can group with others. Once in a group we strive to assert ourselves and be recognised and praised and so on. When basic needs are met we can allow ourselves time for art and culture and eventually 'self-actualisation' – a tendency towards self-improvement, growth, full use of potential and positive change. Maslow called feelings of mastery, happiness, fulfilment and closeness to beauty and truth 'peak experiences', and found them in the lives of 'self-actualisers' like Einstein, Lincoln and Jefferson. His description of the self-actualiser is in fact extremely close to that of the creative personality – creative, problem solving, spontaneous, flexible, tolerant, free-thinking, objectively critical and able to form deep relationships with a chosen few people.

Maslow's model does rightly suggest that the reality we escape from is partly a struggle to satisfy basic needs and the stress that causes. But there are a few problems with it. First, if self-actualisers are fundamentally creatives, then this is not a model for the whole population. In fact, material, realistic people would regard aesthetic needs and self-actualisation as fanciful luxuries, and art itself as escapist. Second, some of the activities people enjoy – like mountain climbing – are opposed to physiological needs like survival because they represent a high physical risk. Third, needs are not the same as pleasure motivations. We need to be healthy but we are motivated to smoke. We need to be fit but we are motivated to overeat and drink. Some of our motivations are perverse, a situation made worse by a consumer society that makes products available that can have negative effects on our well-being.

Escapism, transcendence and escape

Though Maslow constructed his pyramid in 1967 at the height of the LSD and psychedelic movement, and to give him credit he does advocate 'experiencing life as a child with full absorption', he does not include the specifically sixties idea of 'dropping out and tuning in' in his model. Maybe we actually need escapism purely as a relief from reality, something not accounted for in the worthy aspects of Maslow's view and his assertion that self-actualisation is achieved through responsibility, honesty and hard work. What Maslow is really after is the goal of transcendence, the goal of so much of the American self-help movement.

Transcendence is very different from escapism – a way, not of escaping from life's troubles, but of rising above them. It is often a mystical dimension and is closely linked to many religions, cults and sects. It is associated with maturity, though as Berlioz said, 'Time is a great teacher but unfortunately it kills all of its pupils'.[7]

Transcendence has a philosophical base in the works of Nietzsche and others. It can also be a way of politically and socially dominating – Hitler, Genghis Khan. It is a specifically goal-oriented activity, directed towards results and success.

But if you can't transcend a situation, there are times where escape, not escapism, is necessary. The two poles may – primitively speaking – be considered as fight or flight. While fight may require courage and persistence, flight may require more ingenuity and creativity – how to escape, where to seek refuge. If we took a group of prisoners in a prisoner of war camp, we could postulate that escape would be to tunnel under the walls, transcendence would be to try to kill the guards and escapism would be to swallow one's honour, lose sight of the purpose of the war and make matchstick models.

If we place the emphasis on escape, then the tedium and negative quality of the state that is being escaped from seems to provide a good justification. Many people escaped from the former Soviet bloc countries to what they considered was a better life. To them this was an act of courage, and the realities of the escape were often planned and executed very carefully. But escapism is not a synonym for escape – not all escape is escapism. Escapism as a psychological trait or condition is not very conducive to social change and only cements the conditions that caused it in the first place. If no one acts or does something the status quo remains unchanged – if people are not part of the solution they are part of the problem. Escapism is anathema to the revolutionary and even the peaceful protester, since it is seen as negating the need for social change; burying one's head in the sand at the sight of danger. But in another sense – particularly where physical escape is impossible – it can be a sign of social and intellectual awareness, as one political refugee pointed out: 'Escapism is on one level a symptom of dissociation from society. It may say more about the society than the individual. It is not the refuge of the stupid. The higher the perception of the individual the more attractive escapism may appear and the greater the awareness that requires some form of escapism.' Dissociation in this sense can be deeply thought out, as with the surrealists and existentialists. Escape in art and philosophy can be seen in another way as coping with reality, understanding reality better by divergent or lateral thinking, 'thinking outside the box', free thinking, or understanding further levels of meaning not present in society. All the Soviet dissident artists were seen as escapists by the regime, though we would see them as highly motivated artistic experimenters guided by a vision of truth and a refusal to compromise.

Is escapism evasion of moral duty, or of pressing needs?

Transcendence takes us along the path towards the Protestant work ethic, or in a more extreme form, Kant's sense of 'moral duty'. The further we go down this path, the more venomous becomes the criticism of idleness, sloth, frivolity, self-indulgence, hedonism and imaginative pursuits. Kant saw life as a battle between pleasure and duty, to the point where if the moral law was pleasurable, then there was something wrong with it. If you enjoy playing golf, then in Kant's view it would be more dutiful not to do so.

Can we see escapism as a dereliction of duty? Escapism is essentially an ego-driven or hedonistic activity, and as such can be quite irresponsible, since responsibility is not its goal. It can ignore reality, others' feelings and needs, and personal duties and obligations. It can rank personal pleasure above practical issues that need attention, thereby ignoring one's conscience or inner censor. It is probably at the opposite pole to willpower. It would be called by psychotherapist Eric Berne an 'unconstructive use of time' – a pastime, ritual or game that replaces more congruent activity.[8]

But there are some flaws in this argument. For a start, why can't duty be pleasurable? What we want to do can easily be what we ought to do. Aristotle pointed out that a dutiful man might actually like to do dutiful things. A truly generous man, likewise, is one who likes being generous, as opposed to a falsely generous man who forces himself to give out of 'duty' and regrets giving afterwards, or simply gives as a strategy for obtaining a peerage or other reward. There is no harm in pleasure in itself, and surely humans have neither the concentration nor the physical stamina for unrelenting work and moral duty.

Duty, in any case, is a subject that is very rarely raised by ordinary people. It is usually only raised when things go wrong. Retrospectively, we can say 'We should have put more money into the railway track' after a train crashes, but there is less of a moral imperative before a catastrophe. The time when moralists come out of the woodwork is when things have already gone wrong.

The other flaw in the argument is that in practice the human condition is not a daily battle between choices A and B – what we 'want to do' and what we 'ought to do'. Human behaviour, in general, is rarely made from 'choices' because humans rarely deliberate – as was seen by the predominance of Level 2 unconscious thought over Level 1 conscious thought in Chapter 1. Conscious choice usually only happens when things go wrong or where there is a dilemma. Furthermore, a choice can be both rational and irrational. Is a choice conscious or partly conscious? An obvious 'I should be doing this but I'm not going to', or a sort of nagging doubt – 'Somehow I don't feel good about this'?

Can there be such a thing as an 'unconscious choice'? In many people there may be an habitual 'unconscious' course of action, which is occasionally overridden by a conscious choice. If a 'generous man' is normally one who gives generously, there may be occasions where he will refuse to give because he does not support the cause. Choice may be exercised in some cases and not in others. There may be an 'habitual' course of action, and a 'chosen' course of action. With the exception of deliberate procrastination and escapism in times of war or great social upheaval, escapism is rarely a choice or an action arising from a 'moral' dilemma.

On the other hand, escapism can easily be defined as activities that replace a greater or more urgent need, the idea of 'fiddling while Rome burns'. It can be seen specifically as a refusal to recognise a reality need, a kind of denial, as when Chamberlain tried to bargain for peace instead of preparing for war. Into this category would go destroying the ozone layer through an inability to redesign our transport system so as to replace gas-guzzling cars with more sensible options. We lose sight of a greater need, just as if we were sharpening pencils in the cosmic scale of things.

Can useful or goal-centred activities be called escapism?

One dilemma besets escapism – can we define as 'escapism' activities that are either useful or have clear goals? I think we can, in the context of escaping from greater needs that cause more perceived stress. Making gas-guzzling cars, for instance, is a perfectly goal-centred and useful occupation, however unfortunate its consequences. It can be more stressful not to use the car. Another instance of useful activities as evasion occurs in the case of artists like the Norwegian writer Ibsen. Like many writers, Ibsen used to put off writing when he found it difficult – a kind of procrastination familiar to many of us and which we might call escapism. He would fill in the time he 'ought' to have been writing with activities like sharpening pencils. Painters do the same – when they are not caught by the muse they prepare canvasses, make frames and sweep out their studios. Such activities, while useful in themselves, can be escapist in the context of a 'more pressing need' which is more stressful to carry out.

Some may consider it ironic that the arts can be 'purposeful', while making frames and sweeping out the workplace can be 'escapist'. But it is surely reasonable to assume that the arts play a central role in our culture and our self-definition as human beings, and in the form of cave paintings were there at the beginning of man's culture. We can be misled into superficial definitions of escapism when we fail to examine the motivation behind them.

What motivates escapism?

What motivates escapism? It is not, like spin, the urge to deceive (though its practice may involve degrees of self-deception). The most obvious reason for escapism is an increase in personal perceived pleasure. This can be restated as a decrease in displeasure, however temporary this may be. Escape from a state that is unpleasant to a state that is more pleasant – boredom to interest, for instance – carries an increase in satisfaction. If we decide to read a book we carry on until we have had enough, then we are likely to switch to another activity that increases pleasure – having a coffee, going for a walk. Displeasure should trigger a return to reality or a change to another escapist pursuit. But while the pleasurable state continues it generates a better internal feeling, whether through strenuous pursuits like sport or quiet ones like reading.

Since escapism can occur in affluent societies and in fundamentally normal people, it can be exchanging what is already a fairly content state for one offering more intense pleasure. This would certainly be the case with designer or recreational drugs and 'readymade' escapist activities like TV. The availability of such escapist activities would clearly increase the possibility and frequency of escapism.

At some level escapism must offer the psyche some form of fulfilment, satisfaction or other psychological need, either of the conscious or of the subconscious. It may in fact be an acceptable form of expressing suppressed elements of the unconscious, as in those who want to temporarily relieve their fears by acting them out in their imagination through violent or horror movies, the 'catharsis' of Greek tragedy.

Perverse motivations

One problem of defining escapism is defining what people want. Our assumptions of what individuals 'should' want can be frustrated by the apparently illogical behaviour of much of the population. Do all people necessarily want to live a long life? What about rock and rollers who commit suicide or die young? Do all people want to have children to survive them? Certainly not. What about tanning? Doctors say, 'Don't lie in the sun', but people continue to do so. Maybe the reasons for their choices are not health ones – it is more important to them to look good and have easier sexual conquests. People's activities may be a choice, reasoned or unreasoned, wise or unwise. Tanning may be escapist to a doctor, purposeful to a lounge lizard.

As human knowledge changes, activities that appeared purposeful to more primitive civilizations – blood letting, casting out demons – would seem extravagant time wasting to us. In the case of global warming how do we know what is purposeful and what is illusory? Is it entirely man-made or mostly the result of an unavoidable climate shift? Do we in fact have a choice regarding the environment – are the factors involved in climate change accessible to human intervention? How 'purposeful' is the activity of Greenpeace and ecology movements if it is already too late for choice? Maybe the real risk lies elsewhere – it is possible that, after all, the end of the world will come in some huge explosion, some big bang to end civilization, because of man's aggression and selfishness. France and England have been neighbours for hundreds of years, during which time they have been fighting regularly – seemingly man is the only animal bent on self-destruction. How will history look back on the human race – which activities will it see as purposeful and which as a senseless waste of time, an escapism from the real issue?

In retrospect it is so much easier to define activities as 'escapist' than it ever is in the moment of action. The soap opera addict glued to the television by the urgency of following the labyrinthine plots may not see that she is neglecting daily exercise and getting obese until she weighs herself. The football fan who goes to matches regularly with all his mates may not see that he is neglecting his family until his wife leaves him. He may need to see the consequences before he can see that there was any escapism involved, and even then he may choose to lay the blame elsewhere. The question of awareness of consequences is critical to unhealthy escapism.

Towards a redefinition of escapism

Summing up the way that the term 'escapism' seems to be used in modern culture, we would therefore come to a redefinition that would go along the following lines:

> Escapism is the switch from a more pressing need, or a less pleasurable or more stressful situation, self-perception or feeling, to a more pleasurable activity – real or imagined, purposeful or not – which is often recreational and increasingly offered by the mass media and the leisure industry. 'Healthy' escapism may have no negative consequences, while 'unhealthy' escapism, such as procrastination, the addictions and neurotic or irresponsible behaviour may have negative consequences for both the individual and the wider social circle. Sometimes the distinction between one and the other can only be seen in retrospect.

FOUR

Healthy and Unhealthy Escapism

Yi-Fu Tuan, author of *Escapism*, sums up the generally held attitude to escapism:

> Escapism, I will argue, is human – and inescapable. There is nothing wrong with escape as such. What makes it suspect is the goal, which can be quite unreal. And what is wrong with the unreal – with wild fantasy? Nothing, I would say, so long as it remains a passing mood, a temporary escape, a brief mental experiment with possibility. However, fantasy that is shut off too long from external reality risks degenerating into a self-deluding hell – a hell that can nevertheless have an insidious appeal.[1]

Let us take the question 'What is wrong with the unreal, with wild fantasy?' first. This is an argument for experimentation, for creative exploration, or even finding alternate ways of thinking or doing things quite by accident. It is divergent or lateral thinking, or even fantastical thinking. But is it always escapist? Logical convergent thinkers would see taking LSD, for instance, as 'escapist', a way of not dealing with reality. But the Beatles' experiments with LSD formed part of their art, and are reflected in their words and music. Was Freud's use of cocaine escapist, given that he took it experimentally and documented the results? This is a grey area.

The determinant may be, as Tuan says, the extent to which we are shut off from reality. Munch's painting 'The Scream' was created in a strange state, but he was sane enough to carry on painting. Escapism can be the expression of human imagination trying to burst the 'mind-forged manacles' of Cartesian reality, and without some escapist tendencies no creative thought would be possible – civilization and art could not advance. On the other hand, too much escapism – total denial of external reality – is clinical insanity. This is the sliding scale between genius and madness. Good escapism is the expression of the creative artist. Bad escapism is when you stop 'taking care of business' and inhabit a personal fantasy world more or less full time. Artists who go mad at the end of their lives rarely produce much.

'Flight from reality'

Escapism is very close to what psychology calls 'flight from reality' or 'retreat from reality'. This is defined as the use of fantasy and imaginary satisfactions to avoid dealing with a harsh reality, and may be manifested in any number of ways including excessive daydreaming, inappropriate rationalisation or resorting to drugs or alcohol. It is interesting that 'rationalisation' is considered in psychological theory as an escape from 'reality'.

In extreme cases flight from reality is expressed as 'fugue', from the Latin for 'flight', a psychiatric disability which typically manifests itself as a sudden and unexpected leaving of home, where the person assumes a new identity elsewhere. During the fugue there is no recollection of the earlier life and after recovery amnesia for events during it. It is often called dissociative psychogenic fugue to distinguish it from other syndromes that have similar symptoms but are caused by known organic dysfunctions, and has been the subject of several film treatments.

The degree of flight from reality depends on how much escapism is indulged in and how serious is the form of flight. We could add that it depends whether we have a grip on reality in the first place and can recognise what is real and what is fantasy, so that we can both escape and return safely. The danger occurs when people confuse what is real with what isn't and can't get back to reality – the problem with psychotic thinking.

Escape from responsibility

Sometimes we need release from the drudgery of everyday life, particularly if work is less than interesting. Batteries must be recharged. However, if real problems, for example of a financial or emotional kind that must be solved are put aside in favour of escapist activity, then we start on another sliding scale into neglect and social difficulties. Escapism may harm the escapist or those who are close to the escapist and depend on him or her. So another definition of unhealthy escapism – escapism gone too far – is the effects it has on the essential fabric of living – the individual in the context of family, friends and social commitments.

Sometimes it is hard to differentiate between escape and escapism in the social context. Is a teenager escaping from an abusive or violent home to live rough on the streets 'being escapist' or escaping to a marginally better reality? What if the home escaped from is not violent or abusive but mentally repressive, 'something inside that was always denied' as in the lyrics to the Beatles' song, 'She's Leaving Home'? Escape from a situation that is perceived as unpleasant may be as valid as escape from physical abuse. We don't know enough about the 'man from the motor trade' in the Beatles' song to know whether the alternative turned out better or worse. At the time there is frequently no way of knowing this.

How do we look on immigration? It is difficult to consider escaping from a country that does not offer its own citizens the basic freedoms a bad move, and it has been undertaken by thousands upon thousands throughout history who sought better lives in other lands – something that continues to this day. It does not seem to count as escapism and it is not usually temporary – such immigrants rarely go back to their country of origin, since the expected benefits in their new homeland were very clear. Neither is the place escaped to always a bed of roses – starting again in a new country is a long-term uphill journey containing both good and bad, and all the normal reality factors like earning a living and finding food and shelter. It is, however, possible that some depart for foreign lands to fulfil escapist fantasies, an illusion that elsewhere the streets may be paved with gold, only to find that fantasy is not reality.

Positive uses of escapism

As escapism appears to be a natural mechanism, the mind must have a need for it. We could compare it with conscious dreaming. We may need it, also, at particularly difficult times in our life, such as when family members are angry, ill, depressed or chaotic, or when people are in hospital or in prison. In traumatic periods of their life, children may turn to 'constructive' pursuits like making models. They may also turn to destructive pursuits like sniffing glue or joyriding. Later they may well organise their escapist activities with growing self-awareness, joining like-minded people and planning ahead.

People who perceive their life as troubled or who are simply 'sad by nature' or chronic worriers may gain solace from escapism that cheers the mood – laughter, comedy, jokes. Laughter is considered therapeutic in many recent studies (*Reader's Digest* called it 'The Best Medicine' for years and put jokes and anecdotes in every issue), and this includes lessening risks of common diseases and increasing healthy outcome during convalescence.

Escapism may be useful in avoiding acting out, as literally when people in angry states leave through slammed doors or kick the furniture. They are not dealing with a situation in real life because they already perceive that doing so may be dangerous.

Escapist activities in and around the home itself, as in 'changing rooms', DIY, feng shui, gardening and cultivating houseplants increase the feeling of safety and satisfaction in one's physical space, with consequent benefits on one's inner mental space. Such a safe place is important as a bastion against external stresses and fears, as in the expression 'an Englishman's home is his castle'.

Hobbies and escapist activities may also have a vital role in defining the significance of the individual, as Anthony Storr points out:

> An inner world of phantasy [sic] exists in every human being and finds expression in an infinite variety of different ways. The man who goes racing or who eagerly watches football on television is giving rein to phantasy, although he may not be creating or producing anything. Hobbies and interests are often aspects of a human being which most clearly define his individuality, and make him the person he is. Sometimes such interests as the playing of team games are only practicable by interacting with other people, but in Britain every weekend sees the banks of rivers and canals lined with fishermen who keep a discreet distance from one another and seldom converse. The same applies to gardening and to many other interests, whether obviously creative or not, which occupy the leisure of those whose basic physical needs have been provided for. Everyone needs interests as well as interpersonal relationships; and interests, as well as relationships, play an important part in defining individual identity and in giving meaning to a person's life.[2]

Escapism in psychology and psychoanalysis

Anthony Storr is very much an enlightened humanist in the world of psychoanalysis, and stands against Freud's somewhat puritanical vision that proper, mature adaptation to the world was governed by deliberate thought and rational planning:

> Freud would not have countenanced that an inner world of phantasy is part of man's biological endowment, and that it is the inevitable discrepancy between the inner world and the outer world that compels men to become inventive and imaginative. Phantasy, in Freud's conceptual scheme, was linked with hallucination, with dreaming and with play. He considered that all these forms of mental activity were escapist: ways of evading reality which were dependent upon the infantile form of mental functioning which he designated 'primary process', and which were governed by the pleasure principle rather than the reality principle.[3]

Storr is firmly of the opinion that creativity is positive and adaptive, and that

> we should not merely strive to replace phantasy with reason as Freud would have us do. Instead we should use our capacity for phantasy to build bridges between the inner world of imagination and the external world. A race of men who lacked the capacity for phantasy would not only be unable to imagine a better life in material terms, but would also lack religion, music, literature and painting. As Goya wrote – Phantasy abandoned by reason produces impossible monsters; united with her she is the mother of the arts and the origin of their marvels.[4]

Freud was a lover of culture of all descriptions, and it is ironic that his legacy should have devalued art as mere sublimation. The sublimation view is stated by psychoanalyst Ernest Jones: 'When one considers the material used in the five arts – paint, clay, stone, words and sounds – any psychologist must conclude that the passionate interest in bringing an orderliness out of chaos must signify at the same time an extraordinary sublimation of the most primitive infantile enjoyments and the most extreme denial of them.'[5] Creative clients who turn to psychoanalysis can in theory be advised that their art is the problem and that the therapeutic solution is to give it up. This might take the form of avoiding 'sublimation' of personal difficulties into art or creative writing, and solving them in real life. This can not only appear to devalue or question the reason for creative work that can be a personal or economic necessity, but in addition the client may not thank the counsellor for 'feeling better' whilst remaining unable to write or compose, or in the case of a comedian for being better adjusted but much less funny. Much better is the counsellor who accepts the need for fantasy and creative work and concentrates on improving its quality and flow.

Freud himself did value the work of the artist more than Ernest Jones allows. His fundamental position was, indeed, that

> Art brings about a reconciliation between the two principles of Mental functioning – Pleasure and Reality – in a peculiar way. An artist is originally a man who turns away from reality because he cannot come to terms with the renunciation of instinctual satisfaction which it at first demands, and who allows his erotic and ambitious wishes full play in the life of phantasy.[6]

He did, however, go further than this when considering the special qualities of the creative artist's vision:

> He finds a way back to reality, however, from this world of phantasy by making use of special gifts to mould his phantasies into truths of a new kind, which are valued by man as precious reflections of reality. Thus, in a certain fashion, he actually becomes the hero, the king, the creator, or the favourite he desired to be, without following the long roundabout path of making alterations in the external world. But he can only achieve this because other men feel the same dissatisfaction as he does with the renunciation demanded by reality, and because that dissatisfaction, which results from the replacement of the pleasure principle by the reality principle is itself a part of reality.[7]

Baudelaire said a similar thing – *hypocrite lecteur, mon semblable, mon frère* (hypocrite reader, my likeness, my brother), suggesting that the success of the artist lies in clarifying and edifying the very problems we all face with reality.

Escapism and pastimes – how we structure time

Eric Berne was the founder of Transactional Analysis (TA), and a prolific writer on what he calls 'pastimes' and 'games'. Both pastimes and games come within his definition of how humans 'structure time', which he sees as the same as passing time. In *What Do You Say After You Say Hello?*[8] Berne defines ways of structuring time as:

- Withdrawal – no active communication
- Rituals – stylised and predictable interchanges conditioned by social custom
- Activities – as the name suggests
- Work – reality 'adult' activities defined by the material to be worked on
- Pastimes – social activities, partly free, partly programmed
- Games – interactions based on a 'con', a 'switch' and a 'payoff'.

A pastime is an individual or social event, the essence of which is some experience or other that is interesting in itself and has a further dimension of forming the nucleus for social discussions and comparisons. Phrases Berne suggests as typical are 'I had a better time than you', 'me too', 'with me it's different', 'what are we going to do with delinquent teenagers?'. With well-adjusted people a pastime can be enjoyable for its own sake and afford genuine opportunities for developing intimacy. With neurotic people Berne sees a pastime as something nearer to escapism: 'Existentially a pastime is a way of warding off guilt, despair or intimacy, a device provided by nature or culture to ease the quiet desperation. At best it is something enjoyed for its own sake. Each participant uses it in an opportunistic way to get whatever primary and secondary gains he can from it.'

Berne is thus closer to Maslow and the general postwar American therapy movements in distinguishing between positive and negative use of one's time. Where Maslow is more concerned with achievement and self-actualisation, Berne is concerned with what he calls 'intimacy' – a state that is genuine and non-manipulative. Anthony Storr would describe this hunger for social contact as unnecessary to human happiness, and a myth disproved by many happy introverts like Edward Gibbon, author of *The Decline and Fall of the Roman Empire*, who do not so much 'withdraw' as happily engage in solitary activities. Berne is certainly extremely alert to dissimulation, cons and manipulation and his theories cater for all sorts of games in his typical therapy groups. Storr was more an individual therapist and more concerned with individual fulfilment than social games, besides being more naturally introverted by nature.

Escapism as denial

Escapism as denial can range from the relatively benign to the extraordinarily dangerous. A man denying that he has cancer may escape into a world of denial from where he is unable to take effective action against the disease. A world of men acting in denial can propagate tremendous harm. Environmental issues stand as the single most glaring example of the consequences of the denial-based variant of escapism – the truism that 'For evil to thrive requires only that good men do nothing'.

Denial can be the scourge of the egotist, as Canadian theorist Nick Fulford points out:

> Primarily or on a most fundamental level, I see escapism as an attempt to isolate and sustain particular beliefs about oneself and the world. Building layers of psychic plaque to isolate and sustain those beliefs is escapism, continuing to build layers of illusion upon the already deluded part of self that we call the ego. The ego consists of the layers of beliefs and tales that form the identity, the self as a cohesive form. Strongly defined egos often are not very adaptive, and may hold to their world view (or aspects thereof) irrespective of all but the most traumatic of experiences. Depending upon your point of view this can be seen as saintly faith and tenacity or foolhardy lunacy.[9]

The antidote to escapism, for Fulford, is powerful experiences that rip away the veils of the ego:

> In the tarot deck, this archetypical experience is shown in the card, 'The Tower'. The tower is shattered by a lightning bolt, causing destruction and freeing the kernel of self from its isolation. The lightning bolt can take many forms, but the effect is always to free the essential self from the ego's layers and filters. Free of the tower, a person is able to engage the world more honestly and directly. He or she is able to see things with fewer filters, and is able to act with

greater effect, and fewer delusions. Take people and place them in situations where reliance on the ego fails, and they may be broken out of their self-prison. Outward-bound experiences, for example, can challenge young men and women and bring about direct engagement in physically challenging and hazardous conditions. There is no room for ego ruminations in situations that demand direct action. The 'essential' person has resources of courage to draw upon when the ego, the limited or false self, runs in terror. Situations that bring about ego failure provide opportunities to stretch beyond what one believes oneself capable of doing and to accomplish that which seems incredible.[10]

Unhealthy escapism – the addictions

Escapism becomes unhealthy if the escapist activity involves vices or an avoidance of responsibilities, which consequently endangers or compromises the lives of people. When carried too far it is dangerous and can be a symptom of deeper problems in the personality. If milder forms of escape are therapeutic, then the danger can be one of degree – too much, too often, too intensely and for too long. Since there is an obvert element of fantasy in overdoing – which is part and parcel of being who you are not – it is possible to forget the boundary of practical reality.

Too much evasion of reality can lead to too much introspection, isolation and difficulties in social integration. Too many 'virtual reality pursuits' can cause difficulties in adapting to reality. Too much procrastination can result in only a shadow existence rather than a fulfilled life, as opportunities to learn and profit from experience are passed over. Not only are there psychological consequences of over-indulgence, there are many medical consequences, some obvious like obesity through over-eating, some not so obvious such as obesity through replacing active pursuits with 'couch potato' ones like watching TV. The 'glass teat' is cited as the number one cause of obesity in contemporary society, and to some it is the number one problem drug.

The most obvious category of unhealthy activities is the addictions. This includes problems like eating disorders. But while binge eating has escapist qualities, anorexia and bulimia are serious health issues rather than escapist activities. Some of the other addictions, however, are obvious examples of escapism taken too far.

Drugs

'In case you haven't heard yet, drugs have ravaged whole segments of the population. The Black community may not ever recover. Not to mention all whose lives have been snuffed out, who are going through the torture of addiction, and those who have lost everything to drugs.'[11]

The above is a typical argument. Drugs have long been regarded as one of the purest forms of escapism. Instead of confronting the world in as realistic a way as possible, perception is changed so as to reveal a different kind of world – more fun, faster, slower, more relaxing, more exciting – whatever the preference is.

This is a popular but simplistic view. All drugs – medical or so-called 'recreational' – have some effect, as any doctor will point out: 'Show me a drug with no side effects and I will show you a drug that does nothing.' A variety of substances not classified as drugs have strong effects – this applies to foodstuffs and substances like glue. Commonly ingested drinks like tea and coffee have effects. So what is a 'drug'? Is it an illegal substance? Drugs were only made illegal in the 20th century. Before that they were widely used, and even today there are moves to go back to decriminalisation. In the 19th century ether and chloroform were widely used as the 'ladies' remedy' alongside their medical uses. Cocaine was found in a variety of drinks, including Coca Cola, until its use was banned around 1905. In fact it was at one time considered a tonic, and preferable to alcohol, the 'demon drink'.

And how would we classify the experimental use of drugs by figures such as Freud (cocaine) and Sir Humphry Davy (nitrous oxide), who believed that they had to try drugs themselves to verify their effects? Though demonised for his 'addiction' to the euphoria induced by cocaine, Freud did a great deal of accurate experimental work on cocaine, which still stands up to this day. French psychiatrist Moreau de Tours used hashish – originally brought back from Egypt by Napoleon's armies – to investigate states of abnormal thought, and recommended that other psychiatrists should do the same to understand the thought patterns of their patients (a concept akin to Freud's suggestion that all analysts should undergo analysis). And as new drugs like LSD emerged in the 20th century they were again used experimentally and their effects documented in literature, music, art and film. Again, nothing new – when Moreau de Tours popularised the use of hashish and it was taken up by Balzac, Dumas, Gautier and Baudelaire, it emerged in poetry, treatises and even in the novel *The Count of Monte Cristo*.[12]

The problem with drugs is the perennial one of 'how much is too much?'. In a technological age where we routinely drive cars and use complex equipment, we need full control over our perceptions, reaction times and motor functions. The consequences of having less than full control have been repeatedly proven to be dangerous and often fatal. That in itself is enough to ban the use of drugs. Public attitudes to drugs are also influenced by social factors such as the perception that the drugs milieu is an unsavoury underground full of shootings and money laundering, something intolerable in law-abiding, residential communities. Overuse of drugs leads to health problems and lack of productivity – Coleridge, who was a prolific experimenter with drugs, gradually abandoned or failed to finish a lot of his work.

So how, then, do we class mild drug use in fully functioning people with productive careers? How do we deal with the argument that some people may prefer a different perception of the world? How do we deal with artists who claim it improves their work, such as a number of jazz musicians? This is fundamentally the same argument as that for the absence of censorship in art. But arguments for the useful effects of drugs in art may be as overrated as the hypothesis that 'being mad improves creativity' – an argument that hardly appeals to the many artists of all kinds who have benefited from periods of therapy that left them feeling better and with improved creative flow. Rachmaninov, for instance, wrote his famous second piano concerto after treatment to counter a creative block.

Though some artists, like painter Edvard Munch, stated that a disturbed state of mind had a positive effect on their work, the majority of artists rate sanity and well-being as highly as the rest of us. Is it likely, after all, that the use of mind-altering drugs makes us a better survival machine than evolution has done to date? Probably not, but artists have every right to say that the use of drugs makes their work original – as was the case with some very different kinds of expression that derived from the use of LSD in the sixties. This ends up as something of an elitist argument – if you produce something of worth drugs are a means to an end; if you produce nothing they are purely an escapist release. This argument of 'worth by results' has a ring of great familiarity for artists. As one well-known rock musician put it, 'The public judge a musician only by the money he earns. If he's rich he's a great man, if he's poor he's a time-wasting parasite who should get a real job.'[13]

Do drugs tell us more about the society than the individual? Nick Fulford puts it this way:

In an adolescent society, which promotes escapism in its many forms and discourages people from engaging life in its fullness – out of the thought that we may just grow up enough not to be continuously led around by marketers, politicians and the televangelists – it is not surprising that drugs are generally abused. So long as people act as if they are going to live forever, like Peter Pan, and try to avoid those aspects of life which are painful and have a great deal to teach us about ourselves and others, then society as a whole is not ready to use drugs as anything other than an extension of escapism. In the context of an adolescent society, it is not surprising to see the abuse of drugs. A potentially useful tool or sacrament is defiled by those who are using it for no other reason than to get high.[14]

Alcohol

We are all familiar with the 'jester throng at twilight' – groups of people having all the fun in the world, joyfully losing their shyness and inhibitions as they indulge in pure silliness, noise and high spirits. In reasonable quantities such fun behaviour can be positive, bringing together people who might ordinarily be more reserved. But how do we define occasional binges? In Britain 40 per cent of young men binge drink once a week. The object is pure and simple – to get drunk. The 'fun' is often in being deliberately socially irresponsible – displaying hooligan, provocative or just plain silly behaviour. It is an increasingly ritualised evening out, which extends to clubbing, football and trips abroad. A perfectly excusable night out or a step on the slippery slope to addiction? For some it is the former, for others the latter.

Alcoholism is one step too far, as those who have suffered its effects or had to live with alcoholics know only too well. Alcoholism in its more serious forms is a step beyond 'freedom from care' or the chance to 'drown one's sorrows'. The more one drinks the less one copes, so it becomes a vicious circle – the more one escapes responsibility the harder it is to be responsible. Ultimately one ends up being irresponsible – averting blame elsewhere, living in endless denial, leaving tasks undone, ignoring one's family, spending one's resources. 'Alcohol does not solve anything' is an oft-used statement by those 'in recovery' from drinking. One of the main tasks in the recovery process is taking the responsibility to apologise to those whose lives have been affected by the alcoholic's drinking. If anything needs to be solved it is the primary problem of a fragile ego, a life of stress and disappointment and a tendency to escape.

As with drugs, there are socio-economic influences at play in terms of the kind of alcohol available and its cost – London in the days of cheap gin and Moscow in the days of cheap vodka were places where drunkenness and associated health and family problems were widespread. Many countries experimented with prohibition, notably the USA, but also Scandinavia and parts of Europe. Most found that measures to control its use had better results. Alcohol is a particularly good example of a substance that is fairly harmless in small doses – even apparently beneficial in the case of a glass of wine a day – but catastrophic in large doses. Ultimately it is a question of disposition – some get addicted, others do not. There may even be a gene for alcoholism. The fact that it is not particularly mind-altering – in comparison with LSD or hashish for instance – may tend to make people take more than is healthy, and the challenge then becomes how to get back to smaller quantities – self-control or cold turkey. Many experiment more or less successfully with both.

In the arts alcohol has been very widely used, from performers who use it to beat stage fright to writers like Anthony Burgess, who claimed that the subject matter of *A Clockwork Orange* was so painful that he could not write it in a sober state. The alcohol of choice for creative people has even been studied by psychologists, one survey in a north of England university coming up with the beer Newcastle Brown, somewhat unsurprisingly. In the France of the poets and Impressionists it would have been absinthe.

Money

> All progress is based upon a universal innate desire of every organism to live beyond its income.
>
> Samuel Butler, 1835–1902

Escapist activity with money is the clearest arena for studying the complete irresponsibility of the gambler, isolated in the moment of escapism from all sensible material and practical considerations. An all-too-typical story is the following:

A friend has recently been on such a Walter Mitty-like high in his work as an investment consultant that he lost all touch with reality, mortgaging his house and cashing in investments only to lose everything, despite warnings from more detached heads. The greatest danger is probably not the money but the damage done to human relationships, the destruction of one's family and the neglect of human needs. This was how the guy started. He spent less time with his family as he was always somewhere else, neglected his wife and children, plundered the family's income, and in addition became a social bore. He became involved in a web of debt, deception and self-deception. His wife was not aware of the situation until the day before the bailiffs came.[15]

Even more thought provoking is the following:

I once knew a successful lawyer who gambled to the point where he had lost all his savings and was left with nothing but the house he and his family lived in. At this point his wife and children left him. In a desperate all-or-nothing attempt to break his continual bad luck, he wagered his house on an outsider in a horse race. He won. The money enabled him to live comfortably – his wife and children returned. After that he never gambled again and would not even buy a raffle ticket. As with banging one's head against the wall, you realise the true nature of the activity when you stop doing it.[16]

The novel *The Great Gatsby* illustrates the quasi-magical qualities attributed to money. Gatsby has a 'live while you can' belief in money, but also the illusion that he can change the past with it. But *Gatsby* is, as with most gambling, a story about loss. A private swimming pool – the metaphor for money – can be swum in or drowned in.

Another common picture of financial escapism is the able-bodied, intelligent person who has ample talents to earn a good living but who nevertheless contrives to live in borderline penury, and frequently several thousands in debt. We might possibly exclude people like artists and jazz musicians who have their own views of 'art for art's sake', and a black humour to add a little spice to insolvency. We are left with a number of people who bitterly regret their lack of money but do nothing very constructive to get richer – people caught in some sort of vicious circle they may themselves only half understand. Behind it can be an unresolved dependency need – they may still receive money from their families or the state, or they borrow from friends or they get into debt or they spend money on credit cards. The dependency often has a sting in its tail – 'If it weren't for parents/school/something else suppressing my talents I could have done so much better...' This may be a game played out in therapy, with the therapist asked for help and then criticised for not making the situation better.

In these cases escapism can exist on many levels, the primary one being the inner bad feelings about being poor which lead to bills lying unopened and people preferring 'not to know' the extent of their position until their credit, overdraft, telephone or electricity is cut off. On a deeper level the escapism is from responsibility – there is an inability to admit that 'the buck stops with me' and nothing and nobody else can do anything about it. It may well be that previous family life has been good, and siblings are successful. This can make it worse – if there is a refusal to take work below one's perceived station in life then the lifeline of all sorts of possible sources of easy temporary work to stabilise the financial situation will be rejected. And rejected with a note of astonishment as if to say, 'What made you think that a person like me would do that?' Sometimes the person is one of the 'dispossessed' – a family that once had riches in past times and never quite got the hang of what to do about being poor. Procrastination is typical of this kind of escapism. There is always some way out that could be taken, some plan, some dream of riches, but doing something about it could be left for a few days, or until next week... And so the game is played out at a subsistence level, and as with the escapist creation of literature, Oblomov, people may say, 'What a wasted life, and he was as intelligent as anyone.'

Shopping

Shopping is an addiction that has filled houses with extravagant collections of objects. Sometimes it is 'comfort' spending, to provide the illusion of money, worth, attention and luxury. Sometimes it is more 'revolt' spending, to show that nothing about reality – debts, commitments, responsibility, can trap the free spirit. People don't want to be trapped in reality so they cheat – they use credit to escape from reality and live a 'richer' but unsustainable life, often the life they believe they deserve, or the life they should have had if it were not for the twists and turns of cruel fate. Shopping differs from collecting in some ways, though shopping is an essential part of collecting. It may concentrate more on the type and luxury of the shop, the selecting of goods, the paying at the checkout, the smile, courtesy and gratitude of the salesperson, the *élan* of leaving the shop with a branded bag swinging in your hand as you proudly walk down the street in full view of window shoppers still in a state of contemplation.

Yet shopping for the sake of 'hoarding' certainly resembles aspects of collecting. How else do we explain collections of domestic things like clothes and shoes that far outstrip their actual use? John Carter puts it thus:

> When my mother died and I came to explore her rooms I found several vast collections. One was of clothes, more than she could have worn had she lived to be 300. She was 93 and yet she kept buying, coats and shoes, many of which she never wore. Another collection was of household goods, sheets, curtains, towels, even a crate of spray polish. She was a clever woman with a young and agile mind, but she had lived through the 1916–23 Irish 'Troubles', had been bombed out of home in 1941, and had weathered the Great Depression. Having known hard and uncertain times I suspect she found some form of security in collecting domestic things, and I have noticed this in many others of her generation. It is part of the nest-building impulse but also a bulwark against the return of previous deprivations. Collecting is a symptom rather than a disease, and unless taken to extremes it is a harmless and often rewarding pastime, maybe even in itself a 'treatment' that satisfies some inner demand. It can of course be addictive and destructive, but my mother had the means to satisfy her need to have a vast store of 'things', and maybe she was more an 'accumulator' than a 'collector'. Yet I have seen people starve their family and prejudice their future to collect seemingly useless objects at high cost, where the urge to collect overrides all other considerations. Most of us collect as one aspect of our personality but to these unfortunates it can take over the personality. The roots must surely spring from the basic needs for security and self-esteem.[17]

How do we explain buying flowers? Is it collecting? Can one collect ephemera? Elton John is just one of many who constantly buy flowers. Is this compulsive, or just a natural way of re-creating the kind of half-domestic, half-wild environment that geographers call the 'middle landscape'? Is it also a love of smell, as some collect and use expensive perfumes? For those that live their greatest achievements on the stage beautiful arrays of flowers evoke the elegance of the dressing room and the sweetness of their triumph – as the ears melt with the sustained applause, the human senses are massaged with the perfume, the colour and the softness, an experience more opulently sensual even than the rostrum fizz of champagne for Formula One racing drivers or the sheen on the winner's cup in horse racing.

Collecting

Literature has documented the driven, obsessional collector in its various forms, from sinister to pathetic. John Fowles' 1963 novel *The Collector* depicts a psychotic butterfly collector who kidnaps a beautiful art student. The principle character in Bruce Chatwin's 1989 novel *Utz* is obsessed with his collection of Meissen porcelain figurines. Susan Orlean's *Orchid Thief* is a study of an obsessive flower collector who will go to the point of risking arrest to obtain a rare specimen to breed from.

Russell W. Belk, a professor at the University of Utah who studies collecting, believes that new academic research contradicts the idea that collecting represents aberrant behaviour, and shows that in its milder forms it is extremely widespread in developed cultures, affecting about one person in three. This is not even including CD or photo collections, which would make almost everyone a collector. (A 'collection' for research terms is something that is added to or catalogued in a systematic way, and items collected tend to be stored rather than used.)

The motivation of pure collectors is typically nonprofit-making, though collections may well accumulate in value. Some collections are 'virtual' – sightings of birds or train numbers. Even collecting CDs may become ephemeral as music is downloaded from the Net, as reporter Julian Dibbell explains:

> I am unpacking my CD collection. Yes, I am. Not the way Walter Benjamin famously unpacked his book collection, seven decades ago, amid 'the disorder of crates that have been wrenched open, the air saturated with the dust of wood, the floor covered with torn paper'. Not hardly. I'm unpacking my music the way we generally unpack information these days: by setting it free entirely from dust and paper and crates of any kind. By making it immaterial.

Collecting is done equally by men and women and cuts across all socio-economic classes, though it is primarily a feature of developed countries and richer cultures. Paradoxically collecting actually increased during the Great Depression in the 1930s. Even jobless collectors could feel that they were doing humanity a favour by preserving something.

A primary reason for collecting is recreating cherished moments in the past, like opening toys in their packaging (packaging being important in collections), an experience we repeat with the suspenseful breaking of the shrink wrap to signal the return of youthful discovery. Magic moments include discovering the world of musical recordings or books where colours, labels and original condition bring vivid memories back. Sometimes the thrill is not an object but an experience. The first time we hear Beethoven's Fifth can be momentous. Later we have trouble finding that kind of soul-stirring, life-changing experience, but we keep looking, just as drug addicts do when they 'chase the tail of the dragon'. They can't get the same buzz as the first time, but they keep trying, and as the intensity decreases with repetition and the thrill fades it can feel like 'filling a hole with a shadow'. Sometimes the thrill is in the fun experienced with a 'significant other'. Moments recreated can be crucially intimate moments with parents – building a model or hi-fi with father, altering clothes or picking out dresses for a party with mother.

Another motivation is what advertisers call 'anticipated satisfaction', which prompts initial purchases or the constant upgrades of hi-fi gear, computers, etc. Partly this is the endless search for 'something better', which lies deep in human psychology. Partly it is the anticipation itself – there is something deeply satisfying about searching through a catalogue, collecting coupons, making selections and seeing a purchase arrive at your front door. Maybe collecting in this sense goes back to ancient times when man was hunter and gatherer. Mumford describes the granary bin as the village prototype of the library, the resource of 'gathered' objects. The experience of being a collector, equally, entails the love of acquisition, the virtual hunt and also the final mounting of a collection, as hunters over the ages mounted their trophies.

Werner Muensterberger, a New York psychoanalyst, in *Collecting: An Unruly Passion*[18], suggests that collecting also derives from 'transitional objects' used as security against emotional insecurity or pain, as a child fixates on a toy or blanket as a source of comfort when parents are missing. Objects in a collection become a substitute for that absent emotional support, as in Orson Welles's film *Citizen Kane*. Ripped away from his parents as a small boy, Kane becomes an obsessive collector as an adult, stocking Xanadu, his palatial estate, with thousands of objects. But he dies pining for his boyhood sled 'Rosebud', the symbol of his lost childhood. 'Repeated acquisitions serve as a vehicle to cope with inner uncertainty,' Muensterberger writes, 'a way of dealing with the dread of renewed anxiety, with confusing problems of need and longing.'

Reasons for collecting include:

- creating a sense of self-worth;
- establishing an identity;

- offering a potential service to others; and
- striving for a sense of immortality.

'We are creating a small world where we feel secure,' Belk writes. 'We can succeed because we have defined success narrowly enough.'[19] Research by Danet and Katriel into collecting by adults in Israel in the eighties concluded that people who collected were 'striving for a sense of closure, completion and perfection'.[20] Five strategies used by their subjects were:

- completing a series;
- filling a space;
- creating a visually pleasing display;
- manipulating the scale of objects; and
- aspiring to perfect objects, as in restoring a vintage car to mint condition.

The desire for 'completeness' is behind cataloguing, a particular aspect of collecting. In fact, there are those who will catalogue more than collect, who before narrowing a choice down to one item to buy – washing machine, set of golf clubs, hi-fi system – will construct a database of all available options with fields for price, ranking, cheapest provider, etc. 'There is in the life of a collector a dialectical tension,' wrote Walter Benjamin, 'between the poles of disorder and order.'[21] The underlying desire of ordering information is both knowledge and completeness – to make informed choices in life through exhaustive knowledge of all the options. This – like collecting – may even have some genetic component, since it can be observed in several generations of the same family.

What is this feeling of 'completeness'? Is it a positive way of making some mark, is it a displacement – a substitute 'life work', or is it a substitute for a failure of satisfaction elsewhere? If so, a substitute for what? Is it a subconscious magical formula in a Jungian sense? Is collecting a sort of mantra? Will completion bestow enlightenment or immortality? If we have more CDs than the possible time to play them do we think subconsciously our lives will be extended until we can?

Sigmund Freud was a great collector of antiquities and *objets d'art* from the classical world, and before his death had a collection over 3,000 strong which was carefully on display in his consulting and work rooms, and is clearly shown in a Pollock etching of him at his desk. His obsessional aspect showed in confining the objects entirely to where he worked, not his living quarters, and in cataloguing not only the objects but also their exact locations before moving to England so the collection could be recreated intact. Freud biographer John Forrester, author of *The Cultures of Collecting*[22], notes that Freud began collecting just after the death of his father in 1896, a traumatic time in his life, and also 'collected' dreams, case studies and Jewish anecdotes, which he used in his work and writings. Freud rarely referred to himself as a collector, though his disposition for it was obvious.

Werner Muensterberger, himself a collector of African art, does not consider that every collector is neurotic, but nevertheless believes that the seeds of obsessiveness and the impulse for neurosis come from the same place. 'There is an un-neurotic side to collecting: the search for knowledge, the sense of taste, the need for accomplishment,' he said. 'That can border on the obsessional. It can become deviant.'[23]

Do collectors love the actual subject of their collecting, or do they love collecting as an act? Where is the love of the subject in, say, a woman who collects antique snuff bottles, who has never even tried snuff and just 'likes the look of the bottles'? Or someone who collects saddles even though she has never been on a horse? This emphasises the idea that typically what we collect are 'objects'. Objects can be manipulated, sorted, catalogued and potentially used productively. The objects themselves have no choice in the matter – they are, after all, simply objects. They make no demands upon the collector. They are 'uncomplaining friends', as one CD collector put it, adding the dimension of 'friendship':

> That Zubin Mehta recording of the Beethoven 3rd will never be able to make me feel guilty for not having played it for over 10 years. From the time of my earliest collection – baseball cards – the objects I collected were 'like' uncomplaining friends. If women are more people-related in their collecting, and men are more thing-oriented (though there are numerous exceptions where women collect objects) then maybe men do try to personalise their objects in some way.[24]

Collecting is found in children, both naturally and in response to commercially created collecting fads like Pokémon cards and football cards. Children not only get the collecting bug, but they use their collections as demonstrations of peer superiority when they are first to find a particularly sought-after object. Social belonging is another motivation, besides competition, characteristics not uncommon to this age group.

FIVE

What Defines the Escapist?

When questioned in an Internet survey, about a third of people considered themselves slightly escapist. Nearly half considered themselves moderately escapist, and the remaining smaller proportion considered themselves very escapist. Those who considered themselves slightly escapist believed they were aware of the real world most of the time, and that life was not treating them too badly. A typical comment was: 'I try not to "escape" from real problems but seeing a good film, reading a book or magazine, taking time off to do other things than work are, I think, legitimate forms of escapism.'

Those who considered themselves very escapist included those who refused to be tied down or imprisoned in reality: 'just try keeping me somewhere where I don't want to be' said one, who had escaped from behind the Iron Curtain. In a different way it included chaotic personalities who considered they were out of control and unable to function very well in reality. The greatest proportion considered themselves moderately escapist. Reasons given were that they had practical imperatives, like jobs or caring for other people, that kept them rooted in reality, or that they simply lacked the money to indulge in leisure and escapist activities. Moderate escapists considered themselves to be in good control of themselves: 'I'd say that I'm just enough of an escapist to be dissatisfied with reality, but not enough of one to successfully create an alternative reality, package it and market it.'

Defining the 'escapist'

One view is that we are all potential escapists. 'A human being,' Yi-Fu Tuan says wryly, 'is an animal who is congenitally indisposed to accept reality as it is.'[1] This profoundly true statement brings together in one definition all the different processes of transformation that underlie human creativity, humour, art, revolution, innovation and escapism itself.

Another view expressed in the Internet survey above is that there is not so much a personality as a set of situations that need to be escaped from: 'Basically it's the situation you're in that defines the occasional need to break out, unless you're a pathological escapist – a neurotic or psychotic person.' Situations would include all the life stressors listed in 'what are we escaping from' (page 56). A particular description of the escapist as a person unable to deal with situations that need confronting was made by William Stapledon in 1939, at a time of momentous events, with Europe on the verge of war:

> To say that anyone is an 'escapist' is to charge him with shunning unpleasant reality. Instead of recognising and grappling with the facts, he either withdraws into some safe corner where he can live in peace and occupy himself with activities unrelated to the vital struggles of his contemporary world, or else – unable to find actual escape – he solaces himself by constructing a dream world wherein he can live 'in imagination', a world after his own heart's desire.[2]

The escapist can also be partly the product of his or her environment, as in the case of drug and alcohol addiction. There may well be a genetic link in this, but substance abuse still requires such substances to be generally available, and some of these are sufficiently addictive that the casual experimenter may have difficulty kicking the habit. If we are to look for more of a personality dimension than a situational one, then the escapist may not be one distinct personality 'type', since escapism can take different forms. A case can be made, however, for seeing the escapist as a person showing a number of possible escapist character traits.

An introvert

Many see the escapist as introverted – a watcher of life rather than a participant, someone with a rich inner world who is happy in a world of contemplation. Introversion in itself is not pathological or non-functional. There are many happy introverts who enjoy isolation. Introverts find endless solace in walks in the wild, rather than walks 'on the wild side', the purlieu of their extrovert cousins. The ability to enjoy solitude can be considered a sign of inner mental health. Also, introversion is not the same as shyness – extraverts can be shy and introverts can be entertaining social talkers.

Anthony Storr makes a special case for creatives, who often work in isolation:

> The development of imagination in human beings has made it possible for them to use the impersonal as well as the personal as a principal means of self-development, as a primary path towards self-realisation. Many creative people appear to nurture their talents more carefully than they do their personal relationships, demonstrating a human potential which can be found in everyone, albeit in embryo form in most of us.[3]

Here we come back to Maslow's concept of self-actualisation. The contention is that a solitary activity can be purposeful, can develop crucial inner talent, and can in itself supply adequate rewards for it not to be 'escapist' or evasive. Storr argues that, like self-development, 'individualism' is comparatively recent in human history. Tribal cultures, he contends, saw a person as essentially part of the family and social structure. He recounts that when he treated people in Nigeria the whole family would come along to the session and have no idea why a psychiatrist would want to see a patient alone. Such attitudes are still present in traditional village life, and are also typical of aspects of China's social life.

But if individualism and the 'solitude of the individual' are modern phenomena, they are by no means ones that are happily accepted by all. Those who create in solitude may suffer from isolation, and this becomes increasingly relevant with the rise of an Internet culture and people sitting for hours at computers. E-mails are replacing face-to-face conversation in the workplace, and maybe should be renamed 'i-mails' because of their attraction for introverts. Shyness clinics are full of computer programmers seeking help in dealing with their poor interpersonal abilities and their emotional isolation. Even artists and creatives can feel isolated. Feedback from two years of running courses for unemployed people in the arts in London showed they felt the main benefit of the six-week course was not skills training but simply the opportunity to mix with other like-minded individuals.[4]

So what can be considered a better adjustment to reality – following individual interests or socialising? The answer seems to be both, according to some psychological studies of self-esteem. A 20-year longitudinal study into self-esteem in older people found that solitary interest activities and the development of identity were important to self-esteem, but so were social activity levels and relationships with other, non-family, people.[5]

The extrovert, by contrast with the introvert, is more motivated to live in the real world and interact with people. He or she talks more, interacts more, seeks more outside activities and spends less time in solitary pursuits like reading. So is the extrovert less escapist? Not necessarily. The introvert, through contemplation, may reach a better understanding of reality, as philosophers do. The extrovert is more likely to indulge in popular escapist pursuits provided by society – theme parks, group activities and various forms of entertainment that may be fun but which are fundamentally shallow in nature.

A repressed person

One possible definition of the escapist could be a person who fails to act out his or her life, leaving only the imagination in which to contemplate action. This might be a result of early domination by a strong-willed parent or later repression by an employer or bossy spouse. It might also result from a repressive society. The escapist is thus a blocked individual, one who has ample talent and intelligence but is afraid to use it.

The feeling of psychological block can be a result of fear of failure, often through the over-expectations of family or teachers. There may be paralysis of action – even an inability to hold down jobs – while in compensation the imagination may become ever more vivid. The repressed person thus dreams of acting out fantasies but may be unable to do so in reality. A good example of this is Walter Mitty, replete with bossy wife, in the Thurber story.

A close relative would be a disabled or injured person who has had to spend time in hospital or in bed. This was the case with a number of writers of escapist fiction – Thurber (blindness), Cervantes (disabled left hand) and R. L. Stevenson (tuberculosis). Repression can take the form of actual imprisonment, as with Oscar Wilde, Solzhenitsyn or Dostoevsky.

A psychotic or neurotic person

The schizophrenic is in a condition of distorted perception, withdrawal and semi-permanent escapism from life, though in practice this is controlled and lessened by drugs. Psychiatrist R. D. Laing suggested that madness can be a creative resolution of emotional conflicts. This could be presented as a Catch-22 argument: 'if reality is crazy, then it would be mad not to escape from it'. Though the existentialists and surrealists created valid alternative artistic creations to what they considered a crazy world, this is not a path that makes the 'madman' sane, unfortunately, in the eyes of others that have to deal with him. Laing's views, culminating in his conviction that to survive, society needed the '3 Ms — music, meditation and martial arts'[6] — were too extreme even for his friend Timothy Leary. Leary was closer to Huxley in thinking of schizophrenics as 'living neither on earth nor in heaven, nor even in hell, but in a shadowy world of the dead, like the wraiths in Homer's Hades'.[7]

The manic-depressive lives in two worlds — a manic one, which is subject to flights of the most opulent escapist fantasies, and a depressive one characterised by mild to substantial distortions of reality. Depression is like wearing a pair of black spectacles or seeing everything through a distorting mirror. 'Globalised' thinking makes the subject think that everything is hopeless, every day will be bad, nobody cares and nothing will work, rather than 'Tuesday was an unusually bad day but Wednesday should be better'. Even an accident like spilling a cup of coffee can be interpreted as 'I can't do anything right, I'm completely hopeless and always will be'. Though very common in the population, depression is a distortion of perception and — through its moods of apathy and hopelessness — an escape from productive living, and should be dealt with as rapidly and thoroughly as possible.

Those with neuroses exhibit different ways of failing to cope with reality. Neurotics generally live in a state of partially coping with life and partially finding their daily living upset by exaggerated personality deviations. Their imprisonment in their neurotic inhibitions constitutes an escape from normal productive living, and their inflexible behaviour can additionally warp the lives of those partners and family that have to live with their demands. The phobic person has a strong compulsion to escape from the subject of the phobia — spiders, closed spaces, heights — but otherwise can live normally. The exception is the agoraphobic, whose inability to go out is a denial of social living. The hysterical personality feels empty inside and so is compelled to find attention in the world of other people – a kind of escape from the self. The obsessional person creates elaborate rituals, which have to be observed to avoid feelings of generalised anxiety. The original traumas are avoided by progressively more elaborate and far-flung expediencies, rivalling some of the eccentricities of popular superstition. Interestingly, one of these rituals – counting to 10, 12, or whatever to either make a decision or avert some invented catastrophe – can be seen in prominent literary escapist characters like Lafcadio and Billy Liar.

And what of suicide – the ultimate escape from life, and always a potential risk with personality disorders? Most of us would agree with Garrison Kieller about our journey through life to our inevitable death: 'We know where we are going, but it doesn't stop us rowing our boats. We're all like Gatsby – we're all rowing against the current, and we never give up.' In the case of many suicides life is physically so bad that it is too painful to live. For all too many, however, the unbearable weight of life is just a temporary illusion. This sad fact underlines how much of our experience of living lies in our perception of it.

A malcontent or rebellious person

The escapist typically feels a pervasive lack of satisfaction with reality. The malcontent – though similarly unsatisfied – may seek positive and realistic ways out of this situation, for instance by political agitation, revolution, or by escaping from repressive regimes to a freer society with greater opportunities. Such rebellion or escape can, of course, be incubated in long periods of imagination where the time and opportunity of release are endlessly rehearsed. If there is no action then the malcontent may become simply an escapist dreamer.

The rebel has no love for being controlled or influenced, and so escape is central to his or her nature. The force to 'escape' enclosure – whether it be influence, power, social condition or literal imprisonment in a country or system – motivates creative action where it is carried out positively. Where release is impossible, it may simply result in idle daydreams or a refusal to see anything positive in 'establishment' figures or artefacts.

A free or divergent thinker

The problem with the freethinker is that if you are 'outside' morality you may be either better than or worse than it, a liberal humanist or a criminal. The laws of the land are not perfect, and at any point practical circumstances can arise that will 'prove the law an ass'. Before they were repealed in the early 19th century, there were statutes demanding the death penalty for impersonating a Chelsea Pensioner, defacing London Bridge and stealing a sheep, and in practice juries simply found the defendants innocent. So in one way, individual moral thinking is higher than the law, as periodical amendments to existing laws prove.

How do we classify the ecological protester, a member of Friends of the Earth, for instance? If they are truly in touch with reality, they are realists. Yet they stand outside many common activities like driving a car through their alternate views and their courage to stand by them, and they are frequently arrested and tried by current laws for their protests. Avoidance of systematic thought patterns is characteristic of both the criminal who breaks the law and the freethinker who transcends the law. Sometimes it is necessary to do both. Such ethical individualism is defined by the highest level of psychologist L. Kohlberg's stages of Moral Judgement[8], where actions are guided by self-chosen ethical principles, and also by 'the courage to be different', a Scandinavian cultural definition of 'a strong man'.

A slightly different definition of 'thinking outside the box' is provided by psychologists J. Guilford and R. Hoepfner, who made the distinction between divergent and convergent thought. The convergent thinker or 'converger' is more likely to plan logical steps to a desired conclusion. The divergent thinker or 'diverger' is more likely to experiment and try many different ways around something. Psychologist Liam Hudson applied these definitions to a group of schoolboys. His convergers tended to prefer the sciences and excel in tests where there was one right answer, being less good at open-ended exercises where there could be several answers. They also had technical hobbies, showed less interest in people, had conventional attitudes to authority, were emotionally inhibited and rarely remembered dreams. His divergers showed interest in biology or the arts, scored less well at conventional tests and excelled at tasks demanding imagination and fantasy. They were more interested in people, more unconventional, more emotionally expressive and often remembered their dreams.

It is interesting that while many scientists are logical and are presented with a variety of convergent problems which they need to solve, the 'unusual' solutions may come from those who are more emotional, work on hunches and have more contact with their unconscious thoughts and dream worlds. As can be seen from the post-hippie techno generation that launched Silicon Valley, when allied to a keen intelligence this can be a powerful thinking engine. The diverger may also be more of an escapist, tending to jump out of conventional patterns in the search for something more original. The 'lateral thinker', a term coined by Edward de Bono and used in a number of his books on the subject, is a close relative of the diverger, his opposite type being the 'vertical thinker'. The lateral thinker will 'search for the many different ways of doing something, visualising, using chance by acknowledging its value, not interfering, not relying on the arrogance of vertical thinking that prevents the emergence of new ideas'.[9] The escape in this case is from 'the limitations of vertical thinking as a method for generating new ideas'.

Escapism and creativity

The escapist has so many features of the creative personality that they may even largely overlap. The personality factors in creativity are considered to be the following:

- Intelligence – power and scope of thinking
- Sensitivity – awareness of the environment
- Imagination – scope of fantasy and invention
- Competitiveness – motivation
- Critical detachment – creative judgement
- Experimentation – novelty and originality
- Non-conformity – rejection of the status quo
- Self-sufficiency – ability to work intensely or alone.

If we look at this list we see many strong components of escapism – imagination and fantasy, experimentation and non-conformity. The job values of creatives tell a similar story – lowest of all is a predictable routine, while highest ones include variety and experimentation.[10]

Exploring new ways of thinking is a natural process for the creative, because his or her mind is focused on potential, not actuality. Consequently thought processes may jump out of both the present time and the present subject matter. If you put an apple in front of a material-thinking person, he or she would probably think something like: 'Apple, green, juicy, nice-tasting, where did you buy it?'

If you put the same apple in front of a creative thinker he or she might respond with something like: 'Apple, William Tell, Switzerland, skiing, I need a holiday.'

It is obvious that the creative is making a wholly different type of association, and one further out from 'actuality'. The associations are like the subconscious ones that emerge in dreams, and as Freud says, 'the subconscious has no sense of time'. The creative thinker is more likely to make thematic links than temporal ones, and associations can get progressively further away from the original idea until they take on a life of their own. Two creative thinkers may 'click' and follow each other, but the gap with more factual thinkers can become a chasm. By the first or second distant association the two may no longer share any common ground – one is thinking of green juicy apples, the other is off skiing in Switzerland.

Whether we call creative thought 'escapist' is a moot point. Do we, for instance, say that it depends on how much creativity is productive? J. S. Bach was clearly not escapist – he produced a colossal output of music and 20 children. But how do we know in advance that an idea will work? Creative associations can generate productive ideas or they can simply produce a stream of ideas that go nowhere. Creatives will say that some of their best ideas happen while in bed or simply walking about. It can be hard to persuade an ordinarily industrious person that such activity constitutes 'work'.

Creatives are driven to create, driven by restlessness and the desire to transform, change and innovate. The inventive person will spontaneously invent the need for more and better standards. By the time they have reached point A, they are considering points B and C. The goal is always beyond. The grass is always greener somewhere else. The imaginative person will constantly jump out of reality into daydreams, projects, plans and schemes. Potential ideas will then be formed.

How good does an idea have to be in order to be worth carrying out? What gives it the fundamental 'escape velocity' to go into orbit against the gravitational resistance of doubt and inactivity? By 'good' we mean both the intrinsic worth of the idea to the creator, and perhaps even more crucially how the idea measures up to other people's expectations. The 'other people' or 'third party' in the equation can be parents, peers, fellow artists and innovators, audiences, critics or any significant other. While some artists are more hamstrung than others by impossible demands they feel they have to meet, any creative artist worries about the quality of his or her work and is to some extent a perfectionist.

The universality of 'living up to the standards one sets for oneself' was underlined by a recent survey of British musicians, where it emerged as the top stressor in a very long list.[11] Often it is the dearest dreams and the biggest projects that are the hardest to deal with because they mean so much, and their success or failure may be unsupportable for a fragile ego:

> For each man kills the thing he loves
> By each let this be heard
> The coward does it with a kiss
> The brave man with a sword
> For each man kills the thing he loves
> But each man does not die.
>
> Oscar Wilde, *The Ballad of Reading Gaol*

Harold Pinter's answer to an interviewer's casual question, 'Do you ever get writer's block?' was simply, 'Show me any writer who does NOT get writer's block.' Effective therapy for creative artists addresses all the complex issues of creative 'flow', such as following the muse, finding inspiration and finding the best time of day, place and circumstances to enhance creative comfort and ease. The antidote for the stuck creative may be the simple words cleverly used in the Nike advertisements – 'Just do it'. Sportspeople in general are more practical than imaginative and view some creatives as 'making things too complex' and being unnecessarily 'difficult'. Execution without contemplation is like going to sea without a map. Contemplation without execution is like having the map but not going to sea at all. Both are needed by the creative.

Despite existential reasons for creating, like expressing universal truths and leaving something to posterity, creatives can be purely practical in the way they use their skills. Necessity as the mother of invention can be seen clearly when artists have to consider basic survival needs. When the physically ill and impoverished Bela Bartok wrote his third piano concerto in a melodic and accessible style, it was deliberately to create a popular work that would provide his family with some money.

Escapism and procrastination

One almost defining quality of the escapist is avoidance. Avoidance in the sense of procrastinating has been the subject of a lot of recent psychological research into self-esteem.

Psychologist William James originally defined self-esteem as the ratio of 'our actualities to our supposed potentialities'. When there was a discordance, the answer was to either increase actual achievement or decrease expectations.

But later research showed that self-esteem was not one simple equation. People could show both strong positive self-attitudes and strong negative ones at the same time.[12] Also, levels of self-esteem fluctuate constantly, even on a daily basis, and are nowhere near as stable as intelligence or personality.[13]

One effective way of looking at self-esteem is to divide it into three parts. If we consider our 'actualities' as a midpoint that shows what we can typically attain in practice, then there are two dimensions that are 'virtual self-esteem' modes – the superior fantasy (Superman) and the inferior fantasy (Idiot). A person with too much 'Superman' fantasy will harbour the belief that he or she is better than others think, typically leading to some grandiose fantasy like 'I'm an undiscovered genius'. The result may be social isolation – maybe a form of escapism from the real level of one's talents, but not necessarily an impediment to creativity. The person with too much 'Idiot' fantasy, however, lives in the continued fear of not being good enough to satisfy expectations, even of being an undiscovered 'fraud' who may be found out at any time, the potential subject of ridicule for trying to do things above his or her real abilities.

It is this fantasy of things never being good enough that underlies the typical form of procrastination – jobs are put off, auditions, exams, interviews and other forms of assessment are avoided for fear of not being good enough, and acres of time are spent in indecision and avoidance of doing anything that might give others too obvious an idea of one's abilities. Sometimes excuses are harboured for the inactivity, like 'If it were not for... I could do it'; sometimes things are endlessly put off with some construction like 'When I have... then...'.

The sum total is avoidance. This kind of procrastination is something that few people have not experienced at some time, and is broadly speaking a fear of failure, a 'confidence' issue that we all share to some extent.

A saboteur

A close relation of the procrastinator is the saboteur. In this case the fear is of success, not failure. A singer that always manages to get eliminated in the first round of international competitions may really fear the consequences of success – winning the competition would mean having to fulfil a record contract and having to tour the world for a year or so, a scary thought for some. Reasons for fearing success can be various. Often there is a fear of being better than someone close – a partner, a twin or sibling, a parent who 'has to win at everything and always has to be right'. Succeeding would bring the worry of destroying that person. Sometimes it goes back again to the fear of failure: 'If I was really successful I couldn't cope – people would find out that I was really a fraud.'

The mechanism of sabotage is different from procrastination. A pianist may make a fistful of mistakes in the first page of a sonata then play the rest perfectly. The message is, 'Don't expect too much of me and I'll be OK.' Procrastinators put things off; saboteurs constantly take on projects and mess them up. The end result, as in procrastination, is that things that we are capable of don't get done, and this constitutes the same kind of escapism from our real abilities and potential.

The egotist, the narcissist and the psychopath

The egotist is escapist in a social sense – living within the needs structure of other people but not allowing for their needs. The egotist may be a poor listener or may in extreme cases like autism or the psychopath be totally unaware of others' needs or feel no responsibility for them. People with inflated egos like the narcissist may have an obsessive focus on themselves and unrealistic views of their own capabilities, which leads them to seek solace in dreams of success. Egotists may simply not register reality, such is their self-focus, for example Hitler's refusal to recognise the true situation on the Russian Front.

Egotism is a commonly used term, and egotists are normally easy to identify in social groups. Egotists can be fun, talented, entertaining and all those performance gains that result from projecting a strong ego. Their ego involvement, heightened by hedonism and instinctive or intuitive powers, may endow them with originality, humour and the ability to inspire others. Egotism appears to get greater rewards in large sections of the media, and even has a perfume named after it. Is it possible to imagine a perfume called 'Responsibility'? The primal urge to escape responsibility and have fun, possibly at others' expense, is typical of 'youth' broadcasting, where primal behaviour includes shouting, laughing, taking one's clothes off, being exhibitionistic and 'having a go', sometimes on a dare. Game shows pamper the ego and promote 'have a go' competitions, dares and quizzes where the best ego wins.

On the downside, egotists – like children – can be a pain in the neck. Egotists who are aware of their egotism, however, may realise that their inability to empathise with the thoughts and feelings of others and value teamwork results in poverty of experience. While others enjoy a richer world of communication and social reward, the egotist's inability to focus on external realities and the lives of other people like family, friends, partners and work colleagues may result in a crucial inability to organise a successful and productive life.

In particular the egotist may have a weak sense of responsibility – something taken to greater extremes in the psychopath, or as it is now known, the sociopath. One original assessment used to distinguish the disorder was to put the psychopath into a control group, all of whom were wired up to laboratory machines and told they would get an electric shock when the clock in the room reached 12. As the seconds approached 'shock time' (the shock was never given) the controls became anxious while the psychopath showed little reaction, since he was unable to register the implied threat. Equally difficult for the psychopath is understanding the consequences of actions that hurt others and empathising with their pain.

Egotism is particularly pronounced with the narcissist, where the escape from others into one's own ego becomes, as with the psychopath, a personality disorder. Egotism in the arts is somewhat perplexing. Many artists have been insufferable egotists, yet possess an openness to beauty and a sensitivity to the human condition that makes them far from heartless.

Escapism and romance

Escape from lovelessness is the province of the romantic. The romantic typically feels that life without sufficient quantities of love, emotion and sensation is not truly living. If romance cannot be lived out in real life, then it can be indulged in again and again in one's fantasy life by means of reading or viewing 'popular romances'. Such a romance is basically a story of love between a woman and a man, in which a happy ending follows a variety of vicissitudes.

The formula figures to varying degrees in many other genres, in print, films and on television, and maintains the widespread concept of romantic love that has had a pervasive influence on relations between the sexes in the Western and Westernising world. A 'romantic' approach to life ranges from passive escapism into novels and films, to real-life adventures and enthusiastic passions, which satisfy the needs of the 'romantic at heart'. Because of the pervasiveness of romantic hopes and expectations in our society, commercial advertising of consumer goods – lifestyle holidays, cosmetics, clothing – commonly employs the images of romance.

We all have something of the romantic in us, even if it is artificially stimulated by our culture, but some have more than others. The more a person becomes lost in infatuation, the more reality is left to one side. In the great passions of literature – Cleopatra, Anna Karenina, Madame Bovary – the final act, suicide, is one of total escapism. On a lesser scale, infatuation can lead to total addiction to the subject loved and neglect of the realities of life, as many can testify. The only saving grace is that, like escapism, total infatuation tends to be temporary.

Victims of new technology

There was a time when if you were bored inside you went out, and when you were bored outside you came home again. Maybe you read a book or tidied up or found somebody to talk to. All these activities required some thought and some time to put into practice. Fast-forward to the digital age and it all changes. Restless with your TV programme? In a microsecond you flip channels. Restless with the TV? In a moment you are at the computer clicking through Web sites with your mouse. Restless with the Web? Click to a game. Click-game-click-Web site-click-e-mail-click-CD-click-wordprocessor-click-click-click... Welcome to the age of impatience. With a mouse in our hands we don't even have to read information in a linear way, we simply flip out the instant our attention span lapses.

It could be that mass entertainment, games and computer technology are turning all of us into escapists through the use of handheld escapist gadgets – remotes, mice and who knows what else. Once we have the capacity for instant switch, our tolerance for frustration, anxiety and difficulty – all features of the raw, unpredictable real world – may atrophy to the point where escapism rather than transcendence is the option we are bred to accept.

Male-female differences

It is hard to determine whether the extent of escapism is different in men and women, but it may differ in type due to hereditary, personality, educational or environmental factors. The biggest statistical difference between the two sexes remains the tendency for men to be more rational and women to be more emotional and feeling. This is based on the Myers Briggs Type Indicator, whose database shows a two thirds preference for thinking in men and for feeling in women.[14]

Of course the situation is steadily changing in a unisex direction, but up to now men have been more dominant and active in society and have fought most of the wars in history, and they still rehearse their prowess in various competitive games and sports. Women are more likely to read romantic stories and watch soaps. Those left at home – especially without children or with small children – may exhibit escapism that mirrors or could indeed be the first stages of depression:

- Avoidance of social interaction
- Seeking solace in alcohol, pills, other drugs
- Not answering the phone
- Leaving post unopened
- Passively watching 'trash' TV
- Compulsive eating
- Manic house cleaning
- Crying.

In an Internet survey, women were more likely to mention feelings of failure, failed relationships, not being able to tackle their job, financial problems, children who have problems, or things like living with an alcoholic: 'Friends, family and colleagues saw changes in my behaviour and warned me. I knew it wouldn't work but defended the relationship fiercely,' said one respondent. One view is that men and women practise escapism similarly but that the triggering factors are different. In women some of the triggering factors may relate to inferiority feelings, hence the drive to be more attractive or more liked.

On the other hand women talk something like three times more than men – 6,000 words a day vs 2,000 – and so may air and resolve issues in real life much better than men. There may be an argument that men's escapist activities are prolonging activities that belong more to boyhood – sport, train sets, cycling, collecting. Also, until recently men were the major wage earners so they had the financial means to take part in escapist activities. Women, having to do practical things like housekeeping and childcare, couldn't afford – both financially and mentally – to lose themselves too often or too much in escapist entertainment. These days women are in a stronger financial position, which enables them to take on more 'masculine' escapist activities: drink more, get interested in football, go clubbing, buy sports cars and go on adventure holidays.

A typical escapist profile

If we put together the most likely attributes of the escapist we would probably get a profile such as the following:

> The escapist would be imaginative and capable of some original ideas, but a significant amount of time would be spent daydreaming, without putting ideas directly into practice. There would be a preference for spontaneous or hedonistic activity over planning and structured activity, and a tendency to work in binges or at the last minute, doing pleasant tasks before more pressing ones. The career path may be either stable and uninteresting, with a lot of leisure activities, or interesting but erratic, with a number of changes of direction and some foreign travel. Escapists may be self-employed and choose more fringe or experimental occupations than establishment ones – rock or jazz rather than symphonic music, performance art and installations rather than portraiture. At best, results could show brilliance and originality. Achievement may be limited in relation to talent and potential, and there may be times out of work. Money is likely to be a problem. Lack of organisation may mean a messy home environment. There may be one or more persistent time-consuming activity: collecting and cataloguing, playing games, gambling, Internet use. There may be some addictive behaviour – eating problems, alcohol or drug use. There may be periods of depression linked to lack of productivity and financial worries. On the other hand, there may be an original sense of humour. In sum, an interesting, amusing and sometimes argumentative person with obvious interests and gifts, who doesn't seem to be able to really get his or her life together but seems content to potter about doing all sorts of off-beat activities.

SIX

Escapism in the Arts and the Media

The arts and the media are potent hotbeds of escapism. Through their imaginative worlds we can experience, without participating in, activities we would otherwise never want to or be able to take part in – battling with vampires, invasion by aliens, detective mysteries, Napoleonic maritime war stories. In the 'mental moment' it is as if one is there – a virtual escape. A film depicting rich and successful people allows the imagination to carry us temporarily into another world, far removed from boredom and drudgery. The great epic films are good examples of this – *Dr Zhivago, Gone with the Wind, Ben Hur*. Imagination allows us to feel as if we are kings, to marry princesses, possess riches, fight heroic battles, win court cases and solve crimes. Those who watch and enjoy films with violent content like *Die Hard* experience, in the safety of an armchair, a degree of violence that would scare them witless in the real world. Their motivation may be the working out of anger and a sense of personal injustices, so as to see themselves in their imagination as powerful enough to confront and defeat all enemies and those who suppress or intimidate.

Many creatives were adventurers and escapists in their real lives – escaping to exotic lands like R. L. Stevenson and Gauguin, fighting in wars like Cervantes, duelling like Pushkin, indulging in endless romantic affairs. Many, however, were repressed or physically ill individuals for whom their imagination was their whole world. Certainly many were incorrigible hedonists, trying any and every potential form of pleasure and escape and creating a justified reputation for Bohemian living in the demi-monde of the 'Cafe des Artistes'. For a creative artist, the tendency to escapism is a positive, indeed essential, trait. A novelist must be an escapist at heart because the successful novel depends on constructing a credible alternative reality and populating it with well-modelled, plausible characters. A film-maker must do all that with a real-life cast of anything up to thousands.

Escapism in film

The International Movie Database lists 206 entries with the word 'escape' in the title. Eleven of them are simply called *Escape* (plus several more in languages other than English) and four are called *The Escape*, plus there is the film *The Escapist* (1983), directed by Eddie Beverly Jr. The grand total includes 166 films, 24 TV films, two videos, six TV series and two video games. Quite a total. Clearly escape is big business in the film world.

One of the main characteristics of these escape films is danger, or 'jeopardy' as Hollywood loves to call it. The places escaped from are many and varied – locations from *Burma* or *Grizzly Mountain*, to *Glory*, *Paradise*, *Happiness* (aka *Intermezzo*) and *The Sun*. There is both *Escape from New York* and *Escape from LA*. There is *Escape from Planet of the Apes* and *Escape from Mars*, with space typically a hostile environment. There is even escape from *Planet Earth* (aka *The Doomsday Machine*).

Much of the escape is from some form of imprisonment. This includes the films titled *Escape from Alcatraz, Death Row, Devil's Island* and *San Quentin*; the many escapes from enemy capture in war films like *The Great Escape*; and the perennial escapes from the Gestapo, the KGB and so on.

The characteristics of the environment and the means of escape are reflected in many picaresque parables like *Escape by Night, Escape in the Sun, Escape in the Fog, Escape in the Desert* and *Escape under Sail*. Sometimes the means of escape is ingenious, as in the many prison camp tunnel movies. Typically it can be on foot (*Nowhere to Run*), using animals, such as horses, and then inevitably in modern vehicles – trains, lorries, planes, rockets and the ubiquitous car. Usually in a Hollywood action film or US TV cop show there is a car chase involved, normally triggered by the eternal line, 'Let's get outta here'. No surprises in the home of the mass automobile industry – you use the first thing to hand. The hand not carrying the equally eternal gun, that is...

There is also, of course, *Escape to Nowhere*, plus the films that evoke the frustration of being unable to escape – five titled simply *No Escape*. The escape may be one from childhood fears – ghouls, monsters and pursuers – the kind of image that populates escape nightmares where our feet are caught in sand and we are unable to run as the danger comes closer. Some of the escape is from boredom and tedium. The escape may be in our minds, or it may be our own minds that we escape from. Or each other: *I Can't Escape From You* sums it up nicely, together with *Shorty Escapes Marriage*.

Big things – escape from the small realities of life

If the real world seemed petty and humdrum, then Hollywood could be counted on to take us to the opposite extreme – big, bigger, biggest, like *Quo Vadis*, 'the most colossal film you can see for the rest of your life'. But this was simply the filming of 'big things' – huge crowds, vast sets. One irony of this was that actors in these colossal crowd scenes went back to being as tiny as they were in real life. The huge Hollywood sets dwarfed the stars. Douglas Fairbanks Jr initially walked off the set of *Robin Hood*, saying 'What place is there for me?', and had to be persuaded back. So Hollywood made another discovery. It wasn't about 'filming big things', it was about 'filming little things big'. Welcome to the close-up that created psychological cinema and great stars like Garbo. Later, Hollywood discovered something even bigger – space. The concept of 'infinity' was wonderfully caught in the initial scene of *Star Wars*, as well as the end of *Time Bandits* and various other space movies like *2001: A Space Odyssey*. With space, escape from the small things in life was finally complete.

Time is a tyranny that many have longed to escape, and which we are starting to escape in our media world with time shifting, programmes on demand and videotaping. In real life there is a whole raft of recreations of the past – museums, old car rallies, historical air shows, steam railways and historical re-enactment societies (Society for Creative Anachronism, Civil War recreation, Renaissance Fair) with regular weekend events featuring jousting, wenching, pig roasting, smithing and so on. Clearly these escapist activities express people's strong desire to experience life in other times and places – critical times in history like the Battle of Britain or the Gold Rush, where the fate of nations or society was determined by the courage and persistence of a handful of young men, mostly in their mid-twenties. People collect all kinds of things that bring to life such obsessions: books, music, films, software, artefacts, costumes and photos relating to periods and events in history. And for the film and

TV industry the past is not a 'far country' but a permanent set peopled by the heroes and heroines of costume dramas.

A spooky version of returning to the past was created in the film *Westworld*, where holidaymakers could sign up for a real old west fantasy, complete with gunslingers who could actually kill you. Meanwhile, escape from the present into the past or the future has been achieved fictitiously through several different versions of the time machine – from Jules Verne's *Time Machine* to *Dr Who* to the 1985 *Time Machine* TV series to *Time Bandits*. There is a Hindi version of *Time Machine*, a kiddies' version featuring Kevin, a precocious six year old, and a film called *The Time Machine*, currently in production, which catapults Jeremy Irons 800,000 years into the future. Dispensing with the time machine and substituting our own imagination, we then have all the SF films and series like the ever-enduring *Star Trek*.

Escape from societal depression

What do we do with those awkward periods in society when things go wrong? Periods like the Great Depression? Simple – rely on Hollywood to give us Busby Berkeley's babes fanning out in swimming pools like elaborate flowers, and dramatic fantasies like *Grand Hotel*. 'People come, people go,' moans bored Dr Otternschlag at the beginning of *Grand Hotel*, 'and nothing ever happens' – the usual escapist definition of 'reality'. He has obviously failed to uncover the melodramatic lives of the inhabitants of Berlin's fabulous and glamorous hotel, and missed its secret world of romance and intrigue. Otto Kringelein is dying, blowing his life savings and living on the edge. Mr Preysing is desperately trying to merge his textile company before he goes broke. The women – Joan Crawford as an aspiring actress and Greta Garbo as a Russian ballet dancer pining for her homeland and Grand Duke Sergei – vie for the love of the Baron, a gentleman thief who is in the middle of stealing jewellery. As *The Flick Filosopher* says in its review: 'It's all very silly, the ultimate in Depression-era escapism: a piece of Hollywood magic that's impossibly romantic, filled with people who are impossibly elegant, bantering and wisecracking constantly. Its fascinating and diverse characters and a rather dark ending, however, give *Grand Hotel* more heft than any of its hellish spawn such as *The Love Boat* or *Fantasy Island*.'

Escapism through drink and drugs

There are innumerable film escapists in the form of drunks, such as *Arthur* (1981) or *Harvey* (1950), where Elwood P. Dowd faces getting locked up for seeing a two-metre-high rabbit called Harvey everywhere. Generally the drunk is a lovable eccentric, and the number of realistic depictions of the ravages of alcoholism – like *Days of Wine and Roses* (1962) – have been a smaller minority.

Drug use exploded in the sixties and this was reflected in the cinema with a plethora of highly coloured escapist fantasies like the Beatles' *Yellow Submarine* (1968). LSD emerged in a few cautionary tales like *The Weird World of LSD* (1967) and even as a comic character in *The Producers* (1968). The free love and drug culture of the sixties found expression in *The Trip* (1967), *Easy Rider* (1969) and a number of subsequent lifestyle and road movies, whose message echoed popular slogans like 'tune in, drop out' and 'make love, not war'. It is ironic in the case of the Beatles that the creators of the psychedelic 'Lucy in the Sky with Diamonds' also penned tunes like 'Penny Lane' and 'She's Leaving Home', which showed an uncanny observational realism well ahead of its time in popular music. Great experimenters may explore reality as much as fantasy.

Subsequent drug culture movies turned fairly rapidly from hippie free expression to the seedier sides of the underworld, a sinister place of prostitution, gangs, extortion and violence, where the treatment became trite, formularised and nothing more than a backdrop for equally predictable action movies with their inevitable guns, cops and car chases. The focus shifted from any real exploration of the escapism dimension of the individuals involved to the simple illegality and exploitation of the drug scene.

Escape through humour

Sometimes you just have to laugh, as the saying goes. Humour is an escape from gloom and tedium, 'a temporary mental release from reality' as *Webster's* calls escapism. It is our 'manic defence' against reality. We joke about bad things to lighten the burden and the mood. The joke can be farce or burlesque, light or black, frothy or cynical. It may be totally unrealistic or 'super realistic', a way of uncovering a darker hidden reality. At the end of his life Lenny Bruce would simply issue monologues against the system, which became progressively less funny and more real.

Evading the stark nature of reality by making jokes about it is an essential part of human culture. The worse the reality, the blacker the humour, as in *schadenfreude* – humour created out of other people's misfortunes, such as the spate of Internet jokes after any global catastrophe. *Schadenfreude* is admittedly malicious, but reflects a life that, 'if created by divine will', as Jonathan Miller puts it, 'would have seen God in the dock at the equivalent of the Nuremberg trials for gross crimes against humanity'. The 'white' version of *schadenfreude* is genuine levity in the face of tragedy, like the comic send-off given by the Monty Python team following the untimely death of the much-loved Graham Chapman.

The ephemeral nature of comedy

Escapism as a 'temporary release' from reality is very akin to laughter. Laughter is not a state we can escape to permanently. It is a brief moment of relief from care, gone as fast as a sumo wrestling bout. Even comedians themselves struggle for eternal fame. It would be easy for anyone to name any number of famous actors and musicians. It would be harder to name anything like the same number of comedians, and very difficult indeed to name more than a handful of magicians. In fact, in different ways comedy and magic are essentially 'anti-fame'. Comedy, in the sense of laughter, which lasts only seconds, is ephemeral. Jokes are ephemeral. Most comedians are ephemeral. What lasts is comedy writers, whose original scenes and sketches, like Python's dead parrot sketch and some eternally funny scenes from the Marx Brothers' films, have stood the test of time, and the 'archetypes' – unforgettable characters like those created by Charlie Chaplin, Buster Keaton, Woody Allen. The other things that last in comedy are the 'timeless situations' and the double acts – Laurel and Hardy, Abbott and Costello. Like magic, there are some basic 'plots', which are replayed in different forms, like the switches in the 'Drama Triangle' between the three poles of Victim, Rescuer and Persecutor.

The personal psychology of comedians – are they themselves escapists?

Performing for many has been an escape from childhood misery. In many comedians this fundamental misery and sadness never seem to leave them. They commit suicide like Hancock, drink and drug themselves, lead solitary or strange lives and walk around as if in a black cloud, perplexing those who expect them to be perennially funny. Maybe comedians are the very people who have the most need to escape, and in addition possess the rare gift of being able to make others laugh, a gift so rare that Jonathan Miller estimates it is possessed by not more than 5 to 10 per cent of the population. Many people have a sense of humour, even more have a sense of fun and high spirits. Very few are spontaneously funny. A genuine flair for comedy is rare, yet 'a sense of humour' is consistently ranked in the top five desirable qualities of people, 'GSOH essential' being the leitmotif of the personal ad columns.

Are some people physically funny – Steve Martin, Frankie Howerd, Marty Feldman, Tommy Cooper? Or is it timing, use of eyes, particular facial expressions and looks? Comedy is partly innate, partly a learned skill, though good comedians start with an extra knack for constructing a funny situation, seeing an irony, or detecting an unusual or laughable association. Comedian Jerry Sadowitz claims that to do stand-up, 'You have to be funny to start with, then it takes about two years to learn the technique.'

Comedians confess to using comedy to escape from unhappiness, but they also maintain that projecting their 'own truths' is an essential part of what they do. Roseanne Barr says, 'We're unhappy, we're exhibitionists, we use comedy as therapy but we do operate from our own truths.' David Baddiel agrees: 'We have to be as personal as possible – to know how we are funny and how we create humour.'

Where does humour come from?

Where in us does the 'comic' come from? Comedy contains fear, and its suspension through laughter. Surprise is essential, as are switches of plot. Ultimately the comedian should end up being safe, just like cartoon characters who are never allowed to die. Harold Lloyd is not supposed to fall off the clock, however acute the jeopardy. Though they can go through paroxysms of fear and cowardice, as do Bob Hope or Woody Allen, comedians are supposed to survive, as the most menial mortal survives. They are not supposed to commit suicide like Lenny Bruce or get serious as he did. They are supposed to keep happiness as the manic defence against the fears, anxieties and misfortunes of life.

Just as our internal censor protects us against fear we could not endure in our dream world, according to psychoanalytic theory, so comedians censor our fear and transform it into a kind of reverse temporary 'dream world' symbolism where it becomes funny. And like our dreams and nightmares this world is replete with the absurd, the unexpected, the incongruous and the paradoxical. It is a world just like that of Freud's *Introduction to Dreams* with its clumsiness, inversions, puns on words and interpolated characters. But however jumbled and chaotic it may be, it is essentially a human world, which relies on the familiar foibles of mankind. Would humour be funny if it took place in an alien world? Like the potential creations of artificial intelligence, alien humour might be unintelligible to humans. We might simply not get the joke, or any irony that did not refer straight back to ourselves.

The emotions in comedy are certainly the basic and familiar human ones – happiness, sadness, fear, anger. Comedians reflect these – the happiness of Tommy Cooper, the sadness of Chaplin, the fear of Woody Allen, the anger of Lenny Bruce. In addition, comedians are no strangers to love and the lovable. Russ Abbott topped a British 'most loved' poll, Woody Allen succeeded Burt Reynolds as 'America's most attractive male'. Comedy is essentially about the transformation of emotional states, a combination of sadness, anger and fear turned on stage into happiness. Or more precisely, switches between different emotions that leave us in a state of laughter. Anger and hate are the stock emotions behind the venom, sarcasm and bitterness of many stand-up acts, though sometimes the joke is only barely funny.

Chaplin, Laurel and Hardy, Lucille Ball, all the great comedians understood that good comedy often arises from desperate circumstances oozing with fear and that great comedy often balances on the brink of tragedy, as in the old one-liner, 'Outside of that, Mrs Lincoln, how did you like the play?' Harold Lloyd dangling from the clock certainly did that, as did the traditional heroine tied to the railway track in front of an oncoming train, saved in the nick of time. This 'escapist' mechanism in humour seems to be built into us. Why do people who impulsively run across the road in front of oncoming traffic always laugh when they somehow just get to the other side? Timing here is crucial, and all the comic greats understood the vital importance of timing situations to get the laugh.

The transformations and mechanisms of humour are several – another being the contrast and inversion of high and low status, as Chaplin captured in his parody of Hitler. Some comics operate out of high status, appearing cleverer than the audience – Jackie Mason, Peter Cook, Peter Ustinov. Others, like Norman Wisdom, act the fool. Some mix up status messages – Woody Allen is an intellectual who acts like an idiot, Reeves and Mortimer act working class, then humiliate all their celebrity guests. Comedy expresses our own embarrassment at our real or imagined clumsiness and capacity for mistakes, our fear of our human ridiculousness, and in particular the fear lurking at the bottom of our self-esteem that we are all frauds and we'll all be found out one day, transformed in a moment from prince to frog.

Sometimes the inversion of state is between adult and child. Comedy here is an expression of the 'vulnerable human', often with babyish overtones. All the greats are vulnerable, and draw on some of the poignancy of childhood – Chaplin, Woody Allen, Laurel and Hardy, Buster Keaton, Harry Langdon. For all the importance of childhood in humour, the irony is that although children statistically laugh much more than adults in an average day, they are very late developers when it comes to cracking jokes themselves or even displaying the real belly laugh that signifies that they have 'got' a punch line.

Sometimes it is the contrast between the normal human body and various kinds of disability that creates the comedy, like Harpo's dumbness. Often jokes against the disabled or 'misfortunate' – to use a conveniently Irish term – put their finger on that button of dread in us that outputs the reaction, 'There but for the grace of God go I'. The newer generation of alternative comedians had the stated goal of replacing sexist, jingoistic, racist cabaret 'jokes' with an observation of reality that was 'moral' in origin and intent. People were not absurd – life itself was absurd, with its ironies and surreal situations. This existential viewpoint had the craziness of Dada allied to a kind of punk genuineness and faith in human nature. But while one theatre featured the new 'caring' side of stand-up, all the old jokes were getting all the old laughs just around the corner.

Sometimes the inversion is between sanity and madness. Is humour something that happens 'while the balance of the mind is disturbed'? We might think so in the superb scene between Basil Fawlty and his German hotel guests in the *Fawlty Towers* episode 'The Germans'. Through the convenient intervention of a bang on the head, Fawlty changes into a xenophobic right-wing Brit, spouting all the archetypal anti-German platitudes, stomping around his guests' table like a storm trooper and shouting 'Don't mention the war'. The Germans take him to be sane, accuse him of reducing the woman in the party to tears and reprimand him for starting the problem. Fawlty, gliding neatly in and out of sanity, retorts, 'You started it – you invaded Poland.' In the whole scene madness constantly switches with sanity, reflecting the irony that while war is a lunatic state of affairs invoked by healthy people, laughter is a healthy state of affairs invoked by lunatics.

These inversions or changes of status are typical of escapism in general – the poor yearn to be rich, the rich yearn to return to the innocent happiness of their poorer years. The difference between comedy and our natural escapist daydreams is that in comedy the switches are much faster, the contrast between the two states is exaggerated, and the absurdity of the situations we find ourselves in is blown up into farce.

Humour and the brain

Duality in humour is not just the backbone of comedy, it also seems to be typical of the human brain's response to it. Freud believed that a joke had two halves – the build-up of tension and its sudden release. In addition, the best jokes consisted of a puzzle and its unexpected solution. The theory is that the puzzle or incongruity is picked up and processed in the left brain and the solution comes suddenly from the right brain, which is better at thinking spatially or globally. When the punch line arrives it is the forward part of the frontal lobe that becomes most active, showing that this is a crucial location for humour. This is the most advanced part of the brain – which might explain why animals don't appear to get jokes – but hitherto one of the least explained or 'silent' parts. It turns out to be unique in connecting up deeper inner areas like the limbic system with the temporal and frontal lobes, which process emotional expression and problem solving. So the roots of humour may derive from parts of our older or animal brain – the kind that giggle in response to tickling or feel primitive fear and tension – while the interpretation of humour is very modern and sophisticated in evolutionary terms. One of the factors in the healthy release of tension in the brain is that humour appears to join up many parts of brain activity, the opposite of what happens in depression, where there is less co-ordination between the two sides of the brain.

The two-part theory of humour is also very like many descriptions of the creative process. Arthur Koestler called it 'bisociation': 'Any mental occurrence simultaneously associated with two habitually incompatible contexts.' Silvano Arieti summed it up as:

1. Primary process: the need for disorder
2. Secondary process: the need for order
3. Tertiary process: the combination of 1 and 2 into a new order.[1]

This could indicate that the actual makings of a joke or humorous insight may be closely connected with creativity itself. It may also suggest that humorists may be creative and that creative people may have an inventive kind of humour.[2]

Research also suggests that humour is linked to consciousness and our perception of the world. This would confirm an old theory – that life is not funny *per se*; the humour lies in our perception of it. The humour may sometimes be in the very ambiguity between the real and the perceived, as with Magritte's painting of a pipe, marked 'Ceci n'est pas une pipe' or Ben Elton's observation: 'So tell me, why is there only one Monopolies Commission, eh?'

Clearly it does us good to escape through humour, one of the strongest arguments so far for the virtues of escapism. So much so that laughter has been found to improve immune system functioning, boost the body's defences such as antibodies in the bloodstream, and be one of the key factors in longevity of life. In addition it is considered in therapy terms to be one of the best coping mechanisms for dealing with the everyday stresses of life. Ironically, despite the fact that laughter probably does us more good than the rest of cinema put together, only a small handful of comedy names ever acquire lasting fame. This tiny number is absolutely dwarfed by the rest of the famous screen names – sex symbols, romantic leads, sultry enigmas, hot new talents, etc. It seems that comedians are like laughter itself – wonderful for a brief moment, but just a hiccup in the rest of life's serious purpose. Or like the life of the human itself, a 'brief candle', a 'poor player that struts and frets his hour upon the stage and then is heard no more', or 'a tale told by an idiot, full of sound and fury, signifying nothing'.

Escapism in literature – from *Don Quixote* to *Catch-22*

Amazon.com lists a massive total of 1,166 books with escape in the title, though curiously there are very few on escapism. But is literature itself escapist? William Stapledon wrote interestingly on this subject in 1939 for F. R. Leavis's *Scrutiny*, suggesting that 'escapist literature' is a subset of literature in general:

> We often hear it said disparagingly that some writer or other is a mere 'escapist' or that a particular piece of writing is sheer

'escapism'. It is implied that the true function of literature is not to offer escape from unpleasant facts but to help the reader to face up to reality and cope with it successfully. On the other hand we are told by many of those who are interested in the theory of art that the proper function of all art and therefore of literature is 'cathartic', that it should purge the spirit of pent-up forces which cannot express themselves in actual life, that it should afford symbolic fulfilment to our starved needs. Through art these pent-up forces are said to obtain 'release'. Sometimes it is claimed that, by diverting attention from the sordid actuality, art constructs symbols of a deeper reality, more consonant with the spirit's real needs. The need to clarify and develop experience seems to me the essential motive and the essential import of all that is genuine literature. We may distinguish between four predominant types of literature:

- creative literature – where the main import is creative
- propaganda literature – popularisation of facts, ideas and emotions
- release literature – the assuagement of starved needs, the release of pent-up emotions (adventure, sex...)
- escape literature – the main import of which is to protect the mind from some intolerable or unpleasant aspect of reality, to make the fictitious world more attractive and more seemingly real.

Motivation in escapist literature may be mainly unconscious – an unrecognised fear, a perversely creative blindness, which causes an unwitting incapacity to face up to reality. The false fantasy purports to be symbolically true of the real world of men and things. Escape literature may include a great deal of genuine creation, but it tends to distract attention from the need for social change, to prevent the development of experience, to withdraw attention from the inner life and to seek escape from individual moral responsibility by constructing a fictitious world in which individuals are wholly the product of external forces, physical or social. In escape literature there is no self-probing save in safe regions not inflamed by hidden conflict, and no attempt to relate the self's torture to the rest of existence.

Undoubtedly there is a great deal of writing which is escapist in the social sense. Its main import is to persuade the reader and the writer himself that after all there is not much wrong with the existing social order, or that God is backing it, and that certain conventional and outworn ideas and valuations, adequate in an earlier phase of society, are also adequate today. Escapist literature denies newer ideas which are appropriate to a changed social situation.[3]

Possibly the emphasis on escaping a moral challenge was of deep concern to the British in 1939, as Chamberlain's temporary illusion of 'peace in our time' was brutally succeeded by the actual imperative of preparing for a bloody war. Stapledon's criteria are stringent and his judgement of escapism in literature is harsh – 'I judge creation wholly good and escape wholly bad. In the case of propaganda, moral judgement depends on the goodness of the end preached. Release is harmless or actually desirable.' He may have been writing at a time when the 'self's torture' was acute, and the need for moral thought was inescapable. In more peaceful times he may possibly have situated escapism more towards the idea of release, and he admits that distinguishing the two is difficult.

Some great escapist characters

There are certain themes that run through the cavalcade of escapist heroes in literature. First, they have a vivid imagination and tend to confuse facts with lies, fantasy with reality. Second, they live in a drab environment – causing the dissatisfaction and 'need for change' that motivate the escapism. Third, they are surrounded by repressive material people who simply don't appreciate their hidden talent and secret worth. Fourth, they are, in the main, lovable eccentrics with charming and charismatic personalities. Since worries and responsibilities tend to accumulate with age, many escapist characters tend to have a strong childlike component. This may be as obvious as in Peter Pan, or it may be merely a naïve juvenile desire to escape from adulthood and the burdens of real life into a childlike adventure world.

Don Quixote

Don Quixote is the prototype escapist. As strange a hero as Walter Mitty, and no less lovable, he was also the product of a disabled dreamer. Cervantes himself is almost as good an example of the noble but somewhat unsuccessful adventurer as his eternal creation. Originally a soldier, he was imprisoned more than once, often lived in poverty and had high ideals. He remained a sunny optimist despite the repeated failure of his numerous stage plays, and only achieved success with *Quixote* late in life. Clearly he had a very strong sense of humour and an instinct for farce, so his high ideals must have had more than a trace of irony to them. His biographers assume his life was unhappy. Certainly it was hard – poverty, incessant struggle, disappointment and a disabled left hand caused by a gunshot wound, but Cervantes carried within himself the antidote to all these evils. His high spirits, vital energy, mental activity, restless invention and sanguine temperament allowed him sufficient 'escapism' to have remained in a state of optimism. His humour gave him release from failure and pomposity.

The escapism in *Don Quixote* exists on several levels, including, as we have seen with comedy, the inversion of high and low status. For a start, this tale of chivalry is set in La Mancha, the most prosaic and uninteresting province of Spain.

> Of all the dull central plateaux of the Peninsula it is the dullest tract. There is no redeeming feature in the Manchegan landscape; it has all the sameness of the desert without its dignity; the few towns and villages that break its monotony are mean and commonplace, there is nothing venerable about them, they have not even the picturesqueness of poverty; indeed, Don Quixote's own village, Argamasilla, has a sort of oppressive respectability in the prim regularity of its streets and houses; everything is ignoble; the very windmills are the ugliest and shabbiest of the windmill kind.[4]

Cervantes populates this boringly unsophisticated region with a motley assortment of 'agricultural' types. Together with his anti-hero Sancho Panza, the lying conniving realist, the stage is set for a ruthless parody of anything or anyone showing the slightest signs of nobility, ideals and imagination. The representation of the hero as a chivalrous knight had already become outdated in Spain by the time of writing (1605–15), and by the time the book had become popular it died a further death as the grandiosity of knights was popularly ridiculed in the wake of Cervantes' satire.

The punctured pomposity of the humour extends to the language itself. There is a natural gravity and a sonorous stateliness about Spanish, be it ever so colloquial, that make an absurdity doubly absurd, and give plausibility to the most preposterous statement.

The book represents as well as any the tragic-comic struggle between the ideal and the real, between the spirit of poetry and the spirit of prose, between fantasy and reality. Quixote does not have the escapism of the madman – he is sane, and can utter profound things where necessary. His 'madness' is that of an obsession running out of control, as if he takes chivalry to lengths that others take drink or gambling. In addition to this he is either myopic, visually impaired or cognitively disadvantaged. He is, for whatever reason, no stranger to optical illusions.

The moral of the book, so far as it can be said to have one, is

> that the spurious enthusiasm that is born of vanity and self-conceit, that acts on mere impulse, regardless of circumstances and consequences, is mischievous to its owner, and a very considerable nuisance to the community at large. To some *Don Quixote* is a sad book; to some minds it is sad that a man who had just uttered so beautiful a sentiment as 'it is a hard case to make slaves of those whom God and Nature made free', should be ungratefully pelted by the scoundrels his crazy philanthropy had let loose on society. But to others it will be a matter of regret that reckless self-sufficient enthusiasm is not oftener requited in some such way for all the mischief it does in the world.[5]

Sancho's mission throughout the book is to act as an unconscious Mephistopheles, always unwittingly making a mockery of his master's aspirations, always exposing the fallacy of his ideas by some unintentional ad absurdum, always bringing him back to the world of fact and the commonplace by force of sheer stolidity. 'About the ass,' we are told, 'Don Quixote hesitated a little, trying whether he could call to mind any knight-errant taking with him an esquire mounted on ass-back; but no instance occurred to his memory.' We can see the whole scene at a glance, the stolid unconsciousness of Sancho and the perplexity of his master, upon whose perception the incongruity has just forced itself. Sancho Panza – initially the realistic peasant – has some claim to be a secondary escapist character in the second part of *Quixote*, where he becomes an accomplished liar:

> In the First Part he displays a great natural gift of lying. His lies are not of the highly imaginative sort that liars in fiction commonly indulge in; like Falstaff's, they resemble the father that begets them; they are simple, homely, plump lies; plain working lies, in short. But in the service of such a master as Don Quixote he develops rapidly,

as we see when he comes to palm off the three country wenches as Dulcinea and her ladies in waiting. It is worth noticing how, flushed by his success in this instance, he is tempted afterwards to try a flight beyond his powers in his account of the journey on Clavileno.[6]

But who is the funnier – Quixote or the rest of the inhabitants of La Mancha? Maybe they all inhabit a 'middle landscape' – neither mad nor sane. What rescues the book from the merely absurd is Cervantes' insight into the foibles and eccentricities of ordinary human nature. Whereas Byron says of Quixote, 'It is his virtue makes him mad!', Ormsby considers the exact opposite to be true: 'It is his madness makes him virtuous.' Quixote – like Walter Mitty, Peer Gynt, Billy Liar, Oblomov and Peter Pan – has all the lovable qualities that escapists somehow possess, together with some of the Catch-22 of Yossarian. His humanity is an escape from the madness that surrounds him but his sanity imprisons him in his circumstances.

Oblomov

Russian author Goncharov's most famous creation, Oblomov, is an escapist of a totally different kind – the eternal procrastinator, crucially unable to resolve his whims and desires into either decision or action.

> If storm clouds of worry welled up from his soul, his eyes became melancholy, lines appeared in his forehead, doubts, sorrows, fears, flicked over his face but his anxiety seldom took the form of a definite idea, and even more rarely was it transformed into a decision. Every disturbance was settled with a sigh, then dissolved into apathy or drowsiness... He wore a dressing-gown of Persian material, an authentic oriental robe so capacious he could wrap it twice around himself... Lying down was not a necessity for Oblomov as it is for a man who is sick or sleepy, it was his normal state. When he was at home – and he was rarely not at home – he was always lying down, always in the same room that served as bedroom, study and reception room...

So Goncharov sets the scene for one of the most famous escapist characters in literature. Oblomov, in his perpetual dressing-gown, grapples with the task of dealing with realities such as the situation on his country estate, which prompts a succession of letters from his steward. Nothing actually gets done: 'Immediately on receiving the steward's first unpleasant letter several years earlier he had mentally begun to create a plan for certain changes and improvements in the management of his estate. However the plan was still far from being thought out and the unpleasant letters continued coming year after year, prompting him to act and destroying his tranquillity.'

His procrastination continues from minute to minute, hour to hour, day to day, year to year. 'As soon as he woke up he resolved to get up and wash and, after drinking tea, to think things over thoroughly. Tormented by his resolution, he lay in bed for another half hour. Then he decided there would be plenty of time after breakfast. He might just as well have it in bed as usual, particularly since there was nothing to prevent him from thinking while lying down.'

As with Don Quixote, an understandable escapist side of the human character is taken to farcical extremes. His environment has all the characteristic signs of neglect that the untidy among us know all too well and are too embarrassed to admit. He has all the paralysing inertia of the worst procrastinator. Even his servant is indifferent. 'It was indifference to his possessions and perhaps the even greater indifference of his servant Zakhar that made the study look so neglected and untidy.'

Oblomov raises some crucial questions. Was his a wasted life? Is isolation natural or unnatural, good or bad? In favour of isolation, Anthony Storr says, 'The capacity to be alone is a sign of inner security rather than an expression of a withdrawn state.' But how would Oblomov have lived without Zakhar and his many visitors? For like Quixote, Oblomov is a lovable character much cherished, despite his weaknesses, by those who know him. And as in *Quixote*, the humour is played with a straight face, making it much more poignant than the kind of farce where every joke is pointed out by a big stick and copious innuendo. The pathos is in real life — the escapist is all too easily recognised by us as exhibiting embarrassingly familiar human traits.

If we transposed Oblomov into the present and gave him a TV set, he might be little different from the thousands who live at home without going out much. Should we say of them too, 'A wasted life. He was as intelligent as anyone, and his soul was pure... clear as crystal. A noble and affectionate man and... he's gone. What was the reason? The reason... what a reason! Oblomovism.'

Peer Gynt

Peer Gynt is another of fiction's famous liars. Peer is a born liar, or perhaps evader of any truth that might prove uncomfortable or unpleasant. He lies to his mother, even on her deathbed, and spends much of his life skating through existence seeking pleasure and personal aggrandisement without putting out much effort. He even leaves behind the love of his life, Solveig, to avoid any form of commitment. He is totally superficial, as in his self-satisfied remark: 'Metodisk har jeg intet lært' – ('Methodically I have nothing learnt'), a pun that can be interpreted in two ways: 'I have never been methodical in obtaining knowledge' and 'I have methodically sought to remain ignorant', which of course is the underlying irony. When Peer finally returns to Norway a disillusioned old man, it is Solveig – a romantic *deus ex machina* – who saves him from total disintegration and the 'melting pot' into which Death puts all those souls who have never made an attempt to live life fully and properly. In a way he's a bit of a 19th-century yuppie – all grab and no give.

His creator, Ibsen, was a timid but high-minded idealist who was no stranger to evading reality. As a youth, while walking with a girl he was in love with, he fled upon seeing her father approaching. As an author he was a terrible procrastinator and sufferer of writer's block, devising endless rituals to fill in the time he should have been writing. As a Norwegian, he spent most of his life in Italy and Germany. His humour – like the rhymes in his verse – was clever and oblique, and he was strongly critical of much of Norwegian culture, such that when he was finally offered his country's highest award 'on behalf of the Norwegian people' he replied, 'There is no such thing as the Norwegian people – there is merely a population.'

Whilst the hero of his earlier play *Brand* personified Ibsen's idealistic stand against this rural culture and its superstitious conservative attitudes, Peer Gynt as a hero has many of the weaknesses of his national culture. His home, like that of most escapists, is drab and humdrum, 'every second windowpane is stuffed with rags, every fence and hedge is down, nowhere for the cows to shelter, all the meadows lying fallow'. The locals are provincial peasants, and his mother is a nagging materialist whose cynicism he shows scant regard for:

> *Peer:* I'll be a King, an Emperor...
> *Aase:* Now he has finally lost his wits!

Peer: Oh, yes I will – just give me time
Aase: 'Give me time' and I'll crow on a dunghill!
Peer: I was born for a more glorious end than that
Aase: Yes – cooling your heels from a gibbet!

Peer himself is a dyed-in-the-wool daydreamer, whose flights of fantasy grow seamlessly out of reality until they reach farcical dimensions and suddenly catapult back to earth:

Peer: Peer Gynt at the head of a great procession
A glittering company ride behind him
The women are curtseying. Everyone knows
Emperor Peer Gynt and his thousands of courtiers
He rides over the sea, Peer Gynt does
The King of England waits on the beach
And with him all of England's young women.
The King raises his crown and says...
Aslak the Smith: There's Peer Gynt, the drunken swine.

The world Peer inhabits is, as translator James McFarlane states

a fairy tale world of effortless transformations and of disconcerting transformations. For Peer, the return journey from reality to fantasy and back, from the substance to the shadow and return, requires no frontier formalities. Working and dreaming interpenetrate, fact and fantasy fuse, and all distinctions are blurred. The line between appearance and actuality, between fiction and fact, disappears in one great universe of the imagination. Fears are reborn as only nightmares can shape them, desires are achieved as only dreams can fulfil them. The frustrations of one moment become the achievements of the next. 'Black can seem white and the ugly beautiful; big can seem little and filth seems clean.' Peer is intoxicated by make-believe as other men are drunk on brandy. His is a world where wishes are horses and beggars *do* ride. Fantasy worlds counterfeit the real world; the real one mints again the fantastic. Some creatures such as the Woman in Green apparently live a valid life in both worlds; in the case of others appearances change – the village wedding guests become recognisable again in the trolls. Sometimes, as with the sound of church bells, reality penetrates fantasy; at other times – as with the Ugly Child – fantasy invades reality. All is an aspect of a single reality/fantasy continuum wherein fact is a function of fiction, invention of experience, and lies and life are one.[7]

Peter Pan

Peter Pan is probably the best-known piece of literature about escapism back to childhood. It substitutes the endless world of childhood for the inevitability of growing up, with its attendant loss of innocence and magic. Peter Pan is a kind of space orphan – a virtual creation symbolising the childhood of all and every one of us and its mix of adventure and helplessness, where the infant hero has not yet outgrown his need for mothering and someone to 'do the spring cleaning':

> As you look at Wendy, you may see her hair becoming white, and her figure little again, for all this happened long ago. Jane is now a common grown-up, with a daughter called Margaret; and every spring-cleaning time, except when he forgets, Peter comes for Margaret and takes her to the Neverland, where she tells him stories about himself, to which he listens eagerly. When Margaret grows up she will have a daughter, who is to be Peter's mother in turn; and thus it will go on, so long as children are gay and innocent and heartless.

At the same time as embodying gaiety and innocence, however, Peter Pan lives in the 'heartless' world of the child, where adventures carry within them the darker, crueller sides of the child's primitive fears – dangerous animals, imprisonment, pursuit by frightening hordes – and the wish of the child to take on these demons and fight them. As an exploration of the archetypal child's unconscious, the book – like all great literary creations – contains some innate realism in that it is rooted in human experiences and emotions, but the idea of never growing up is purely escapist. Barrie admits as much in the first sentence of his book, and in so doing introduces his creation: 'All children, except one, grow up.' The justification for his fantasy is not long in following: 'Mrs Darling put her hand to her heart and cried, "Oh, why can't you remain like this for ever!" '

As in all the typical escapist classics, the 'real' world is a humdrum place inhabited by frighteningly boring people. Mr Darling's reaction to having children is a farcical criticism of those who put money above life itself: 'I have one pound seventeen here, and two and six at the office; I can cut off my coffee at the office, say ten shillings, making two nine and six, with your eighteen and three makes three nine seven, with five naught naught in my cheque-book makes eight nine seven...' His inhuman reaction at the birth of Wendy and his calculations as to whether to keep her or not are just as heartless as anything in Peter Pan's world: 'and so on it went, and it added up differently each time; but at last Wendy just got through, with mumps reduced to twelve six, and the two kinds of measles treated as one.'

Barrie starts his story in foggy, habit-bound London, a mundane world peopled by awful adults whom you long to fly away from, and then keep on going. The escapist imagination in *Peter Pan* is like the layers of the onion in *Peer Gynt*, or the layers of time in *Time Bandits*, as in the description of Wendy's mother: 'Her romantic mind was like the tiny boxes, one within the other, that come from the puzzling East. However many you discover there is always one more.'

The lure of escapism is that wherever the frontier is, we can always go past it; wherever the future lies, there is always another future beyond it. It is like the riddle of the infinity of infinities – a Hilton Hotel of the Skies where even if the infinite number of rooms it contains are filled with an infinite number of people, there will always be room for the nocturnal traveller or the busload of virtual tourists. In the world of *Peter Pan* there will always be room for one more child... in the world of children's escapist fiction there will always be room for the next Harry Potter.

Lafcadio – the existential escapist

Lafcadio, one of the key characters in *Les Caves du Vatican* by André Gide, is an interesting example of the escapist, since he personifies the dilemma of how the individual is to achieve mastery over his actions inside a society for which that individual has no respect. Part escapist, part motivated by transcendence, he seeks some resolution. The same theme, of arbitrary murder as an 'intellectual act', features in Hitchcock's film *Rope* (1948).

Gide, in *Prométhée mal Enchaîné*, says, 'that which distinguishes man from animals is the "acte gratuite", a gratuitous action which is motivated by nothing – not any interests, passions, nothing – an action without vested interest which simply occurs. It is an act with no goal, no master, a free act'. The person who thus acts without reasoning can be called free. Such a person can accomplish anything, even an action that is completely absurd.

In *Les Caves du Vatican* Gide makes one of his characters carry out such an act. The young Lafcadio is travelling to Rome by train and finds himself in the same compartment as an old man called Fleurissoire. Suddenly, as the old man is standing by the train door, the idea occurs to Lafcadio to push his travelling companion out. He decides that if he can count up to 12 before the train passes a set of lights on the track, he will take no action. But on the count of 10 they pass a light and he carries out his act. The action is one accomplished without any foundation to it, as a result of an arbitrary decision that emerges by accident out of a purely mental caprice.

The underlying philosophy of the existential movement was a lot more profound than the tawdry and emotionally bankrupt act of the unlovable Lafcadio, who is as much an anti-hero as a hero in a French intellectual game which loves nothing better in life than a double paradox. Gide, the 'sombre casuist', had long been accused of labyrinthine thought and while his vision of the society that had condoned the awfulness of the First World War was as bleak as that of the other existentialists, the *acte gratuite* was more a piece of escapism than a moral solution – more a sullen reaction that 'if society can be so absurd, how can its inhabitants not be equally absurd?'.

Gide's belief was that

> the individuality of Man was the only thing of intrinsic worth in the universe, and that apart from Man and his works everything was absurd, chaotic and meaningless. Man's destiny, therefore, was to revolt against the outside world, to develop to the full his latent powers and so contribute to the uniqueness of the human race. Man's function is self-creation, his aim is to release through 'authentic living' the God that is within him.[8]

Like Nietzsche, Gide sees Man as his hero, his God – a force of nature different in kind to animals and the rest of life. But in attempting to deify man he runs across the familiar problem that the history of mankind is stained through and through with absurdity, cruelty and animal behaviour – not so much of an intellectual riddle to a Darwinist, of course. Unlike French poet Max Jacob, who postulated that man was fundamentally absurd ('une personnalité n'est qu'une erreur persistante') or Rimbaud, who chose to live a life of absurdity (a 'déréglement de tous les sens'), Gide was left with the attitude that since man had to be god-like, the absurdity had to come from somewhere outside him – maybe from society, or something else about the human condition.

In the majority of escapist literature, everyday life is humdrum but not weird, and the escapist escapes through imagination and dreams of adventure. For Gide – wrapped up in his intricate intellectual knots – everyday life, though equally empty, has a more profound absurdity, and his attempt to escape from it is a perpetual attempt to return to some kind of authenticity. Lafcadio tries to escape, however, only to enter a world even more disturbing and chaotic than the one he is attempting to transcend – something close to the world not of the freethinker but of the criminally insane. By this period of French literature and the arts one thing was for sure – the rigidly scientific deterministic 'reality' proposed by Descartes, where there was no room for absurdity – was as warped and out of shape as the clocks of Dali. In the aftermath of the First World War, Gide shows us absurdity without humour and an escapist with no lovable features, reminding us of Sherlock Holmes' observation that there is but one step from the grotesque to the horrible.

Walter Mitty

A creation of American humourist James Thurber, Walter Mitty has become the cultural figurehead for escapist fantasies. The character type of Mitty was even taken up by a psychologist, and 'Walter Mitty Syndrome' was put forward in a British medical journal as a clinical condition, which manifested itself in compulsive fantasising. Thurber himself had a rich fantasy life, partly because after his brother blinded him in one eye with an arrow playing William Tell he could not participate in the usual games and activities with other children. His difficulties continued as he had to drop out of university, and he later went almost totally blind. His poor eyesight made him the frequent victim of clumsy mistakes, adding to his rich sense of the absurd.

The story by Thurber, *The Secret World of Walter Mitty*, is very short, and its flavour is well captured in the following excerpt:

He picked up an old copy of *Liberty* and sank down into the chair. 'Can Germany Conquer the World Through the Air?' Walter Mitty looked at the pictures of bombing planes and of ruined streets.
   ...'The cannonading has got the wind up in young Raleigh, sir,' said the sergeant.

Captain Mitty looked up at him through tousled hair. 'Get him to bed,' he said wearily, 'with the others. I'll fly alone.'

'But you can't, sir,' said the sergeant anxiously. 'It takes two men to handle that bomber and the Archies are pounding hell out of the air. Von Richtman's circus is between here and Saulier.'

'Somebody's got to get that ammunition dump,' said Mitty. 'I'm going over. Spot of brandy?'

He poured a drink for the sergeant and one for himself. War thundered and whined around the dugout and battered at the door. There was a rending of wood and splinters flew through the room.

'A bit of a near thing,' said Captain Mitty carelessly.

'The box barrage is closing in,' said the sergeant.

'We only live once, Sergeant,' said Mitty, with his faint, fleeting smile. 'Or do we?'

He poured another brandy and tossed it off.

'I never see a man could hold his brandy like you, sir,' said the sergeant. 'Begging your pardon, sir.'

Captain Mitty stood up and strapped on his huge Webley-Vickers automatic.

'It's 40 kilometres through hell, sir,' said the sergeant.

Mitty finished one last brandy. 'After all,' he said softly, 'what isn't?'

The pounding of the cannon increased; there was the rat-tat-tatting of machine guns, and from somewhere came the menacing pocketa-pocketa-pocketa of the new flame-throwers. Walter Mitty walked to the door of the dugout humming 'Aupres de Ma Blonde'. He turned and waved to the sergeant.

'Cheerio!' he said…

Something struck his shoulder. 'I've been looking all over this hotel for you,' said Mrs Mitty. 'Why do you have to hide in this old chair? How did you expect me to find you?' 'Things close in,' said Walter Mitty vaguely.

Much of the fame of *Mitty* comes from the film starring Danny Kaye. In the film, Walter Mitty, like Don Quixote, is the 'escapist adventurer' – a daydreaming accountant with an overprotective mother and a possessive girlfriend, whose flights into unreality feature himself experiencing great adventures as various macho hero types – great surgeon, RAF pilot, riverboat gambler, brave sea captain. His dream becomes true when he accidentally meets a mysterious woman who hands him a little black book. According to her it contains the locations of the Dutch crown jewels, hidden since the Second World War. Mitty soon finds himself in the middle of a complex conspiracy and finds out that dreaming of adventure is one thing but living it and trying to be a hero in real life is a whole different story. In the book, of course, Mitty's derring-do occurs uniquely in his fantasy, so making anything real is not exactly in the original spirit of the creation, and contradicts the absurd dimension of Thurber's vision.

Part of Thurber's art is that 'reality' is a movable feast. Plenty more of Thurber's characters, in fact, become convinced of the impossible in the course of another short story. In *The Day the Dam Broke*, the entire citizenry of the East Side of Columbus flees from a non-existent tidal wave. In real life he described his grandmother's 'groundless fears', including 'the horrible suspicion that electricity was dripping invisibly all over the house', an image reproduced in one of his cartoons. Other cartoons continue this spooky sense of fantasy. One of the best known shows a couple in bed, and the irritated wife snapping, 'All right, have it your way – you heard a seal bark!' Unreality increases in *The Moth and the Star*, where a moth spends each night trying to fly to a star he thinks is 'just caught in the top branches of an elm'. His father ridicules him: 'All your brothers have been badly burned flying around street lamps!'

Billy Liar

A modern escapist hero is Billy Liar, an ambitious but lazy young man caught in a dull job routine and a dreary home life, who spends most of his time daydreaming about a land where he is a hero. A number of minor indiscretions cause Billy to lie in order to avoid the penalties. As these events start catching up with him, he finds himself telling bigger lies to cover his tracks. Finally, when his life is a total mess, and nobody believes a word he says, an opportunity to just run away and leave it all behind presents itself, and Billy has a difficult decision to make.

The literary creation of Keith Waterhouse (and made into an excellent film starring Tom Courtenay), Billy Liar owes much to his escapist antecedents like Peer Gynt and Walter Mitty, as can be seen in the very beginning of the book:

Lying in bed, I abandoned the facts again and was back in Ambrosia.

By rights, the march-past started in the Avenue of the Presidents... One by one the regiments marched past, and when they had gone a hush fell over the crowds and they removed their hats for the proud remnants of the Ambrosian Grand Yeomanry. It was true that we had entered the war late, and some criticised us for that; but out of two thousand who went into battle only seven remained to hear the rebuke. The war memorial was decked with blue poppies, the strange bloom found only in Ambrosia.

I put an end to all this, consciously and deliberately, by going 'Da da da da da da da' aloud to drive the thinking out of my head. It was a day for big decisions.

The book also makes some surely conscious references to Oblomov – it begins with the hero daydreaming in bed and even refers to an oriental dressing-gown: 'I put on the old raincoat I used for a dressing-gown, making the resolution that now I must buy a real dressing-gown, possibly a silk one with some kind of dragon motif.'

The prosaic middle-class drabness of Billy's surroundings is a now-familiar backdrop: 'Hillcrest was the kind of dwelling where all the windows are leaded in a fussy crisscross, except one which is a porthole.' Breakfast was equally ritualised: 'Ay Yorkshire breakfast scene. Ay polished table, one leaf out, covahed diagonally by ay white tablecloth, damask, with grrreen strip bordah. Sauce stain to the right, blackberry stain to the centre. Kellogg's corn flakes, Pyrex dishes, plate of fried bread. Around the table, the following personnel: fathah, mothah, grandmothah, one vacant place.' The 'personnel' have the familiar tone of materialistic nagging:

Gran chipped in: 'He wants to burn that raincoat, then he'll have to get dressed of a morning.' One of Gran's peculiarities, and she had many, was that she would never address anyone directly but always went through an intermediary, if necessary some static object such as a cupboard. Doing the usual decoding I gathered that she was addressing my mother and that he who should burn the raincoat was the old man, and he who would have to get dressed of a morning was me. The old man interrupted:

'And what bloody time did you get in last night? If you call it last night. This bloody morning more like.'

I sliced the top off my boiled egg, which in a centre favouring tapping the top with a spoon and peeling the bits off was always calculated to annoy.

Billy tries to escape from his environment at the very end, and in a fit of exhilarating bravado nearly makes it – only to be dragged back by a curious version of the *acte gratuite* in *Les Caves du Vatican*:

> I took out the ticket and looked at it... I could not think except in confused snatches. I began to count 10; at the end of the count I would oblige myself to answer one way or the other. One. Two. Three. Four. 'The train now leaving platform three is the one thirty-five for London, calling at...' Five. Six. Seven. There was no need to count to the end. I picked up the suitcase, feeling deflated and defeated. I walked out of the waiting room and across the booking hall to the ticket barrier. I did not wait for the train to leave. I transferred the suitcase to my left hand and walked out of the station... and then I began the slow walk home.

Yossarian

The character Yossarian presents a particularly interesting view of the escapist, because the backdrop for Joseph Heller's novel *Catch-22* is not humdrum life but a dangerous war zone. As we have seen, the ways out of a difficult situation are transcendence, escape and escapism. The accepted patriotic reaction to war is transcendence, but this assumes that a war is logical and necessary. Heller lampoons the idea of transcendence in the constant escalation of the missions the airmen are ordered to fly and the ludicrous prioritising of 'neat' patterns of bomb explosions by Colonel Cathcart. Like the great realistic war poets he sees war as dangerous, loud and fearful and he feels pity for its protagonists, such as the blown-to-bits Snowden ('where are the Snowdens of yesteryear?', punning on François Villon's achingly beautiful line 'mais ou sont les neiges d'antan?'). As Wilfred Owen wrote, 'the subject of it is war and the pity of war. The poetry is in the pity'.

Yossarian is Heller's mouthpiece for the ordinary soldier caught up in war, and he 'tells it like it is':

> The only thing going on was a war, and no one seemed to notice but Yossarian and Dunbar. And when Yossarian tried to remind people they drew away from him and thought he was crazy...
> 'They're trying to kill me,' Yossarian told him calmly.
> 'No one's trying to kill you,' Clevinger cried.
> 'Then why are they shooting at me?' Yossarian asked.

'They're shooting at everyone,' Clevinger answered, 'they're trying to kill everyone.'

'And what difference does that make?'

Yossarian is fully aware of the power of patriotic spin that has turned his fellow soldiers into unthinking fighting machines, and has to hold on determinedly to his view of reality: 'It was all a sensible young gentleman like himself could do to maintain his perspective amid so much madness. And it was urgent that he did, for he knew his life was in peril.'

The madness of the war operates on different levels – first, the basic level that war, ie attacking and annihilating our own species, is madness; second, the level that all this is validated by government propaganda and third, that it divides humans into 'heroes' who are prepared to throw their lives away and 'cowards' who obey the natural human instinct for preserving their lives:

It was a vile and muddy war, and Yossarian could have lived without it – lived forever perhaps. Only a fraction of his countrymen would give up their lives to win it, and it was not his ambition to be among them. History did not demand Yossarian's premature demise... That men would die was a matter of necessity; which men would die, though, was a matter of circumstance, and Yossarian was willing to be the victim of anything but circumstance. But that was war.

Heller fully exploits the paradoxes implicit in the situation, and the title, *Catch-22*, is the ultimate paradox in an insufferable reality where the protagonists should have already been sent home for fulfilling their 40 missions but are being forced to fly more and more purely to satisfy the vanity and desire for promotion of Colonel Cathcart. Flying these missions is madness, so you can be medically grounded for insanity. However, once grounded you are no longer insane and therefore fit for duty, so you are put back on missions. There is no escape, as Yossarian finds when he puts the question to Doc Daneeka:

'Is Orr crazy?'

'He sure is,' Doc Daneeka said.

'Can you ground him?'

'I sure can. But first he has to ask me to. That's part of the rule.'

'Then why doesn't he ask you?'

'Because he's crazy,' Doc Daneeka said. 'He has to be crazy to keep flying combat missions after all the close calls he's had. Sure, I can ground Orr. But first he has to ask me to.'
    'That's all he has to do to be grounded??'
    'That's all. Let him ask me.'
    'And then you can ground him?' Yossarian asked.
    'No. Then I can't ground him.'
    'You mean there's a catch?'
    'Sure there's a catch,' Doc Daneeka replied. 'Catch-22. Anyone who wants to get out of combat duty isn't really crazy.'

On the face of it Yossarian looks like an escapist   his avoidance of unpleasant reality, his fanciful excursions like walking around naked, his vague liver condition enabling him to walk in and out of hospital, and his surreal censoring of the men's post, which he signs 'Washington Irving' or 'Irving Washington' as the whim takes him. In fact, almost the whole cast of the book are escapists in different ways – Major Major, who flees from his fellow troops out of the back of his tent and can only be 'seen' when he is out, and Colonel Scheisskopf, who ignores the reality of his wife's adultery in his escapist addiction to parades:

It was the despair of Lieutenant Scheisskopf's life to be chained to a woman who was incapable of looking beyond her own dirty, sexual desires to the titanic struggles for the unattainable in which noble man could become heroically engaged.
    'Why don't you ever whip me?' she pouted one night.
    'Because I haven't the time,' he snapped at her impatiently. 'I haven't the time. Don't you know there's a parade going on?'

Heller's whole message, though, is that in a crazy world only the 'crazy' – who reject it and try to escape from it – are sanc. To make this point he deliberately turns everything around: 'The Texan turned out to be good-natured, generous and likeable. In three days no one could stand him.'
    The text is full of such reversals. But the core of the book is the reversal of war and peace, and the madness and pity implicit in a situation that has to be endured because there is no apparent escape and no alternative – a metaphor for life itself.

Dunbar loved shooting skeet because he hated every minute of it and the time passed so slowly.

'Do you know how long a year takes when it's going away?' Dunbar repeated to Clevinger. 'This long.' He snapped his fingers.

'A second ago you were stepping into college with your lungs full of fresh air. Today you're an old man...You're inches away from death every time you go on a mission. How much older can you be at your age? A half minute before that you were stepping into high school, and an unhooked brassiere was as close as you ever hoped to get to Paradise. Only a fifth of a second before that you were a small kid with a 10-week summer vacation that lasted a hundred thousand years. And still ended too soon. Zip! They go rocketing by so fast. How the hell else are you ever going to slow time down?' Dunbar was almost angry when he finished.

'Well, maybe it's true,' Clevinger conceded unwillingly in a subdued tone. 'Maybe a long life does have to be filled with many unpleasant conditions if it's to seem long. But in that event who wants one?'

'I do,' Dunbar told him.

'Why?' Clevinger asked.

'What else is there?'

Hugh Hefner – the sexual escapist

Hugh Hefner – a publisher rather than a literary figure – was the symbol and figurehead of sexual escapism in the 20th century, basking in his artificial world of smiling and compliant big-breasted young models and starlets, bunny images of women called 'pets' and a 'womb couch' where all your needs are met by a pet at the touch of a button. Feminists hated it all and with good reason – women were reduced to cartoon figures and spread over gatefolds for men to stick on walls and locker doors and to keep under the bed or in some mouldy brown box at the bottom of the cupboard away from the prying eyes of girlfriends or mothers. When his publication *Playboy* was accused of lacking any depth or reality, he would vigorously argue that every issue contained some profound political comment, some interview with a leading intellectual figure, some new short story by a well-known writer of the time. The women, of course, remained exactly the same, and the rabbit's ears stayed on.

The escapism was exactly the kind that Stapledon criticised: 'Escape literature tends to distract attention from the need for social change, to prevent the development of experience, to withdraw attention from the inner life and to seek escape from individual moral responsibility by constructing a fictitious world in which individuals are wholly the product of external forces, physical or social.'[9] Porn images isolated the sexual dimension from the rest of the person, delayed social change – where were the rabbit's ears on the men? – and offered a comfortable escapist environment where sexual relief could be obtained in virtuality with no questions asked and no intervening reality of a physical person with needs, feelings, preferences and points of view.

Hefner was one of very many men, including Bob Guccione and Peter Stringfellow, who made a lot of money out of sex in the 20th century. The claim was always of liberation from the hackles of convention and conservative sexual attitudes, and that the women who were paid for what they did somehow also did it willingly and enjoyed every moment of stripping off. There is some truth in the last part, since a number of women enjoy being looked at by men, and a smaller number want to be looked at so much that they enjoy taking their clothes off. But the question waiting to be asked is why such women invest so much of their attraction in their physical bodies that they become unsure of the strength of their intellectual and emotional identities, as indeed many are. The 'hysterical' patient in psychiatry is the most likely to feel empty within, seek excitement in the outer environment, and feel that life isn't 'real'. So what might seem on the surface a win–win situation – guys who like to look and girls who like to be looked at – may contain a more profound emptiness. Neither money nor attention nor sex is the same thing as loving, or even liking a person.

PART III

Simulation

SEVEN

Simulation and Creativity in Human Evolution

Can you have intelligence without consciousness? I don't know.
                                                    Arthur C. Clarke

To sociobiologist Richard Dawkins, consciousness derives from man's capacity to simulate, the evolution of which is something he considers the most profound mystery facing modern biology; consciousness, he speculates, arises when the brain's simulation of the world becomes so complete that it must include a model of itself. We have – in robots and artificial intelligence – evolving models of ourselves. Such artefacts are ingenious, but they are still far from achieving the consciousness that humans uniquely possess.

The third part of our exploration of the 'virtual worlds' we live in deals with simulation, the process of invention and the products of our simulations. Just as we have seen that the escapist is very close to the creative personality, so simulation – the creation of a new model – is very close to creativity. The word was originally used in its meaning of 'pretence' – to imitate, to counterfeit or to fake an emotion. In man-made products like simulated fur, it then meant to resemble the real thing, a meaning very like 'virtual'. When it became used in science and technology its meaning became specifically that of 'modelling' something. In psychology it was used for modelling human behaviour, in the City for financial modelling and in the aviation world for modelling flight behaviour. It is used also in music for simulating different sounds, in physics for modelling stresses due to, for example, frost action and in computing for modelling cognitive functions (as in the General Problem Solver (GPS)).

Only a few centuries ago it would have been said that what separates us from the animal world is our capacity to reason. Reasoning has surely helped to shape our culture, but a more powerful force in human development is imagination and the urge to create. Creativity is related to reasoning ability, but if we allow for a good level of reasoning as a basis, then the creative personality is different from the purely rational. In particular, it tends to think more symbolically and make more daring jumps between one subject and another. Such imaginative thinking gives us several alternative possibilities, from the meaningful and useful to the frivolous and totally fanciful. These alternatives or 'abstracts' can then be compared with the present state of things. In evolutionary terms abstract thinking has been facilitated by language, leading us to concepts and the foundations of thought. Out of concepts we get simulations – models of how things behave. And out of simulated models we get all the artefacts of our new technology – machines to knit wool, bicycles that go faster than our legs can, computers that perform calculations, and eventually robots, artificial worlds run by intelligent systems, cloned animals and artificial intelligence itself.

Our ability to conjure up many alternatives makes us uniquely adaptable to our environment, unlike creatures lower down the evolutionary scale, which are largely governed by pre-programmed patterns. An animal's basic needs for survival will be provided for as long as the environment remains constant, but if the environment does not, it cannot easily adapt to changing circumstances. Humans do have a range of built-in responses in order to ensure survival, but their unique advantage is the ability to learn. And when environments are as different as that which is found on the moon and other planets, man's ability to exist in such alien worlds – maybe one day to conquer them – is proof of enormous innovation, ingenuity and skill. The whole key to such sophisticated exercises in survival is the replacement of innate programmes with adaptive and creative thought.

Imagination, the double-edged sword

But imagination is a double-edged sword – it creates both instruments of destruction like the nuclear bomb, and instruments of salvation as in radiation treatment for cancer. The very gift that can destroy our environment is the one gift that can offer some kind of lateral thinking that might save us. We need imagination to save us from our own imagination: 'The human species uniquely confronts the dilemma of a powerful imagination that, while it makes escape to a better life possible, also makes possible lies and deception, solipsistic fantasy, madness, unspeakable cruelty, violence, destructiveness and evil.'[1]

In another, more emotional way, imagination also lies behind the 'divine discontent' humans feel: 'Imagination, it is safe to say, is more highly developed in human beings than in any other creature. It is clear that the development of human imagination is biologically adaptive; but it is also the case that we have had to pay a certain price for this development. Imagination has given man flexibility, but in doing so has robbed him of contentment.'[2]

The double-edged sword of imagination, to Anthony Storr, contains the unavoidable disappointment of man's environment never perfectly meeting his needs or fulfilling his desires for perfect happiness. Even transcendental experiences of happiness, like falling in love, are transient. Dissatisfaction with what is, or 'divine discontent', is an inescapable part of the human condition. This is a view echoed by Yi-Fu Tuan, who considers the human being as 'an animal who is congenitally indisposed to accept reality as it is'.

Storr puts it thus: 'Man's extraordinary success as a species springs from his discontent, which compels him to use his imagination and thus spurs men on to further conquests and to ever-increasing mastery of the environment.'[3] Freud introduces a further element with his concept of wish-fulfilment – the idea that it is unhappy people that fantasise: 'We may lay it down that a happy person never phantasises [sic], only an unsatisfied one. The motive forces of phantasies are unsatisfied wishes, and every single phantasy is the fulfilment of a wish, a correction of an unsatisfying reality.'[4]

Storr considers Freud's view of fantasy as 'essentially escapist, a turning away from reality rather than a preliminary to altering reality in the desired direction', and prefers the view of imagination as a positive adaptive force. He criticises Freud in that

> he seems to assume that the real world can or should be able to provide complete satisfaction and that ideally it should be possible for the mature person to abandon phantasy altogether. Freud was too realistic, hard-headed and pessimistic a man to believe that this ideal could ever be reached. Nevertheless he did consider that phantasy should become less and less necessary as the maturing individual approached rational adaptation to the external world.[5]

Storr is heavily inclined towards imagination as the engine behind some of mankind's most spectacular achievements, and a force that was often misunderstood as absurd by conventional pattern-bound contemporaries:

> Newton's notion that gravity was a universal which acted at enormous distances was a leap of the imagination which must have seemed absurd until he was able to demonstrate it mathematically. Kekule's discovery of the ring structure of organic molecules originated from a dream-like vision of atoms combining in chains which then formed into coils like snakes, eating their own tails. Einstein's special theory of relativity depended upon his being able to imagine how the universe might appear to an observer travelling at near the speed of light. These are examples of phantasies which, although originating in imagination, nevertheless connected with the external world in ways which illuminated it and made it comprehensible.[6]

He adds a cautionary reference to 'phlogiston', at one time considered the material principle of combustibility and later revealed – as many other failed theories have been – to be pure delusion. Imagination is clearly a hit or miss phenomenon, proved only in hindsight. But without it successful theories would not be possible. To Storr this bridging of the inner and outer world remains the key to the evolutionary value of imagination:

> There are good biological reasons for accepting the fact that man is so constituted that he possesses an inner world of the imagination which is different from, though connected to, the world of external reality. It is the discrepancy between the two worlds that motivates creative imagination. People who realise their creative potential are constantly bridging the gap between inner and outer. They invest the external world with meaning because they disown neither the world's objectivity nor their own subjectivity.[7]

Incubation in creativity

The discrepancy between the actual and the ideal may motivate escapism or it may motivate the desire for mastery. In the creative personality it is likely to initiate a state of 'incubation' where the problem is considered quietly in the unconscious, even in sleep, until new pathways are found and ideas emerge into consciousness.

There is abundant evidence of the value of 'incubation' in creativity, and it has been described by creatives as varied as Einstein, Kekule, Henry James, Housman and Mozart. In a survey of 83 Nobel Prize science and medicine laureates, 72 strongly implicated intuition in their success.

Michel Brown (Medicine, 1985) said: 'We felt at times there was almost a hand guiding us, because we would go from one step to the next and somehow we would know which was the right way to go; and I really can't tell how we knew that...'

Konrad Lorenz (Medicine, 1973) agrees that incubation in its own time can be superior to conscious trying: 'If you press too hard nothing comes of it. You must give a sort of mysterious pressure and then rest, and suddenly BING!... the solution comes.'

This is supported by evidence that 'trying' restricts choice, while spontaneous inspiration increases the variety of solutions entertained. Data on creatives from the Myers Briggs Type Indicator™ confirms this – spontaneous creatives were found to be those most respected by their peers in terms of talent, though in the real world structured and planning personalities with convergent attitudes tended to be more successful in routine activities. As it says in Ecclesiastes, 'Wisdom comes through leisure – he that hath little business shall become wise.'

Psychology – which was much taken by creativity in the sixties – has taken up again the idea of 'the intelligent unconscious' and the neglected faculty of intuition. With this comes a questioning of the established tenet that explicit articulate thinking is the most powerful form of cognition, to be taught in schools and universities and used in areas of problem solving or decision making. Popularly used forms of alternate thinking are referred to as 'mind mapping', indicating that creative thinking is back with us and that the mysterious 'creative flame' offers something beyond pure rationalisation.

Incubation in sleep

'Higamus hogamus, woman is monogamous; hogamus higamus, man is polygamous', wrote that pioneer of psychology, William James, in a moment of sleepy inspiration that turned out to be something less than earth shattering the next morning. Nevertheless, invention can be strong in the middle of the night. After the first part of deep sleep, there is lighter sleep where one can wake up with useful thoughts, even a productive flow, as it were a magic golden thread. Some of a writer's best work is done after deep sleep and in the early hours, when the cosiness and warmth of one's bed beckons but the mind is unavoidably drawn to write. There is something about that time of the morning when invention is at its purest and the noise of the world is at its weakest. Commercially, the music industry has created the truism that there is no money in silence (well, maybe a little in John Cage's *4'33*), but for invention, silence is indeed golden – the goose that lays the golden eggs. The analogy with birds is not entirely fortuitous – research from the University of Chicago suggests that birds spend their nights dreaming up new songs and rehearsing them to become pitch perfect and try out new melodic variations.

We seem to have some innate capacity for working things out in our sleep – there is as much truth in the adage 'sleep on it' as there is in Freud's idea of censored desires. Sleep is a miraculous 'undiscovered world' – to sleep, perchance to dream, perchance to create. Dreams that fade in the light of day seem sometimes so profound that we may feel like Wordsworth in his *Ode to Immortality*, that consciousness 'is but a forgetting' and that 'the soul that rises with us, our life's star, cometh from afar'.

Science fiction

> We science fiction writers never attempt to predict. As my friend Ray Bradbury said, 'We do this not to predict the future but to prevent it.'
>
> Arthur C. Clarke

One question humans have never satisfactorily answered is 'Why do we exist?' We have a lot of information on how we exist and when we existed, but the fundamental riddle of existence remains unanswered. Theories have been supplied by science, religion, even poetry. But in a way, the 'cosmic yearning' of the imaginative soul has found some of its best expression in the simulations and future modelling of science fiction writing.

Science fiction writers rightly see their genre as much more serious than 'escapism', and certainly not the avoidance of reality through fantasy or other forms of diversion. They see their vocation as the chronicling of present and future reality through fantasy; not avoiding reality but rather seeking to illuminate the human condition by examining it in circumstances that could not occur in our day-to-day lives, so providing unique and provocative insights. SF may not be able to prove 'why we exist' but it does attempt to give us some plausible alternatives to ponder.

As a term, 'science fiction' originally comes from the mid 19th century, and was revived in the late 1920s by Hugo Gernsback, an American magazine editor who featured the stories of greats such as H. G. Wells and Jules Verne. To Gernsback, a science fiction story was 'a charming romance intermingled with scientific fact and prophetic vision'.[8] The expression 'scientific romance' was used by Wells and has survived in the relationship between some genres of SF and Gothic romance, though later writers moved SF increasingly into the pure and life sciences such as physics, sociology and psychology.

As advances have occurred in science, SF has been consistently used to explore their 'applications', to use a technical term. In an era of rapid scientific and technological development, it explored the human consequences of industrialisation, the implications of Darwin's evolutionary theory, Einstein's theory of relativity, and the second law of thermodynamics concerning the ultimate entropy of a closed system like the universe. Its exploration of these phenomena mainly took the form of storytelling, and this – together with a cast of colourful and strange characters – underlies its popular appeal.

Is it fair, with a genre that is inherently about simulation and projection, to say that SF 'lacks literary realism' or 'lacks character depth', as has been argued? Its greatest writers have, in fact, striven for and achieved both depth of character and a quasi-realistic depiction of the future using familiar elements understood through the present. If the future is a dehumanised technical society, then the roots of this can be found in the present. They would also argue that exploring the direction in which we are evolving as a society is a valid way of exploring the fundamental question of 'What constitutes the human?'

The duality of the real and the virtual, the interface between man and machine, is central to both SF and real-life computer technology like VR. One of its first and greatest expressions was in Mary Shelley's *Frankenstein, Or The Modern Prometheus* (1817). The whole ethical debate around artificially created life gained sudden momentum from this startling creation, which predated laboratory-created life like Dolly the sheep by nearly two centuries. *Frankenstein* expressed not only the duality between romantic hero and machine that characterised much later SF work, but also the confrontation between one form and the other. How should we think of an alien form – as something deserving to be understood, or as a mere monster? And who is alien to whom? Humans themselves are 'aliens' to other life forms, and planet Earth is just one tiny part of the cosmos. We have already come far from the grandiose historical concept that the stars revolved around the earth, and that lower life forms revolved around the supremacy and mastery of the human race.

With the work of Wells we see a blueprint for a lot of the SF that was to follow. Starting in the last decade of the 19th century – the time when Freud was making his most famous discoveries about the nature of the human mind – Wells's novels *The Time Machine* (1895) and *The War of the Worlds* (1898) provide models for a range of subsequent SF and a good many film and TV spin-offs. To him we owe time travel, pseudo-scientific discourse, sociological criticism and prediction, confrontation with the alien, the death of the world, interplanetary war and invasion by aliens.

As we move into the more modern period of SF, we start to see the distinction between the utopians and the dystopians. The romantic stream of SF continues with the mythical and spiritual world of C. S. Lewis and its angels instead of space ships as a means of interplanetary travel. The cynical and satirical view of the future, where man's social, political and technological experiments are responsible for a series of disasters, is more the realm of Aldous Huxley's *Brave New World* (1932), George Orwell's *Nineteen Eighty-Four* (1949) and John Wyndham's *The Day of the Triffids* (1951).

Some of the concepts used in SF were simply updates of ideas common in great literature. Wyndham's *The Kraken Wakes* (1953) and *The Midwich Cuckoos* (1957) depict catastrophic disturbances of the natural and social order in a way that Shakespeare had already hinted in his tragedies. *The Day of the Triffids*, with its doomsday scenario of a small band of survivors marooned in an arduous environment that they need to adapt to to survive, harks back directly to Daniel Defoe's *Robinson Crusoe* (1719). One virtue of this is that the old and familiar are used to guide the reader into the worlds of the new and strange.

'Cosmic yearning' is the flavour of the writing of Arthur C. Clarke (b. 1917), who continues the tradition of Jules Verne – meticulous technological detail combined with a romantic vision of man striving to transcend his environment. This proved just what Hollywood was looking for, and as the cinema began to take up the work of the great SF writers, he went on to write the screenplay for Stanley Kubrick's film *2001: A Space Odyssey* (1968). TV series like *Star Trek* continue this transcendental view of man's enormous powers through his mastery of advanced technology. Brian Aldiss mirrors the romantic nostalgia of *Star Trek* and the theme of imagined catastrophe, adding exotic images and the Heraclitic realisation that everything changes and nothing stays the same, that we can never step twice into the same river.

Futurists continue to be divided between the utopians and the dystopians, and hardly any SF rings a hollower note than that of J. G. Ballard (b. 1930), who brings to SF a kind of black desolation, full of strange visions and paradoxical thinking. One of the most psychological of all the SF writers, the inner landscapes of his motley crew of characters are as unsettlingly alien as the surreal outer landscapes they populate. He is a disturbing writer, with a bleak cynicism reflecting his traumatic experiences in the Far East during the Second World War, and his catastrophe novels, like *The Drowned World* (1962), *The Drought* (1965) and *The Crystal World* (1966), have none of the romance or optimism of mainstream SF. His tales of urban dissonance, like *Concrete Island* (1974) and *High Rise* (1975), are disturbingly modern, suggesting a theme we have encountered already with other SF writers – that the irrevocable roots of catastrophe are already growing in our culture. He is filmable in a different genre, his novel *Crash!* (1973) being closer to the cult underground than the Hollywood epic, more punk than utopia.

The future is a shared destiny of both sexes, unless something surprising changes our evolutionary path, and a much-needed female perspective was brought to the genre by Doris Lessing, already a widely read feminist author. The cynicism and vision of the decline and breakdown of society in *The Four-Gated City* (1969) and *Briefing for a Descent into Hell* (1971) are, however, as strong as her explorations of gender and spiritual awakening. A writer on the grand scale, she interweaves the mystical and the psychic into her utopian worlds assailed by the empires of evil. *The Marriages between Zones Three, Four and Five* (1980) offers a potentially more positive future role for women, and goes beyond the typical marginalisation of women in SF, paradoxical for a genre that started with Mary Shelley. A growing number of women are now involved in the genre – Michèle Roberts, Zoë Fairbairns, Sarah Lefanu, and the list will lengthen as women become more familiar with new technology from their use of computers and the Net.

151

Just as 'convergence' is the buzz word of entertainment culture on the Internet, so science fiction and science fact are converging as 'theory' meets application and computer culture rapidly becomes more sophisticated and takes a stronger place in modern culture. New terms like 'cyberspace' and 'cyberpunk' entered the SF vocabulary with William Gibson's *Neuromancer* (1984), called by Fredric Jameson 'the supreme literary expression if not of postmodernism, then of late capitalism itself'. Jeff Noon continues cyberpunk in *Vurt* (1993) and *Pollen* (1995), intermixing the tradition of the human/machine duality with another familiar piece of literature – the old-fashioned detective and suspense story. David Brin, with a Ph.D. in space physics and four years' experience as a research engineer, is uniquely placed to impart realism to the cutting edge of space travel, and his novels, such as *Startide Rising* and the *Uplift* trilogy have won several awards.

As SF moves from book to screen, more up-to-date metaphors evolve. In the film *The Matrix*, virtual reality is explored in the vision of a human race reared like battery hens literally to form a huge battery or energy source. Because they live in a virtual reality something akin to Plato's cave – with no knowledge of anything more 'real' than what they experience, they do not realise their true condition or the point of their existence. This is an update of a very old question – how do we know that our environment is 'real' or in fact anything other than what we perceive it to be? Even mainstream film-makers like Woody Allen have experimented with 'impossible' distortions of reality, like morphing one person into another in *Zelig* (1984), cryogenics in *Sleeper* (1973), the violation of the fourth wall in *Annie Hall* (1977), invisibility in *Alice* (1990) and Tom Baxter walking out of the screen of the film he is acting in, into the cinema in *The Purple Rose of Cairo* (1985) – an intriguing study of moving between actuality and virtuality.

Robots and androids

So much for fiction – but how far has the human/machine and the real/virtual duality come in real life? We are far from the ideals of SF, but we are steadily advancing with robots, intelligent systems and artificial intelligence. The word 'robot' comes from the Czech for 'slave', and this is an adequate description of their function to date, the 'master' being the human control centre. They are used for building cars, performing mechanised tasks, exploring space and hazardous environments, keyhole surgery – the list goes on and on.

The most intriguing (though not necessarily the best technically) examples are androids like Terminator or Robocop – robots built on the model of the human body. Primitive androids have been with us for 300 years in the shape of clockwork automata performing simple functions. Contemporary designs like the plastic-bodied androids with miniature electric motors built by the Honda research laboratory in Japan are still a very long way from Robocop, but are becoming increasingly more functional.

There are huge problems to overcome. One is reproducing the fine control of the human hand, which has 9,000 sensors per inch and needs the use of a strain gauge to avoid crushing delicate objects. Another is balance – 98 per cent of the earth's surface is not flat so movement is a traditional challenge to technology, whether it be via wheels or legs or something else, and further requires the use of a gyro or integrated gyro-function chip to create a horizontal reference. The Honda team is experiencing ongoing problems with feet and limbs and has had to develop sophisticated ankles and knees to absorb irregularities and avoid frequent falls. The situation is even more complex when the robot has to carry unequal weight on either side or front to back. And then we come to all the feedback mechanisms we as humans have through our senses – hot and cold, far and near, loud and soft – of which robots need at least some to avoid collisions and burn-up.

So are androids, in fact, the solution? It may be simply a fortuitous feature of evolution that the most sophisticated form of intelligence on earth has a human-shaped body. Remember, also, that dolphins – second to man in intelligence – have a totally different shape and set of functions. Experiments with non-human shapes confirm several advantages. Four or six legs like those of insects are much more stable, and can be used with suckers for climbing vertical walls. Multi-leg robots like Dante are already used for dangerous tasks like defusing bombs and for entering radioactive environments like Chernobyl. Maybe we will see millipedes with intelligent legs or flying insect-type robots in the future, or even shapes not mimicked anywhere in the animal world. There are already birdlike robots like the aerosonde, a type of miniature unmanned plane used for obtaining data in dangerous environments. Operationally, compressed air is a useful alternative technology to electrical impulses for limbs. And other forms of energy besides human food are likely to be superior, though many – like batteries – are considerably heavier than the human stomach.

Remote robots like Dante are used by NASA for hazardous terrain like the insides of volcanoes, and are also the present technology for space exploration. In space, the robot needs considerably less life support than the human – solar power can be used and there is less need to depend on atmosphere, food and drink and the fragility of the human body. One difficulty is time delay in controlling a robot in further-off locations, but this may be partly helped by the robot assuming more independent functions.

As mentioned, robots are also used increasingly in keyhole surgery, the advantages being precise control and a much smaller incision. Again, this technology can be used in remote locations – a skilled surgeon can operate from another room, another town, another country – possibly, one day, another planet.

Remote robots have caught the popular fancy, as witnessed by the fights between survival machines in *Robot Wars* on TV. What started with remote-controlled cars, boats and aeroplanes has developed into a gladiatorial struggle for dominance. Not cutting-edge technology, perhaps, but useful in educating children and 'kidults', and something we are destined to see more of. Parallel to this kind of action technology is the development of robot dolls like Hasbro's 'My Real Baby', another popular usage where the focus is on reproducing credible emotional responses to cuddling and holding. All these popularisations introduce the idea of robots as 'likeable' technology. Additionally it is assumed that intelligent toys and dolls will change children's responses to play, so that there will be less imaginative projection and a more demanding attitude to what toys are expected to 'do'.

The problems with robots are similar to those of artificial intelligence (pages 158–62) – complexity is hard to develop. Presently robots can do programmed tasks but lack any real flexibility. The android requires a sophisticated programme simply to open and go through a door, let alone circumnavigate a two-storey house with a multi-level garden. As for replication, a simple robot has been made in Brandeis University that can design and build other robots. At this stage the offspring are just little plastic trusses propelled by pistons and controlled by elementary neural networks.

But one startling fact is that robots have got as far as they have in a hundred years or so, compared with the millions of years of human evolution. The principles are different – evolution is a different paradigm from conscious creation and research, and of course the development of robot technology has been done not by robots but by humans in a parallel process to the development of human knowledge, but the time scales remain interesting. And robots potentially – allowing for the fact that few mechanisms are problem-free – have all the indestructible properties of Terminator, and its awesome ability to go on and on, 24 hours a day, seven days a week, as long as parts work and there is a source of power.

Cyborgs

A slightly different concept is a being that is part human and part machine. The word was coined in the middle of the 20th century, and implants have kick-started the idea in recent years. The interesting part is 'intelligent' implants like those proposed to restore sight to the retina, and above all microchip implants that can be linked up to other circuits. The prediction is that cyborgs could be possible in the next few decades. By then, the number and type of implants may have increased to the point where humans are going that way anyhow; even now it is estimated that around 10 per cent of the US population has an implant of some kind, if we include contact lenses.

Nanotechnology – miniaturisation to a very small scale – will help with the engineering, and advances in robotics and materials will help with the design and production process. The theoretical frontier is whether we can make a quantum shift in technology from electronics to some kind of biotechnology. The core of this technology is nanotechnology, as VR pioneer Mike Pesce suggests:

> Two of the most crucial and, as yet, unbuilt devices in nanotechnology are the nanocomputer and nanoassembler. The nanocomputer is a molecular machine capable of executing a string of instructions and producing a result. Once the nanocomputer exists, it becomes possible to create a nanoassembler, a device constructed at the atomic level, which can arrange atoms precisely into almost any desired form. A nanoassembler could simply 'pluck' atoms from a 'bin' and, like a post-industrial loom, knit them into position. In our cells, ribosomes do something similar, copying DNA into RNA, and then gathering the correct amino acids to create the proteins which make up our physical nature. The nanoassembler translates instructions into molecules and is the Holy Grail of nanotechnology; once a perfected nanoassembler is available, almost anything becomes possible. Once you have a single

nanoassembler you can make as many as you might need. But it also means that a nanoassembler is a perfect plague. If a nanoassembler were released into the environment, with only the instruction to be fruitful and multiply, the entire surface of the planet — plants, animals and even rocks — would be reduced to a grey goo of nanites in little more than 72 hours. The 'grey goo problem' is well known in nanotechnology, where it acts as a check against the unbounded optimism which permeates scientific developments in atomic-scale devices. But despite the dangers, molecular nanotechnologists study how to build machinery up from the atomic scale, while molecular biologists study how to 'strip down' the organelles of the cell into atomic-scale devices. Given the immense commercial pressures of the biomedical industry, it seems unlikely that molecular biologists will stop learning how we work, so one way or another, it seems, we'll soon know enough about nanocomputers and nanoassemblers to construct both.[9]

Expert systems and simulated worlds

Moving up a level from the robot to the system, we see similar progress being made. Software simulating management of resources — from Football Manager to Sim City — is now starting to introduce young gamers to the real-world challenges of how to create and manage a system, whether human or eco. As children spend hours on their computers constructing and maintaining cities and ecosystems, they are preparing themselves for the larger simulations science will pursue in the future.

Expert systems already have a sophisticated role in our society, and *Would-be Worlds: How Simulation Is Changing the Frontiers of Science*, by John L. Casti, investigates aspects of this computer modelling process.[10] He documents areas like economics, where modelling has been used in programmes like Sugarscope to predict the global economy and so deal more profitably in stocks and shares. Major banks already use complex modelling systems, and US academics are developing more specialist applications. Casti examines how we can experiment on a smaller, simpler version of the world market as a prototype for larger extrapolations.

As yet there is no general theory of complex systems. But already, in fields like mathematics, evolutionary biology, bird flight, biochemistry, economics, logic, literature and meteorology we are shown how a few simple rules can make possible a whole complexity of solutions. Modelling is already applied in familiar real-world areas like weather and election forecasts, sport analysis and transportation. TRANSIMS, a model of the city of Albuquerque, New Mexico, is an example used to reveal the root causes of events like traffic jams and accidents.

Casti tested out some of his theories by trying to predict the outcome of a Super Bowl, choosing an adequately powerful computer game program to play a series of simulated games.[11] The results of his experiments using the 1995 opponents, the 49ers and the Chargers, made basic points about computer simulations and models, and went on to suggest areas of uncertainty where either actual games were flukes or the program contained flaws. As with artificial intelligence, absolute prediction may not be possible, and it is the success and integrity of the theory and how one deals with limitations and paradoxes in the system that is useful for ongoing research.

Actual applications where modelling needs to be used are many. They include situations where experimenting in real life is costly or downright dangerous (drug tests in medicine, flight patterns over busy airports) or where existing circumstances are so distant or uncommon as to provide scant data (planetary motion, meteor collisions with Earth). The cutting edge is neural networks, which attempt to simulate the structure of the human brain. Theoretically neural nets could do tasks as complex as reconstructing the beginning of life itself on Earth. The initial promise in the early nineties was of a forecasting tool that learned as it went along, like AI, giving better and better matches to the real world. In practice it got bogged down all too often and didn't get much past the demonstrator stage, though the technology has been used with some success in stand-alone forecasting and text recognition.

A real-world practical challenge is modelling political crises so as to try to steer peaceful outcomes, and Casti uses game theory to try to explain the denouement of the Cuban missile crisis.[12] The laboratories of the future will increasingly turn to modelling, be it computerised petri dishes growing digital life forms, or complex space research. One of the most exciting territories being mapped is the exotic new frontier of 'complex, adaptive systems', systems involving living 'agents', which continuously change behaviour in ways that almost defy prediction and measurement – examples being environmental and economic ecosystems and evolution itself. Casti gives the example of Tierra, a 'computerised terrarium' in which biomorphs – artificial life forms –

grow and mutate, providing new insights into natural selection and evolution.

A wonderful future perhaps. One thing that is being developed at present is the intelligent house. Potentially a 'dream house' with everything at the touch of a button, experiments like the 'UbiComp' in the Georgia Institute of Technology have so far got little further than wiring up all the rooms with cables and filling them with TV sets, microphones and cameras. Dream or nightmare? In case this sounds like *Big Brother* replicated everywhere, there is a good reason for making the home ready and that is the whole future of converging digital entertainment, which will see a large gateway server for each householder fed by the telephone network, satellite, wireless or broadband cable. A hub will then distribute data links to PCs, TVs, music systems, home theatre and smart appliances, each controlled by a mixture of keyboard, direct or remote controls and voice activation. Content provided will then be everything from music, broadcast material, films and the Internet to virtual reality, 3-D holography and telepresence. Home sweet home.

Artificial intelligence

Thought by some to be the final frontier, artificial intelligence – AI for short – is divided into two distinct types:

- Weak – AI that uses programs as psychological theories
- Strong – AI in which psychological properties actually apply to the AI models themselves.

Clearly, strong AI is the 'final frontier' – machines that can think, though whether they have 'consciousness' is another matter.

Research into AI is done primarily on computers, which are useful tools for psychologists because they provide ways of testing AI theory. Creativity, for the purposes of designing a model, is defined as the ability to generate novel ideas and artefacts that have value. A distinction is made between two types of novelty in creativity:

- P-creativity – ideas novel to the mind of the person, the basic form of creativity
- H-creativity – ideas novel to history as a whole, though not

necessarily of great human importance. These by definition start off as P-creative.

Since the process is in its infancy, it is not likely to match great examples of creativity such as the works of Shakespeare or Bach. Consequently, models of AI typically address the question of P-creativity. H-creative ideas have emerged, however, and have even been awarded patents, eg designing a three-dimensional logic gate on a silicon chip.

For the purposes of AI, three types of creativity are considered:

- *Combinational* – novel combinations of familiar material, eg poetic imagery, jokes (the JAPE joke generator came up with 'What do you get when you cross a sheep with a kangaroo? A woolly jumper')
- *Exploratory* – novel versions within a familiar conceptual frame, eg jazz, science, art
- *Transformational* – new conceptual invention, eg 12-tone music, Kekule's ring molecule.

Sometimes it is hard to distinguish exploratory from transformational, and often exploratory creativity follows within the new dimension created by a transformational leap like that of Kekule. But truly transformational creativity creates whole new structures.

The effect of new structures can be shock and amazement – an 'impossibilistic' surprise felt by the creator as well as the observer. The problem is that new structures may be so surprising that they are unintelligible or pass unnoticed because we lack the parameters to see them. They may simply be rejected in the first instance, as the Impressionists were relegated to the *Salon des Refusés*, and the tectonic theory of moving plates on the earth's crust was greeted with disbelief. The main point with the current development of AI, however, is not to label new ideas and programmes as creative or not but to try to model existing theories of creativity into new software and computer environments, and to see in what way programs may show elements of creativity.

With weak AI, we are probably at a stage where the programmer can set up a conceptual model, which the computer can then develop or refine. What seems a greater challenge is for a program to transform itself in any major conceptual way, and even more to be able to 'reflect' on the results of transformations and self-evaluate them. The jokes generated by JAPE, for instance, depended largely on pre-programming joke structures and types of words that could be used.

D. R. Hofstadter prefers a more flexible representation of concepts, which could allow more unpredictable results – closer to human creativity.[13] Unfortunately, much of the present work is still based on computational concepts that generate numerous variations within a given style, eg architectural drawings, fugues, jazz improvisations, story plots, electronic parts or chemical molecules. Fortunately, a number of these computer creations have proved very useful, and have been patented and sold. But this still leaves the challenge of exploratory creativity. One cynical observation is that

> despite years of development and millions of dollars of funding, artificial intelligence researchers still haven't built a robot that could survive for long outside a laboratory. Even the smartest ones don't have the instincts of an insect, much less the common sense of a human being. They tend to perform poorly when taken out of their structured environments because they can't adapt to an unprogrammed world.[14]

Storage capacity in computers is clearly a relevant factor, since human creatives in art and science have huge amounts of learned information at their disposal, both primary to the task and secondary in terms of general knowledge, which might be introduced into new concepts. In the case of innovatory composers like Bach, Beethoven or Stravinsky, imitation after the event takes no account of the transformations they made to the musical thought of their time, and a computer that 'thought like an innovatory composer' would have to innovate not imitate.

Sheer number-crunching capacity lies behind chess computers like Big Blue, which beat Gary Kasparov in 1997, but this is largely a computational task within a given set of chess rules. Or is it? Was Big Blue's move 36 in game two against Kasparov 'magic' or just accurate analysis of where to put the queen? Kasparov, for one, was taken aback by a computer that could produce such an elegant trick 'out of the blue' and this surely unsettled him in the games to come. Humans get miffed at being beaten by machines. Super-humans get super-miffed.

So what of the future? Increases in storage capacity and computational power can be taken for granted, but what about conceptual progress? One area of ongoing research is genetic algorhythms (GA), programs that can alter their task-relevant rules at random. This mimics the kind of mutational processes that occur in genetics, and in the same way such mutations can be productive or unsatisfactory. Crucial to these more advanced programs are ways of self-evaluation, for example 'generations' of rule sets that learn from 'parent' solutions and thus show some form of evolution.

At present humans intervene at critical stages and select more promising variations to pursue. The challenge is to minimise such intervention while still producing results of value, a difficult task when one 'family' of results may be quite different from its precursors. Too much change can easily revert to random uninteresting results, and since the computer itself cannot evaluate even remotely as well as humans, it becomes more human-dependent. So it may be necessary for computers to develop self-critical procedures before creative procedures can have any real value.

A further step into the future would be computers that could make real H-creative advances. This opens up a whole new dimension to human understanding. If artificial intelligence were to come up with a paradigm for existence so different from ours that it was unrecognisable, then it would not only have to invent something that was a step further than our comprehension, it would have to have 'powers of persuasion' strong enough to show humans why such initially alien models were valuable to us, or indeed made sense at all. If such artificial intelligences were created by us, how could we program them to 'persuade' us of things we cannot – in the process of programming them – understand? We could program them with a methodology we understood, and which could output a new model, and then presumably we could understand that new model if we tested it with our familiar scientific methods.

But how could we program an artificial intelligence to output a new model of existence that could only be properly tested and validated by a new model of testing that we don't possess, or by some way of understanding alien to us? This paradigm breaks the bounds of our anthropomorphic comprehension, and is similar to the more advanced concepts of virtual reality, where we inhabit not androids but alien forms in a virtual environment, like the avatar transforms in the ACCD VR world of Michael Heim, without gravity or horizon. These AI conceptual shifts are not even close at present, and they test our powers of comprehension to the limits. Even in the more anthropomorphic world, programs showing motivation or emotion in the psychological sense seem similarly distant.[15] So what do we have for Christmas 2000? AIBO – Sony's 'intelligent' dog, a sleek electronic gadget defined by techno-journalist Brian Clegg as 'perhaps rivalling a bluebottle with a migraine'.

But can we speculate on a time when robots with artificial intelligence may become as 'gods' to us – when they can do things we simply cannot, and when we cease to understand them? 'When robots pass beyond our understanding they may come to look like gods. Understanding robot science would be like testing the gods. We could not possibly understand what they do or why without a shared folk psychology, and we can hardly expect that our folk psychology will apply to robot behaviour. So what robots do may become invisible to us, as they become as gods.'[16]

The new genetics – cloning, biotechnology, genetic modification

We now have Dolly the sheep, to be closely followed by a variety of other cloned animals. Part of the current goal is to preserve species from extinction, such as the gaur, and partly it is to reconstruct extinct species like the Spanish mountain goat, the bucardo, which became extinct in 2000. In the wings are the Sumatran tiger and the giant panda. Present technology makes such cloning possible, but it is still far from straightforward. Ironically, much-loved pets such as cats and dogs, which their owners want cloned, are some of the most difficult.

In the next decade or two there might be genetic mutations to humans to confer resistance to HIV or protection from high cholesterol. Goals with humans, naturally, include increasing cognitive ability and longevity. If we add in selective cloning for particular qualities then we raise the whole issue of eugenics – breeding towards a 'super race' and eliminating problem gene combinations. We could even in theory have 'pure bred' human species, who would interbreed with themselves rather than the normal gene pool. Since the Sun will burn out one day, many theorists postulate that humans will leave Earth and colonise another part of the cosmos. The most obvious interim target for colonisation is Mars, and in theory humans would start mutating to suit such an environment. If there is one eventuality that would make sense of our whole evolution towards the capacity of 'simulation', it is the idea of a complete environment with robots and intelligent systems that could be reconstructed in another place for man to continue his survival.

Should scientists play God? Genes may be the final frontier, but the problem is that down here on earth, the greatest human god is greed. Commercial enterprises that develop genome research will want to hoard it, stifling further study, or shackle society with expensive products. Scientists are not moral as such – they develop products. And they do so usually on behalf of funded laboratories, which then have a political role depending on their funders. We should not expect altruism in a business where 'if it does not make a profit, it is not a business', and of course humanitarian applications to drug companies to give free medicines to disaster areas like central Africa or Kosovo have met with little more than a grudging agreement to reduce prices by up to 80 per cent – a move considered by some as too little too late in the case of Africa's AIDs pandemic.

Biotechnology is clearly dangerous – modifying a virus used in lab experiments in Australia has produced a new strain, 'Mouse Pox', which, though it does not appear to cross the species barrier, is so dangerous that it has triggered calls for the strengthening of world treaties controlling biological weapons. On the other hand, diseases deriving from gene defects are exactly those that could benefit from gene technology.

'ANDi', the product of an Oregon lab, is a monkey, the first genetically modified primate, altered with genes from jellyfish. Genetically modified monkeys are used in the USA for experiments to find cures for common diseases. Popular reaction was predictable – animal lovers and doomsday theorists warned of 'opening the floodgates' and of all the dreadful consequences seen in SF tales of human-induced global catastrophes. Scientists are considered 'arrogant' for going ahead without consulting the public. One thing we will see more of is the backlash against genetic engineering. Organic or GM-free food is but the tip of the iceberg.

EIGHT

Games

Man would never have risen to the top of the evolutionary tree without the ability to dominate his fellow creatures. Not the fastest or the strongest, man was by a very long way the cleverest of the animal kingdom. His capacity for simulation gave him something unique – weapons. His increasing sophistication in hunting gave him a sense for strategy. All this took him beyond the simple competitiveness of other animals. In time man developed a whole variety of activities that simulated his survival battles. These days we broadly classify these strategic, simulated competitions as 'games'.

The term 'games' comprises quite a number of possible activities. The Olympic Games, for instance, encompasses many physical activities that we usually call 'sport'. Games as a whole are typically interactive, sometimes played by two participants (chess, boxing), often by teams (rugby, football). Sports are either team-based or competitive, solitary activities like shooting, archery or ski-jumping, done against the clock or on a points basis. Where we put ice-skating, ballroom dancing and synchronised swimming in the pantheon of 'games' is another story – the common feature seems to be simply that there are winners and losers. On this basis maybe we should include international piano competitions in today's anthology of games.

Historic contests

The concept of 'games' in ancient times was often a bloody one – a gladiatorial conflict involving skilled fighters, slaves, foreign captives,

Christians, lions and other beasts – whatever could provide the gory spectacle of a desperate life-and-death struggle. Admiration and prizes – not least life itself – were accorded to the strong and skilful. Much the same kind of violence continued through the Middle Ages, with its jousting, fistfights, dog fights and cock fights. The winner survived – most of the time. The loser often did not.

Death is fairly rare in modern games, but it happens in a variety of them – rugby, car racing, boxing, bullfighting. The occasional death is presumably seen as simply a statistic. Debates continue about dangerous sports, and changes periodically take place – tyre walls and runout areas in Formula One, more sophisticated medical facilities in boxing. But still such games and sports continue.

Strength games are still played, as in contests to find the world's strongest man. But skill soon came to be an integral part of the spectacle, and the factor that uniquely distinguished winners. Skill games often demand some combination of mental and physical aspects – more mental than physical in the case of snooker, more physical in the case of rugby and football. Finally, skill games such as chess developed where the winner's prowess was exclusively mental. Physical games are the realm of youth; mental games like chess, draughts and a variety of board and card games are for all.

Then there are the managers, the trainers, the sponsors and all the peripheral trappings of public contests. The 'executives', to use a word from the film *Rollerball*, control the games but do not star in them. Sometimes they are ex-players. Cynically – as in *Rollerball* – they protect their position by proposing that the game itself is more important than any of the players, whilst inwardly burning with envy that they are not the young players whom the public idolise. In real life some executives amass huge power bases, like Bernie Ecclestone in Formula One racing, or Don King in boxing, while others – like the England football manager, come and go seemingly on a whim. Sport is full of financially powerful people – another simulation of winning.

Quizzes and panel games

One popular development of games is the media quiz or panel game. Quizzes and riddles have had substantial popularity over the ages, but the media version brings in a wider public of vicarious winners and losers who simulate the competition at home, shouting out the answers in a room full of people, thus creating a supplementary quiz. Where there is money involved, they can also simulate winning it: 'I would have won £64,000 on that quiz', the clever viewer may say, except that, of course, he was not there and he didn't. But with a 'willing suspension of disbelief' quizzes are interactive viewing. The same vicarious pleasure of winning happens with crosswords. Even if most people do not send away their prize crosswords, they can simulate winning a prize by the act of finishing the crossword: 'I could have won it, it could have been me.'

Games as simulations of aggression

Biologists are well aware of the competitiveness and simulated fighting of the litters of several species, not least our immediate ancestors the apes. Gregory Bateson describes studying this at Fleischhacker Zoo, and also observing the way animals are able to signal to each other the nature of the interaction:

> What I saw at the zoo was a phenomenon well known to everybody: I saw two young monkeys *playing*, ie engaged in an interactive sequence of which the unit actions or signals were similar to but not the same as those of combat. It was evident, even to the human observer, that the sequence as a whole was not combat, and evident to the human observer that to the participant monkeys this was 'not combat'. Now, this phenomenon, play, could only occur if the participant organisms were capable of some degree of metacommunication, ie of exchanging signals which would carry the message 'this is play'.[1]

This phenomenon of safe competition is central to evolution, since it enables us to simulate combat without hurting ourselves. We need combat skills, but we also need to survive. Combat games were among the first games in human culture. Early games like chess ranged one army against another, and are still played alongside other more recent strategy games like Risk. As technology became more sophisticated, computer games with graphics gripped us, and the next major step will be virtual reality games and photo-realistic figures. In essence the same principle, in execution miles apart.

Combat games may offer the opportunity of experiencing a 'symbolic victory' when in fact real life is difficult or contains a lot of tension. This can be a form of escapism, with the added benefit of a simulated boost to self-esteem. An interesting instance of this is reports of cases where the playing of Space Invaders increased fourfold (or more) just before the onset of marriage – similar to the state of 'computer catatonia' reported by other researchers.[2] Maybe the approaching loss of independence triggered the need for a rush of morale-boosting symbolic wins.

If we see combat games as escapism, then they fit comfortably into the use of escapist games as a method or process of temporarily reducing dissatisfaction. Simplistic forms are substituted for the real and complex forms and processes that are part of life outside the escapist activity. Combat games also provide a means of indulging in activities that in the real world would have horrific consequences, like mass murder. In this type of escapism the form is limited and idealised in the sense of providing an environment where the fight or flight of adrenalin is experienced, and anger and hostility are projected onto 'evil' virtual opponents, which one can then in good conscience blow to smithereens.

Games and pastimes

To Eric Berne, the definition of a game is something with a twist in its tale. 'The great bulk of social intercourse is made up of engagements', he writes, and continues that 'engagements are of two types – pastimes and games. A pastime is straightforward. When dissimulation enters the situation a pastime becomes a game'.[3]

Berne's technical description of a game includes certain obligatory elements:

- A gimmick – some weakness or 'handle' to hook into (fear, greed, irritability, vanity)
- A switch – a change in position, eg from victim or rescuer to persecutor
- A cross up – a moment of confusion resulting from the switch
- A payoff – feelings that the game arouses in both the agent and the respondent.

Games are, for Berne, social transactions more than simulated combat. The requirement for a 'con' would rule out sports like athletics and track and field where individuals compete in a largely straightforward way to the limits of their ability. They would also rule out a large number of games where the competition is quite open on both sides, though subterfuge would come into several games as part of tactics. A game of poker would be closer to Berne's definition, but would not fit it exactly unless we considered it as a repeated succession of 'games', each involving trickery, deception, switches, cross-ups, etc.

Again, Berne's context for games is that of successful, intimate social interaction against unsuccessful or 'gamey' structuring of time in ways where intimacy is avoided. The evolutionary cadre for games is much closer to combat, a compelling urge to test ourselves in the arena of gain – monetary, intellectual, sexual, power, political. 'Society' in this sense is a gene pool, and the 'game' is one of ensuring a high place in the survival competition, a maximal chance of replication, where we exercise our ability or our fantasised ability to be the fittest to survive.

Can there be altruism in games?

The British have a tradition that it's not whether you win but 'how you play the game'. Altruism in the biblical sense is the ability to love one's enemy. In games it can be the ability to respect opponents. All are useful in terms of living to fight another day. Whether altruism is strictly possible in sociobiology is disputed – Dawkin's 'selfish gene' theory maintains that though altruism seems to occur in the animal world, it may be an illusion that has a simpler explanation in the mathematics of maintaining gene survival. Human culture is considerably more complex – altruism could be as much a learned cultural phenomenon as a genetic trait – and so sociobiologists have turned increasingly to game theory to try to decipher behaviour. Popular games, however, remain very much simpler than the computations done in labs, though simpler versions of the latter, such as the 'prisoner's dilemma', can be played experimentally.

Altruism conflicts with the desire to win in obvious cases like parent–child games. Many sportsmen and women were initially trained by a parent, and frequently a parent like Tiger Woods's father, whose words must surely resonate with any proud parent: 'I vividly remember when Tiger first beat me at the age of 13, though the way he tells it he was nine.' As with Bart and Homer Simpson, there is an implied intimacy heavily hidden under several layers of competition. Within a family there is a strong imperative for sustainable competition – a child shares half its genes with any parent, the strongest bond you can have outside identical twins or cloning.

Winners and losers

Win culture is expressed in all sorts of ways – growth in business, the pursuit of excellence. Best is defined again and again – best lists, books or records, richest lists. We spend little time defining average or worst. Even most leisure activities are centred around being 'better'. We improve our cars, our homes, our hi-fi systems. Improvement is the governing word. Our media world is expressing this concept of better with increasing frequency and strength. Commercially better, through better advertising. Financially better, through winning. Cleverer, better in ability or knowledge. Quizzes are all for points and about winning.

The loser may be the environment. If we want more fish there will be less in the sea. If we use more oil there is less in the earth, and so it goes on. There is no planetary free lunch – the earth is not renewable, and there is only one earth around these parts. Species vanish at an alarming rate, but as long as humans carry on winning…

In sociobiological game theory more is gained by collaborating than by dividing the available resource pool into winners and losers. There is a growing movement to take winning out of education and substitute debate, team spirit and collaboration. Thought by many to be faddish in primary education, it is nevertheless getting into high-level business training courses, where 'team spirit' is a buzzword and team games away from the boardroom are increasingly being built into corporate life. Some of these games are simulated war games involving both co-operation and winning, and these are growing in popularity.

Simulated combat games

An interesting development is the playing of 'simulated' war games. Brunel is one of many universities that has a Gaming Society, which organises various 'campus games'. One example is LARP – Live Action Role Play, where combatants play live 'death games' on designated campus areas excluding 'safe' areas like the library, lecture theatres, laboratories and the bar. Variations are Vampire, Mafiossa and Circle of Death. The actual combat and killing is of course simulated, though the game is carried out in real life, with water pistols, cap guns and various makeshift weapons.

Real-life risk displays may be steadily losing out to computer games, at least such is the belief of India's travelling circus acts, which resort to motorcycle wall-of-death displays to earn a living. As more gaming is simulated, however, real-life experiences may return as a welcome contrast.

Computer and video games

The first computer game – the 1972 table tennis game known as Pong – opened up a huge new market that started to bloom with the arcade game Space Invaders in 1979. By 1981 the diverse array of games included Pac-man, Galaxian and Donkey Kong, and since then the games business has exploded in variety and sophistication. Games come in various categories, and a useful guide to these has been given by psychologist Mark Griffiths:

- Sports simulations – golf, athletics, etc
- Racers – a type of the above, it features various motor sports and downhill skiing
- Adventures – fantasy settings where players escape to other worlds and take new identities
- Puzzlers – games requiring problem solving, eg Tetris
- Weird games – more aptly called miscellaneous games, like Sim City 2000
- Platformers – running and jumping games with platforms eg Mario 64, Sonic
- Platform blasters – platformers also blasting everything in sight, eg Robocop
- Beat 'em ups – games involving physical violence, eg Street Fighter, Mortal Kombat, Tekken
- Shoot 'em ups – games involving shooting and killing using various weapons.[4]

The four platforms for games are handheld, PC, video console and arcade machine, sales going up as much as 700 per cent in 1991 alone for handheld games. In the USA 9 out of 10 adolescents have played computer or video games at one time or another, and their growth in popularity is a worldwide trend. In Britain, more money is now spent on computer games than on either the cinema or video rental. Adolescents and pre-adolescents are the biggest players, and research from the Broadcasters' Audience Research Board suggests that peak interest occurs at age 10 to 12. This continues until the early twenties when interest drops off, though the computer continues to be used for other purposes. Solo play, as opposed to play with friends, was rated by one study at around 43 per cent.

Male and female participation

As little as 5 per cent of boys state they are not interested in computer games, while for girls this figure can be more like a quarter. The male stranglehold on computer games continues to those who design and produce them – they are predominantly created by males for males. One analysis of 21 common games showed that none had exclusively female images, while 12 contained exclusively male images. Attempts to artificially change this with the introduction of Ms Pac-man and Game Girl have so far failed dismally.

While the significant association between males and computer games has been well documented, the reasons for it cover several hypotheses. Some of these are:

- Women have not been encouraged to express aggression in public, so may be more cautious of playing in front of others. Evidence shows that many go along to arcades to watch and support their boyfriends.
- Boys have slightly superior visual and spatial skills, so girls may feel disadvantaged.
- Game content is more biased towards males, who play to master the game and for competition, while girls prefer more whimsical, less demanding and less aggressive content.
- Games are currently designed by males according to male stereotypes.

Gillian Skirrow has taken a psychoanalytic approach to the adolescent male's obsession with computer games and hypothesises that the male infant, confused at having a different body to his mother, has a fearful desire to re-enter the mother's womb, seek primal knowledge there and fight an Oedipal battle with his father.[5] She sees evidence for this theory in common features of games, like a quest structure, the centrality of battle and the recurring imagery of womb-like spaces such as caves, tunnels, the interior of space ships and dungeons. To her, the 'story' in VR games holds the promise of a new creative narrative as the player partakes in the creation of the game. Birgitta Hosea speculates that the *yearning* for VR could be not the desire to fight and dominate but the desire to explore the mother's body – the pleasure of immersion in virtual worlds being akin to the exploration and feeling of engulfment in the matrix from whence we all came.[6] Since many females are passionate about this field, we can look forward to a more balanced exploration of new technology than that offered by male aggression alone, including types of computer game that really do appeal to girls and women.

Positive uses of games

Many see computer games as enhancing problem-solving ability. Research supports this. In one study parents, by a small margin, believed that the use of games was more likely to increase problem-solving skills than aggression.[7] This view was age dependent – the younger the parent, the more they believed in positive effects, over 55s with less actual experience of games continuing to believe that aggression was the dominant response. In this study the 'benefit' of computer games was calculated as problem-solving response minus aggressive response. Using this calculation the positive effect of games came out as 27 per cent for boys and 25 per cent for girls, problem-solving responses being 6 per cent higher in boys than girls. Research shows that, at present, games users are of above average intelligence, so this appears to confirm some level of difficulty involved in playing them.

Games encourage skill development, which can improve hand–eye co-ordination, attention span and reaction times, something by now well documented. Such skill development, through simulation games like Flight Simulator, can make a positive contribution towards 'preparation for reality'. The US army and navy, for instance, use games to train gunners, and are reputed anecdotally to scour arcades for new recruits, offering them bigger and better 'games'.

The ability to use new technology like computers and the Internet is seen as useful training in itself. Associated with this is the argument that children familiar with new technology feel self-confident in relation to their peers, in addition to the sense of accomplishment they experience from their capacity to master the actual games themselves.

Indirect benefits include presenting educational material through fun activities. Fun can be broken down, for instance, into motivations like curiosity, challenge and fantasy, all of which can have positive educational possibilities. This idea is already behind software used in schools – including Sim City – and similar titles like Football Manager, which teach strategy, decision-making and the realisation that in real life there are choices and there are consequences. The wish that all commercial games were equally educational or altruistic, however, largely falls on deaf ears when profits are considered.

Computer games can be used in therapeutic contexts for observing child play or putting children at their ease, for helping in the rehabilitation of stroke patients and also in assessing mental and motor skills. Whether computer games encourage social skills is a moot point – some claim that competition improves social skills, others that preoccupation with computer games may be depriving children of real-life interaction with their peers. One cynical argument is that children preoccupied with games may do less damage in reality, something akin to the observation that criminals in prison are *ipso facto* not on the street committing crimes. The other side of the coin is that children might otherwise develop more general knowledge of life and a saner attitude to society than can be derived from blasting cartoon figures to smithereens, including the realisation that violence in real life results in considerable damage and human pain.

Video games and aggression

A central debate has always been whether computer games are detrimental to a young person's healthy development, particularly since children of certain ages find playing games more interesting and absorbing than watching TV. This debate has partly grown out of the debate over the consequences of violence in broadcasting and videos, since both media feature entertainment value, violent content and plot and action resemblances. The content of games – like that of action movies – certainly includes violence, death and destruction. Up to 85 per cent of games are of this type, and other surveys indicate that as little as 15 per cent do not include some violent content. These statistics, however, ignore the fact that a lot of the best-selling games have been non-violent, including several platformers like Sonic and Super Mario and an increasing number of sport titles.

Research into this subject has been accumulating since the eighties, and Mark Griffiths has done substantial work reviewing the evidence from several sources.[8] His findings show that experimental studies – potentially the most reliable – produce little significant evidence of an increase in violence, violent games producing no more changes in cardiovascular response than other games. It was even found that a more hostile playing style could be caused by increasing the temperature of the room. One interesting finding, though, was that priming a group of gamers for co-operative behaviour produced a less hostile playing style (fewer kills) than shown by a group primed for competitive behaviour. Such studies are theoretical, for the obvious reason that it would be unethical to set up experiments in real aggression towards people.

Observational studies have examined the free play behaviour of children of various ages subsequent to playing violent games. The findings included observations that:

- Girls in the age range 9–10 showed an increase in aggression in free play while boys remained the same.
- Both girls and boys in the 4–6 year age range showed increased aggression in free play.
- Children tend to mimic the character(s) in the game in subsequent play.
- Boys aged seven and eight showed more aggression after violent games than non-violent games.

In these observational studies, observers consistently noticed some increase in aggression.

Another way of collecting evidence is report and self-report studies, where subjects give information about themselves that can be correlated with other factors. For instance:

- Boys aged 9–11 who were rated high on aggression by teachers also showed increased gaming activity.
- Boys aged 10–16 showed a correlation between aggressive attitudes (eg pro-war) and the amount of time spent playing aggressive games.
- Teenagers reported that playing aggressive games made them feel more aggressive, and this was highly correlated with the amount of time spent playing.
- Undergraduates showed more anxiety and hostility after playing very violent games than after playing mildly violent ones.
- Other studies showed no significant correlation.
- One study showed that aggressive video games had a calming effect.

Such studies not only show contradictory results, they also do not establish whether it is the aggressive type of child that plays such games or whether games make children aggressive. There may, of course, be a mixture of these factors. Further to this, deprived socio-economic backgrounds were not directly considered, though these are known to have links with increased aggression.

Meanwhile theoretical arguments are consistently made in favour of retaining 'fantasy violence' as an essential process in rehearsing and understanding human feelings, an argument put by games designer Theresa Duncan:

> Child psychologist Bruno Bettelheim, in his opus *The Uses of Enchantment*, argues that violent themes like patricide, murder and cannibalism are vital to fairy tales for children. Fairy tales, he says, speak to the young child on the 'enchanted' level and safely give vent to the confused and troubling emotional states that he is not yet able to understand and describe. Bettelheim argues that children are aided by the tales' reassurance that the difficulties they experience in their lives are commonplace, and that by overcoming violent and destructive impulses they can develop into adults of good character. Critic and historian Marina Warner, in her recently published *No Go The Bogeyman*, devotes 400 pages to understanding the human impulses that have given rise to the invention of ogres, giants, demons and monsters throughout history. She seeks to examine 'the forms we put on our fears' and discovers that we enjoy being disgusted and frightened. Warner concludes that our variously gory cultural products – video games, slasher flicks and scary children's stories – serve to give rise to latent fears so as to soothe and quell them.[9]

Other effects of video and computer games

Some negative physical effects of gaming have been discovered, one being the possibility of repetitive strain injuries due to rapid and repeated finger and thumb movements. Associated with this are various elbow, skin, muscle and joint disorders. In one survey 65 per cent of arcade players complained of various ills including blisters, sores, calluses and numbness in hand and elbow, and others have found problems with raised blood pressure and over-arousal. More worrying are cases of epileptic fits and seizures, with potentially fatal results.

As with the Internet, concern has also been expressed that games are addictive, and some of the injuries described above speak eloquently enough of bingeing and overindulgence. Video game addiction, according to Soper and Miller, is comparable with other addictions in exhibiting:

- Compulsive behavioural involvement
- Lack of interest in other activities
- Association largely with other addicts
- Withdrawal symptoms like the shakes.[10]

Attempts have increasingly been made to classify games machines, the Net and television as addictive, but a sizeable body of hard evidence is yet to be accumulated. One suggestion is that players get addicted through the production of increased levels of dopamine in the brain – something akin to taking amphetamines. A study by Dr Paul Grasby at Hammersmith Hospital in London using PET scans determined that playing video games triggers the release of dopamine in the brain to double the levels usually found in normal activity. Taking this a level further would lead us to speculate that ordinary life activities like school might appear boring in comparison with such increased excitement levels, so that fundamental psychological attitudes might become shifted, including impatience and an urge to speed things up.

However such addictive behaviour takes place, it is not necessarily a bad future prognosis of adjustment. A study by Margaret Shotton found that self-reported games addicts were actually of superior intelligence and five years later had gone through university into good jobs.[11] This might possibly be because computer games in their infancy attracted a special breed of techies who were in the forefront of experimentation, but the opportunities for such techies are still out there. Debate still centres around the question of whether games attract subjects of limited imagination who need ritualistic entertainment, whether it attracts the curious and imaginative, or whether it attracts both in different ways. It is assumed that players enjoy states of arousal and the chance of winning and dominating situations.

What is less certain is whether games addicts are oral, addictive or dependent types. One theory is that games consoles are like friends for lonely or depressed adolescents, though the fact that players frequently talk to the game while playing does not necessarily prove the existence of a 'relationship' of any kind. There is some anecdotal evidence of cases where compulsive playing stopped when family troubles had been successfully resolved.

Games and film

To begin with, games followed film – martial arts, sports, action movies, etc. As the two genres progressed, however, more developed parts of the gaming genre crept back into film. This became an inevitable commercial reality when the same corporation syndicated their product across different media. The film version of Mortal Kombat included all the platform games, characters, morphing, sound effects and features (fatality, animality, brutality) of the computer game. What was added to films was live actors, and in the case of *Mortal Kombat* – so far the best of the genre – the very effective Christopher Lambert. What was taken away was much of the gore – with live actors violence becomes more real and therefore more potentially offensive to viewers.

Since the genre of game-films is in its infancy, it is hard to predict how successful it could become. The first examples have been frankly poor as films, attracting comments like 'the most pathetic excuse for a movie that I have ever suffered through'. The general consensus remains that they are mainly of interest to gamers wanting to see their characters on the big screen.

One aspect where games have influenced films is the high-speed chase, with films increasingly trying to emulate animation's high-speed explosions as the hero weaves in and out of impossible situations. Simple movie car chases have been upstaged by the excitement of arcade games, so the cinema has had to spend a lot of money and use a lot of stunts to keep up. Cinema loses out again in terms of not offering the chance of slow motion replay to savour particular moments. But purists would say that interactivity would destroy the cinema's essential 'art' – that of a created work that stands or falls on its merits, whereas games are interactive and depend on the input of the player.

This is the same anti-convergence argument that futurist writer Douglas Rushkoff uses about TV and the Internet:

> The rush to converge the Internet (a communications medium) with television (a programming medium) is ill-founded and ill-fated. TV is TV and the Net is the Net. Never the twain shall meet. I don't want to watch TV at my desk, and I don't want to send e-mail from the couch. TV could be considered a 'yin' experience – a passive acceptance of entertainment programming. The Internet is a 'yang' experience, where we sit at our desks and type out our thoughts and feelings.[12]

TV and games may simply appeal to different psychological states in us. There are times when we want to simply chill out and flop on the sofa to watch TV rather than get mentally speeded up playing games. The real convergence, according to Rushkoff, is more likely to be between games and the Internet: 'If networking is about contact, and entertainment is about content, then how can the two be combined? So far, the best examples of networked entertainment I've seen are interactive gaming sites. Players of computer games like Doom or Myth can log onto networks and play with or against one another instead of the machine.'[13]

Are games and film compatible bedfellows? Gary Dauphin, a film critic at *The Village Voice*, believes that you have to go a lot further than simply grafting bits of one on to bits of the other if the goal is a really creative synergy:

> The balance of cinematic invention and character development is tricky to maintain, and some of the highest profile attempts are ultimately cautionary tales. Take Nintendo's Zelda 64: Ocarina of Time and Squaresoft's Parasite Eve. Both Zelda and Eve are stunningly rendered 'cinematic' games that require players to take meticulous walks through the wilds of character building in exchange for the privilege of viewing lengthy visual rewards. In Zelda (which has no FMV), the main character Link literally grows from a boy to a man against the backdrop of some of the most finely rendered scenery this side of Industrial Light & Magic. Expanding on the 360-degree camera-control first introduced with Mario 64, Zelda effectively lets the player direct his own film and watch it at the same time. The details are impressive. Zelda even mimics compound-lens flare when Link looks into a bright light, offering the player the ultimate in faked verisimilitude. But play these games and you'll be bored out of your skull. The long-awaited Zelda is a true case of designers missing the forest for the trees, a brilliant but empty game that's at best a high-end demo for the Nintendo 64 platform. While the game's code might constitute a formal quantum leap, not even 64 bits of eye candy can overcome Zelda's sheer on-screen stupidity. At the other extreme, Parasite Eve is a kind of FFVII gone wrong, a massive investment of labour and capital that, like the worst of big-budget Hollywood, isn't about anything except its own scale.[14]

Shigeru Miyamoto, designer of pioneering games like Mario, believes that though there is a lot of cross-fertilisation, the formats of games and films are, in the final analysis, dissimilar:

> Novels, movies, and games for primitive game machines can't completely express the creators' ideas (including the NES), but nonetheless make use of people's imaginations in order to successfully stimulate their minds. Thanks to the recent technological evolution, games' visuals now come closer to that of movies. In response to that, we have been trying to learn a lot of modes of expression from movies. The camera system adopted in Legend of Zelda: Ocarina of Time is something new. It combines movie methods and techniques we created in making interactive videogames. Will videogames surpass movies? Videogames and movies each belong to a completely different genre, so they cannot be compared. It's like asking, have movies surpassed novels?[15]

Gary Dauphin points out the obvious – for games to surpass movies they need great artists of the stature of some of Hollywood's legends: 'Gaming has plenty of Máliàs and Muybridges but no Griffith, and no Welles. It's time for a game or game maker that radically breaks from the medium's precedents and rivals other entertainment. Technologically speaking, the stage is set. What are they waiting for?'[16]

Death in games

How much death can people tolerate in games? In the cinema deaths occur in films about sports like motor racing, and in sci-fi films like *Death Race 2000*, a black comedy about a car race across the USA where the winner is the driver who kills the most pedestrians along the route. In *Rollerball*, a futuristic gladiatorial contest set in what looks like a speed cycling track, the statistic for maximum death count in one game is nine, and the theme is similar: the use of brutal sports as an opiate for the masses. In the case of *Rollerball*, one of the leading characters says at the end 'this isn't a game'. Only a minority of computer games players actually want 'final' death in their games, because they want to play again and again. Also, it takes a fair amount of setting up to get a character up and running to a viable fighting level, and to do that over and over again because of real death would bore most gamers into quitting. However, the shock of true player death is considered by some players to add a spice to a match that makes it heart pounding, but the number of fights that the average player would want to risk his or her life on are probably very few and far between. Players would either back off or not fight so often. One way of doing it – and keeping the raised level of arousal – is to have a final duel between players where death eliminates the character the player has created, with all its kudos and history, so the player has to start again with a different character. Again the death is simulated, but there is more sense of finality.

The gore factor in games gets more shocking as the realism increases, as with Quake 3 Arena. VR guru Mike Pesce felt sickened when he tried it:

> I had expected the high-octane realism of the visuals, but when my 19-inch monitor (running at 60 frames per second – double the speed of your television) displayed a torso blasting into a gelatinous ball of viscera, raining torrents of blood, and studded with the impacts of various limbs, one horribly predictable thought ran through my mind: Columbine. Quake treats violence as if it were as boundless as cyberspace itself: there are few limits and no consequences; you can blast apart as easily as you regenerate. It's not the gore, then, that troubles, but the specific way Quake detaches that violence from the usual moral universe that surrounds it – an ironic trait for a product that so prides itself on verisimilitude. And the question I kept asking myself was: How much of that violence was somehow imbedded in the original technologies behind virtual reality, and how much has been foisted on it by subsequent explorations? It's easy to dismiss Quake as a corruption of VR's otherwise innocent roots, but what if the seedlings of Carmack's carnage had been there all along?[17]

Ultimately, the gore factor in games is likely to parallel the prevailing gore tolerance of society. There are signs that combat is getting more extreme in real life. Simulated gladiatorial fights are commonplace on TV, but more worrying is the rise of 'Absolute Fighting' or 'extreme sport' in various forms, from bare-knuckle fighting to fighting in barbed wire rings or cages. It might be claimed that such no-holds-barred fighting has always had an underground existence, but it is gradually coming further and further to the surface. Absolute Fighting is gaining popularity in Russia and the USA, where it is filmed for pay-to-view TV. It is played out in front of up to several thousand adrenalin-seeking spectators – including a section of the underworld – who are jaded by existing limits on fighting. With only head butting, eye gouging and biting forbidden, the capacity for injury is considerably greater than anything regulated by the Queensberry rules, and of course there have been serious injuries and death. An advert for one video promises 'teeth knocked out, sprays of blood, bouncing skulls, dislocated arms, broken jaws' – and bear in mind that this is for 'Cage Fighting Women'. Maybe an echo of video games' packaging proclaiming 'As easy as killing babies with axes' or 'More fun than shooting your neighbour's cats'? As in *Rollerball*, the fighters are treated like royalty and are well paid. The future now? Maybe the slippery slope at least.

The future of computer games

After the major advance in realism of Sony's PlayStation 2, we are currently waiting for Microsoft's X-Box, which promises 10 times the performance of PS2, bringing it close to the frontier between computer-generated simulation and near photo-realism. Big players are involved in this 'battle of the Titans' – Microsoft is joining with Intel and upstart video-chip developer Nvidia in an attempt to definitively see off Sony – for now. A quarter of Sony's revenue comes from the PlayStation, and almost half of Microsoft's revenue comes from home computer users, so a lot of money and power is riding on the playoff between the two. One reason Microsoft may win is that no platform fees need to be paid by software developers, presently the largest revenue chunk for Sony, Sega and Nintendo.

Equally interesting is the beginnings of 'intelligent' computer games, which require creativity to set up and run, and which can even learn and develop themselves – 'God games' as they are colloquially referred to:

> Over the coming months, two of the most ambitious and anticipated 'God games' will hit the market after years of development in England. Throughout Peter Molyneux's Black & White, gamers divine everything from weather to manna for groups of tribal villagers, and, for real fun, create a beast that personifies their evil or benevolence. In Evolva – a kind of hybrid shooter/God game – by designer William Latham, players genetically mutate and then command squadrons of troops in a war for intergalactic control. Meanwhile, on these shores, two legends

of God gaming, Will Wright, creator of the Sim City series, and Sid Meier, designer of the hit Civilization games, have topped charts with their own recent releases, The Sims and Alpha Centauri.[18]

'We play as we develop,' says Meier. 'It's a very organic evolutionary process. We focus on making the story interesting, as opposed to the goal. The journey is the reward. We want you to have fun throughout the process as opposed to only at the end feeling satisfaction.'[19]

Some of the augurs of these creativity games are positive. Writer David Kushner says:

> Black & White allows you to be whatever kind of God you want to be, from very evil to very good and everything in-between. What has emerged is that while most people playing start off with the premise that they are going to be harsh and nasty Gods, in reality most people do not have it in them to be really truly nasty for a sustained period of time to either the villagers or their creature − so the players' worlds tend to be grey as opposed to either black or white.[20]

NINE

From Cartoon to Virtual Reality

'Experience the magic', Walt Disney repeatedly says, using this slogan to persuade us to use its products. A simple advertising exercise maybe, but the first cave drawings were, in fact, both cartoon and magic: 'The Palaeolithic artists who drew and painted animals on the walls of their cave dwellings were not making works of art in order to express their personal way of looking at the world, but were attempting to work magic.'[1]

Germain Bazin agrees: 'The primitive artist was a magician whose drawing had all the virtue of a magic spell, an incantation – early man used painted and carved forms to ensure the fertility of his prey, to entice it into his traps or to acquire its strength for his own purposes.'[2] While for Bazin the 'first creative act' was naming things, the second was drawing them, something that additionally helped in the formation of concepts. The image grew to serve other purposes, such as to keep alive in the eyes of the people their departed heroes – to cheat death in a form of magical representation.

Such a 'magical representation' of things is, according to Freud, typical of the world of the child:

Perhaps we may say that every child at play behaves like an imaginative writer in that he creates a world of his own, or – more truly – he arranges the things of his own world and orders it in a new way that pleases him better. It would be incorrect to say that he does not take his world seriously – on the contrary, he takes his play very seriously and expends a great deal of emotion on it. The opposite of play is not serious occupation, but reality. Notwithstanding the large affective cathexis of his play world, the child distinguishes it perfectly from reality, only he likes to borrow the objects and circumstances that he imagines from the tangible and real world. It is only this linking of it to reality that still distinguishes a child's 'play' from daydreaming. By dealing with things that are small and inanimate, he can master situations that to him are overwhelming.[3]

Cartoons can have the comfort of what psychoanalyst D. W. Winnicott calls 'transitional objects' – things that offer some solace and intimacy and help negotiate difficult situations, like Linus's blanket in *Peanuts*. 'The interaction between inner and outer worlds is easily seen when we observe children at play. Children make use of real objects in the external world, but invest these objects with meanings which derive from the world of their own imagination. This process begins very early in the child's life. Many infants develop intense attachments to particular objects.'[4]

So cartoons can be seen as a simple version of life with some added layer of comfort. Real people are too complex for small children, who fail to relate to them on TV until later in their development. So instead, people are reduced to 'cartoon essentials' – bare bones or 'mono ideas' with prominent features. Pinocchio is, for example, either honest or dishonest and the length of his nose shows what state he is in. Cartoon characters in films do have the usual range of emotions – happiness, sadness, anger and fear, but these are simplified and exaggerated, as is everything else.

Complexity is out, and the plots are simple and predictable, with all the frequent switches of the drama triangle. The persecutor becomes the rescuer, the rescuer becomes the victim, the victim becomes the persecutor – just like the perennial *Tom and Jerry* cartoons, whose eponymous stars are the most popular film heroes of all time. The pursuits and other plot elements take the place of psychological depth in these miniature 'action movies'. Maybe ordinary movies have borrowed from the success of cartoons – Forrest Gump as the 'idiot savant'. Or in these style-conscious days maybe it would be more correct to refer to the 'idiot chic'.

Another use of cartoons is as teaching tools for children, and in fact for adults if a message needs to be simplified and endowed with fun. Life reduced to its essentials, like parables. And since the essentials predominate in an exaggerated way, cartoons in magazines and newspapers have over the ages been perfect for lampooning popular and unpopular figures of the time.

Just as they can be put to magical use, cartoons are equally good at conveying the grotesque. But then the fearful and grotesque are just as much part of the enchanted world of the child, as the villains in fairy tales amply illustrate. And for the younger age groups it is not so much plots and suspense that cause fear as the actual shape and size of the images – something cartoons with their two-dimensional simplification and their exaggeration of features are perfect for.

Simplification of character brings us into the world of Jung's 'archetypes' – figures that tug at a deep sense of the familiar in us. Archetypes may be further simplified into animal shapes, the type of animal indicating its properties – the donkey as hardworking, the lion as proud and fierce, the fox as cunning, the wolf as hungry, the crow as vain. Such archetypes help younger children navigate the complex world of adult behaviour and help older children digest difficult emotional or social issues, as in larger cartoon productions like *Animal Farm* or *The Lion King*. Cartoons are a useful way of depicting a large part of the dark aspects of humanity central to fairy tales in a way that escapes the censor's cut. Even something as simple as *Little Red Riding Hood* is, when dissected and analysed by Eric Berne or Bruno Bettelheim, a sinister tale with many unexpected twists. Is the wolf the persecutor or the victim? Why does granny deliberately live in a forest full of wolves – what's her script? Why does mummy send her daughter alone into the forest to visit her – what kind of mother is she? Why does the girl wear red?

Cartoons can be used experimentally, as in *Fantasia*. They can be used as 'kidult' entertainment, as in *The Simpsons* and *South Park*, where boundaries are constantly shifted, swear words and violence abound and Kenny is killed in every episode. Politically, they can be 'vigilantes against hypocrisy', vehicles for puncturing pomposity. We love to see important people pilloried when they fall from grace as we exhibit some sort of tribal feeding frenzy to close in on the kill once the victim is maimed and weakened. Long-pilloried senior Labour statesman Tony Benn thinks they are influential in shaping opinion. Cartoons can't be 'spun', so politicians loathe them, and if they turn on the cartoonists, they bite back even more sharply. Cartoonists can 'interpret' spin and see through it. And cartoonists are allowed to misbehave, and don't have to apologise. Adult cartoons like the *Furry Freak Bros.* even managed to graphically depict the sixties drug culture – something that was illegal in practice.

Puppets and cartoons

The classic 'rag puppet' is a rag that can be made to 'dance' as if it is human. The puppeteer makes the audience believe that inanimate things come to life – one of the typical fantasies of the toddler, who believes dark cupboards are inhabited and objects turn into people, as in Ravel's musical comedy *L'enfant et les Sortileges*, where teacups talk to grandfather clocks. Puppetry is like 'animating the toy cupboard' – making toys live. How else can Barbie dolls and Action Men sell in such huge numbers when they don't even move, let alone 'act' without being moved by the imaginative hands of the child?

Stage puppetry is three-dimensional, adding the third dimension that cartoons lack, though its simple forms like *Punch and Judy* are virtually two-dimensional and enacted in front of a flat background. Puppetry uses the very young child's fascination with hands and how they can move and suggest shapes and animals, a trick also used by ventriloquists. The movement conveys all kinds of emotions and suggestions, from fast and scary to delicate and charming. In three dimensions stage puppetry, which has a long tradition in Europe, can 'direct' the sight and focus of attention of the audience, and so perform tricks.

The creative human mind works with whatever 'contingencies' are there at the outset. Earth colours and cave walls are replaced by pen and paper, film and finally digital technology. The cartoon image, as a facsimile of real life, is a 'fundamental', but its realisation changes as the materials change. Cartoons are the precursors of computer graphics, and these days cartoons themselves are made on computers. Puppets, meanwhile, are the forerunners of virtual reality avatars, and have contributed significantly to the technology of movement. As the transition has been made between these forms, some have emerged in 'mixed modes', interfacing cartoon and real worlds in films like *Who Framed Roger Rabbit?*, or interfacing holograms and androids with real figures in the cult TV series *Red Dwarf*.

Computer graphics and animation

With the introduction of the mouse – that popular cartoon figure – spatial travel around our computer screens became possible. The windows metaphor then made cyberspace a 3-D space. Interfaces became graphical. With each advance in technology, the interface, the hardware and the software has shaped our perceptions and expectations in new ways.

With the development of computer graphics, the early number-crunching machines were transformed into vehicles for entertainment and new culture. With enhanced detail, line drawing and colour, computer art packages started to become useful in the real world, and when images and photographs could be inputted and manipulated the new technology became indispensable to art departments and publishing. Computers were soon used as creative tools in design itself.

Non-interactive graphics originally produced just one image, like charts and graphs from tables of data. Next came taking a start picture and an end picture and drawing a series of images moving successively away from the start and towards the end (known as 'inbetweening' in the animation industry). A further version of this is 'morphing', where one shape can turn into another, for instance a human into a cow. Then came combining different images, as in *Star Wars*, to produce backgrounds for scenes using models. Computer simulation is becoming common in films, like *Titanic* or *Jurassic Park*, as the industry and in particular its special effects departments embrace the new technology with gusto, making increasingly lifelike images from fractals. No less influenced were the art and design worlds – both commercial as in advertising, and pure art, some artists choosing to work exclusively or primarily in a computer-generated medium.

Interestingly, the development of the images in a film like *Toy Story 2* goes through the whole history of cartoons. A storyboard frame will first be sketched by hand by artists. The next step is to transfer it to computer and make a crude realisation of the characters as wire frames or outlines. A rough rendering check will then be made using coloured polygons, typically tiny triangles and quadrilaterals. Finally a complete rendering will be done at movie screen resolution, in which all the lighting and texturing will be put in. Shading and lighting are crucial to realism, and the advances made between *Toy Story* and its sequel are easy to see.

Three-dimensional graphics have enabled the expansion of CAD (computer-aided design) to produce designs and manipulate them in various dimensions. It is particularly useful in allowing creative departments to model designs rather than using expensive prototypes. Together with live data, CAD can also be used for testing that is complex or indeed dangerous. Nuclear tests in the Pacific provided data enabling future weapons to be tested by computer simulations. In the business world CAD can allow clients to view early prototypes and cost different variations, or customers to view applications like kitchen and room design.

Digital imaging firm Digimask is already popularising this technology by offering to create a 3-D head from a user's photo. This 'cyberself' can then be used in all kinds of computer applications – not only games but also for viewing oneself in 3-D to assess the visual effect of wearing different shapes or colours of spectacles and other fashion accessories.

Animated graphics opened the way for a huge expansion into film and games, with further spin-offs into training and eventually the sophistication of virtual reality. The present limitation of such systems is the complexity of the images, requiring not only large storage capacity in terms of static memory but also speed of download when loading or streaming images, so faster computation is being driven forward by all sectors of the industry.

Virtual Environments (VEs)

Zebras in the California desert, a crocodile in the Loire, a buffalo in the Alps. Welcome to Frank Horvat's computer-enhanced world, his 'Virtual Zoo'. Native habitats become irrelevant as animals appear in alien settings, where they nevertheless seem to blend in comfortably. Taken in zoos and then digitally manipulated, his pictures explore theoretical boundaries of the environment.

For a more design-oriented approach to virtual environments we can turn to architect Peter Anders's *Envisioning Information in Cyberspace*, which describes cyberspace art and architecture, and also provides unexpected unions of reality and virtuality and visions of challenges and opportunities as yet unexplored. The book questions cyberspace's impact on physical, cultural and social reality, and the human-centred 'anthropic cyberspace' principles of its design. Anders states:

> We think with space. Using our mind's ability to dimensionalise information, we reduce complexity to manageable units or objects of information. Computers can help us by presenting information in ways that capitalise on this skill. 'Mythic Space' offers a communal mind space, a shared but non-physical environment. Traditional mythic spaces convey meaning on many levels. Noah's Ark is simultaneously a wooden vessel as well as a refuge for the innocent. Eden is both a garden and an origin of humanity. Cyberspace has

not yet achieved this cultural richness – the effort so far has been technology-driven rather than guided by a vision based on human aspiration. We should now take the time to describe the cyberspace we want. Anthropic cyberspace could allow dynamic motion through information, letting us rely on our instincts rather than memorised rituals of interaction. It could assist us in the navigation of information using our innate, spatial literacy.[5]

VE technology can go both forwards and backwards in time, and one of its intriguing uses is in the field of virtual archaeology. *Re-creating Ancient Worlds*, by Italian archaeologists Maurizio Forte and Alberto Siliotti, looks at ancient worlds through the eye of VE simulations.[6] It recreates how people actually lived, rather than what we are presently used to – the usual collection of fragmented pots and pans. Studies of computer-assisted archaeological work on 70 sites give us a nearly global survey including a great deal on Italy, central Asia and Japan. The computer is used to generate maps and graphics of how famous and some not so famous sites originally looked, including the pyramids at Giza, Abu Simbel, pre-Inca Peru, Troy, the biblical city of Ur in Mesopotamia and Stonehenge with the sun in various positions. Faded frescoes are restored, eroded walls rebuilt, gaps filled in and the authenticity of the recreations is checked against aerial photos and original research. The 3-D re-creations of ancient Rome, Cahokia, Stonehenge and Pompeii give a fascinating taste of the full-scale VRML (virtual reality modelling/mark-up language) walk-throughs that may lie in the future.

Avatars – cyber androids

Virtual environments need virtual people. 'Avatar' in its Hindu origin means the incarnation of a deity, as in Vishnu taking the identity of Krishna in the Sanskrit poem the *Bhagavad-Gita*. In its cyber android form it refers to three-dimensional electronic representations of people in cyberspace. A simple element in a technological space? Surely, something created in the image of man should have more mystical dimensions than that. Michael Heim, creator of the Active Worlds VR Web site, certainly thinks that if we consider all the rich cultural and magical history of the mask as a representation of the self, then androids are potentially all that and more:

Placeholders for real-time human presence, animistic spirit vessels in a vast system of digitally encoded events. Avatars tap into the age-old magic of transformation. When we put on our avatar, we also put off the habitual self, shifting our shape in order to be who we are in different forms. We lay aside the illusory fixity of being a hard ego encapsulated in a shell of flesh. Avatars allow us to engage a playful self who revives the human capacity to laugh at oneself.[7]

So how easy is it for an average computer user to experiment with avatars? Easier than one might think, it seems. The technology for creating cyber androids is already well established, and can be tried out in avatar worlds on the Web. These are a good introduction to virtual reality because they are accessible to millions of users, and the technology is already in existence for builders to experiment with them and express their own individual visions. Hundreds of people log on each day from their PCs to don an avatar and enter virtual worlds. They chat with one another, express themselves through movement and gesture and build and design their own 3-D environments.

Handbooks like *Guide to 3-D Avatars*, by Sue Ki Wilcox, take computer-literate novices through the necessary technical steps − 3-D graphics, rendering, texture mapping, VRML and technology using the voxel, a 3-D version of a pixel.[8] There are already several avatar construction sets (Avatar Maker, People Space, Avatar Builder, Dancer, Cosmo Worlds, Poser, 3-D Assistant, Oz Avatar Editor, *Le Deuxieme Monde*, Figure Sculptor and Onlive) that can be incorporated with prebuilt bodies such as ergonomic avatars, virtual humans and 3-D clip art avatars. Animating avatars requires motion capture technology, using tools like CyberMask and LifeForms to develop animated photo realistic versions of cyber androids, which can be either fantasy heroes and heroines or computer representations of oneself.

Avatars!: Exploring and Building Virtual Worlds on the Internet, by Bruce Damer, goes on to explore virtual worlds where your avatar can play on your behalf − environments both real and surreal. In his eight virtual world systems (with names like World's Chat Space Station, The Palace, Virtual Places and Oz Virtual) he shows how to interact with different cultures, what responses can take place, the nature of 'digital etiquette' and the amusing or strange things that can happen when virtual and real worlds collide. The companion Web site greets us with the news that an avatar is 'your body double in Cyberspace, your presence in the virtual communities growing inside two- and three-dimensional virtual worlds online – you can now leave simple chat rooms behind and venture forth into the true frontiers of virtual world Cyberspace'.[9]

A whole new area of avatar technology is going to be copyright. Realistic portrayal of humans is getting closer, with the most realistic so far being Sebastian Caine in the film *Hollow Man*, the graphical recreation by Sony of actor Kevin Bacon. So who is going to own graphical representations of real people? Will it be the actors themselves, with their agents taking a cut? Will it be the big studios? After the success of *Toy Story*, real actors are getting nervous. Graphical images won't need to command huge fees, won't throw tantrums and can be available on several different sets at once, if other actors are hired to wear the bodysuits and do the physical acting that creates the animation. Woody in *Toy Story* owed a lot to the actual acting of Tom Hanks, so the realistic portrayal of an actor goes some way beyond a mere voice. Total credibility is still a long way off, however, since an image would have to convey consciousness, emotion, sophisticated physical gestures and personality. Plus it would have to act and have charisma. However, we have clearly come further with graphical humans than with androids, since in the robot world androids are still having difficulty opening doors.

Humanoid or non-humanoid avatars

As with robots, we seem so enamoured of our own physical shape that we tend, in the first instance, to use ourselves as prototypes. When people enter virtual worlds, they choose their avatar, which determines how they will appear to themselves and to others in the world. Many humanoid parts exist in avatar kits, and these can be assembled piecemeal into customised identities. The initial design of these parts strongly affects the final look and feel of the avatar. The other element that affects the choice of avatar is the type and feel of the world it will inhabit.

An average world in Michael Heim's ActiveWorlds

clothes its real people in humanoid forms, which tend to replicate gender types and character stereotypes found in pulp culture. A world will have avatars like 'Surfer Dude', 'Tourist' and 'Tanya' – these avatars share in common a biped, humanoid form. With some few exceptions, the avatars prior to 1998 fit perfectly in a flat-earth world, replicating as far as possible us two-footed creatures who actually walk the earth.[10]

But in a virtual environment we need not be limited by any of the features of our actual world. If we depart from a typical human environment with gravity and a horizon and enter more liberated worlds, then avatars can change accordingly. In Heim's 'ACCD World' (Art Center College of Design)

> the first important design decision was to reject the usual implementation of gravity that assumes a single horizon with a flat earth. This decision held profound ramifications for every other design decision, including the type of avatars that belong to the world.
>
> Because of the absence of gravity, ACCD World has multi-layered building levels. You can float up or down to enter different structural levels. Some areas do not reveal themselves immediately upon entry. 'Memory Chamber', for instance, first appears as a large black-and-white photo out of childhood's past. As you approach the photo to see it more closely, other photos begin appearing next to the first, until you realise that you are completely surrounded by old photos, ambushed, as it were, by memories from the past. One of the first avatars to be mounted in ACCD world were [sic] Tweek and Sqaak – giant bird-like avatars. These giant birds are appropriate vehicles for navigating vast stretches without gravity. Free-flying avatar birds are not just birds but transforms where the fantasy and fun of the virtual add something to real presence rather than simply replicate it.[11]

Current avatar design, for Heim, falls into three general categories:

- humanoid;
- non-humanoid; and
- humanoid transforms.

These three general classes of avatar design fit into a broader design issue, one that harks back to the question of representation in art. Representation is often contrasted with 'abstract' or 'expressionist' art, which suggest either formal patterns abstracted from matter or creations that reveal the artist's individual feelings. But non-representational designs, such as humanoid transforms, still remain under the sway of real-world reference, no doubt because many new visitors feel a need for familiar navigation and because current software places certain limits on imagination.

In the process of 'transform', writes Heim,

the self expands to incorporate the avatar identity, and the avatar identity penetrates the user identity. This process of transformation into online avatar is fairly novel, but we can already see some general features of avatar identity that may guide speculation. Avatar identities present both a positive transfiguration as well as a less wholesome transmogrification of the human being. These virtual worlds show the first stages of an evolving 'transubstantiation' of life. They could even be called an 'ontological shift in the tectonic plates of culture' – the virtual world is only now beginning to absorb the other media, and so we cannot know yet how far culture will go into the virtual dimension. Design issues for avatars go beyond the 'merely aesthetic' issues because in the virtual, to create is to exist, and to conceive is already to design.[12]

Virtual reality

Virtual reality is, along with artificial intelligence, the most exciting element in a potential Brave New World. Where AI is the brain, VR is the body in its environment. The term 'virtual' in *Webster's Dictionary* means 'being in essence or effect, but not in fact'. Whereas reality is a real event, entity, or state of affairs, virtual reality can be said to be the illusion of participation in a synthetic environment. Participation is a key element, though VR in its initial stages also includes external observation of such a world. What you see and what you do looks and feels real, but is only a computer simulation of the real situation.

This new artificial or 'hypothetical' environment, often called 'cyberspace', either simulates the real world or creates realistic fantasy worlds. The body is mapped onto the X, Y and Z grid of Cartesian coordinates, and we use 3-D coordinates when we represent ourselves as avatars in a virtual world. We are provided with sound and images through headsets or 'visors', into which are built two small screens, one for each eye, giving a three-dimensional view of the computer-generated environment. Movement is provided by sensors in the visor, manual controls and special gloves known as 'data gloves' that allow the user to move objects in the environment by making hand movements. The images and sounds thus change in response to the movements of the user, giving the impression of a realistic three-dimensional environment that the user not only experiences but controls.

Uses of VR technology are expanding, and already include military applications such as training pilots in flight simulators, the recreation of history and other cultures such as the now-ruined abbey of Cluny in central France, medical technology like moving around the human body, and remote control. Used as part of CAD systems, VR enables customers to not only view new products and building layouts, but to even 'walk through' the VR model and move elements of the design like doors and windows before any modifications need to be translated into expensive new drawings and blueprints. An exploding market for VR is that of computer games, where the player's movements may be mirrored by a character in the computer-generated world.

At its simplest, VR merely reproduces the essentials of primary reality – creating a home, walking about and meeting people, shopping, playing games, planning a commercial project or experiencing culture containing sound and image. As such it is not expanding our horizons in any H-creative way that would cause too much intellectual discomfort. The September 1999 world conference in VR (http://www.outerworlds.com/worldcon/) is a good example of this:

> Cybertown is a futuristic off-world city accessible via the Internet. Our multinational citizens inhabit and socialise in richly detailed 3-D Bladerunner-type worlds using 3-D avatars to represent themselves. Citizens can immerse themselves in these virtual worlds by owning personal 3-D homes, obtaining jobs, forming clubs and much more. Cybertown also provides special programming for its members through entertainment and educational formats including contests, celebrity chat, parties, classes, town meetings and more. Cybertown is always growing and evolving and will soon include such features as customisable robots and pets, member-owned stores in the Mall, personal avatar creation software, increased personalisation of homes and a new Entertainment Complex. WVRR – Worldcon Virtual Reality Radio – broadcasts specifically for VR audiences. FURCADIA is the magical world where the Beasts have learned to walk upon two legs and speak – the multiplayer online game with 3-D rendered animated graphics, magnificent music, whimsical games, a friendly atmosphere and an exciting setting for role-play and adventure.[13]

The original pioneers

'For as long as engineers have dreamed of building faster and more powerful computers,' writes Fred Moody in his opening to *The Visionary Position*, 'some among them have dreamed of displaying computer-stored and generated information in three dimensions, with users walking through information landscapes the way they walk down grocery-store aisles and city streets.'[14] Nearly a quarter of a century before the term was coined, the chief focus of this book – Dr Thomas A. Furness III, an electrical engineer with the US Air Force who designed cockpits in the Vietnam war – began research into VR, eventually leaving in 1989 to attempt to 'turn his new interface into a powerful weapon of moral and social change' in the pioneering Human Interface Laboratory at the University of Washington.

Moody (author of *I Sing the Body Electric*[15]) chronicles how his work there stirred up attitudes and contrary positions amongst academics, programmers and financiers in Seattle's expanding techno-culture. Some of the young computer whizz-kids he assembled to develop civilian applications for his ideas were eccentric and ego-driven, with more loyalty to their own visions than the laboratory, but they did move forward several aspects of the technology, like developing the VRD – a device to project computer images directly onto the retina, instead of using the usual headset. The all-too-obvious collision is between the venture capitalists and entrepreneurs representing 'market forces' and wanting quick returns on research and those whose goals were beyond mere consumerism.

Ironically, it has been said of VR that, 'In the world of VR, imagination has replaced money as a unit of currency.' True in theory maybe, but not in practice, as one looks at the companies that mushroomed around Seattle in the late 20th century – Virtual i/O, F5 Labs, Microvision and Zombie Virtual Reality Entertainment. At the turn of the millennium there are approximately 400 companies in the United States working on virtual reality products in business, medicine, exercise, gaming, the Internet, communications and mass entertainment.

A developing technology

The complete hardware for VR is expensive and still under continuous development – HMD, body suit, gloves, etc. Hence VR also comes in a cheaper version for the PC, where movement is achieved through a mouse or joystick, as in computer games. This abbreviated version is called 'non-immersive' – as opposed to the 'immersive' version using the full kit – but can be improved by larger screens, darkened environments and stereoscopic glasses.

VR is a rapidly developing technology, both functional and escapist, and potentially offers a wondrous parallel universe of unlimited possibilities, as Timothy Leary describes: 'Suited in these electronic star-suits the individual human being is enabled to cross the Merlin Wall and realise our most noble dreams of joy, freedom and fair play.'[16]

Ivan Sutherland, the pioneer of VR, described, in 1965, where he thought VR was going: 'The ultimate display would... be a room within which the computer can control the existence of matter. A chair displayed in such a room would be good enough to sit in. Handcuffs displayed in such a room would be confining and a bullet displayed in such a room would be fatal. With appropriate programming such a display would literally be the Wonderland in which Alice walked.'[17]

At the time of writing not even the most powerful supercomputers can currently generate photo-realistic images in real time, so the creation of photo-realistic detail through faking a convincing illusion, a believable virtual stage set, is the role of the artist. Sensory body stockings and plugging the computer directly into the brain *à la* William Gibson's *Neuromancer* are still not remotely possible.

Psychological and humanitarian uses of VR

Psychologists Rose and Forman consider that their profession has been slow to appreciate the great potential of VR:

> The ability to isolate people from their normal sensory environments, and to substitute computer-generated environments which are infinitely flexible, entirely controllable and within which behaviour can be monitored in great detail, must be of interest to psychologists. Virtual environments may be seen as the next step in experimental psychology – a complex large-scale environment allowing active interaction rather than passive observation.[18]

So what types of research can benefit? For a start, the brain can be mapped during 3-D tasks, giving direct measurements of neural activity and offering clear benefits to neuroscience research. Spatial learning is improved in a 3-D environment, and can be facilitated by colouring in routes or highlighting features. So after computer games, the greatest emerging area is training, where the ability to download virtual environments from the Net or from CDs and DVD offers great operational flexibility.

In *Virtual Reality: A Door to Cyberspace*, Ann E. Weiss hints at future humanitarian uses with a description of a boy with cerebral palsy learning through VR what it's like to ride in his wheelchair over different kinds of surfaces and around a neighbourhood.[19] Others have trained people with learning difficulties to navigate supermarkets or practise bus routes. Weiss deplores the current emphasis on lucrative entertainment and military uses, which emphasise violence, when there are so many more worthwhile possibilities in the fields of industry and medicine. She anticipates that while VR is already being used to treat phobias, it has the potential to help a whole range of rehabilitation needs such as severe sight problems, Parkinson's disease, eating disorders, sexual dysfunction or brain damage, where it could aid recovery. Virtual environments can be tailored to the needs of users, for instance by being blurred to correspond to sight deficits. All the indications are that VR could also be a sophisticated tool in assessment, combining both realism and scientific control. First explorations of this are in the realms of cognitive function.

The principal barrier to progressing beyond the plentiful hype surrounding VR is the unavailability and high price of hardware and software, but surely this will improve. There still remains the high cost of training, programmer time and support systems.

The key issues of VR

The origin of the term 'virtual reality' is ascribed to Jaron Lanier, who wished to 'contrast this technology with "virtual environment" systems, where you focus on the external world but not on the human body or the social reality created between people. The human body and social interaction between people are the primary indicators that one is alive, on an everyday basis, and that the external, architectural environment is secondary'.[20]

VR is an expression born in paradox, an oxymoron built of 'virtual' and 'reality' – surely opposites? The term encases many of the problems that perception theory has with reality and illusion. The word 'virtual' was used in optics at the beginning of the 18th century to describe the refracted or reflected image of an object and is still used in physics to describe the enigmatic behaviour of subatomic particles, which can be said at the same time to exist or not exist, depending on how they are defined. Virtual reality, as a form of computer-generated imagery, is a state in which the object is simultaneously a representation and an experiential phenomenon. Literally speaking it is the computers we interact with. Figuratively we interact with the software. Imaginatively we interact with the artificial world it creates.

Birgitta Hosea defines the key properties of VR as follows:

- a fictional or hypothetical space created by computed data;
- three-dimensional spatial information;
- immersion;
- interaction or play.[21]

Aukstakalnis and Blatner suggest three stages of VR, which can be seen as three points on the spectrum:

- Passive – the subject moves through the space but has no control, eg rides
- Exploratory – the virtual space can be navigated, eg architectural virtual models, ski/snowboarding/motor racing/surfboard simulators
- Interactive – the subject can walk through the space and interact with it through the use of the four primary input devices: data gloves, voice recognition, body input with a data suit and three-dimensional mice.[22]

Michael Heim defines 'three Is' of VR:

- *'Immersion'* – 'a complex and elusive phenomenon', is the psychological effect deriving from devices that 'isolate the senses sufficiently to make a person feel transported to another place'. The degree of immersion or engagement achieved can presumably vary with the subject (as in hypnosis) and the sophistication of the technology.
- *'Interactivity'* – which Heim sees as 'the computer's lightning fast ability to change the scene's point-of-view as fast as the human organism can alter its physical position and perspective.' This requires computers powerful enough to handle data conversion from a person's sensory input to virtual world output, and back again.
- *'Information intensity'* – Heim suggests that 'a virtual world can offer special qualities that show a certain degree of intelligent behaviour',

such as telepresence, the ability to carry out operations in remote locations while remaining immersed in a simulated environment.[23]

Duality

So what do we do with the actual human body in VR? Leave it in the locker room, according to Simon Penny: 'One does not take one's body into VR, one leaves it at the door, replacing the body with a body image, a creation of mind – as all objects in VR are a product of mind. As such it is a clear continuation of the rationalist dream of disembodied mind, part of the long Western tradition of denial of the body.'[24] Descartes's view in *Sum Res Cogitans* was that 'I am a being whose whole essence or nature is to think, and whose whole being requires no place and depends on no material living'. This conception of duality, an 'incorporeal mind lodged mysteriously in a mechanical extended body', a mere 'ghost in the machine', is present in many aspects of modern society. For instance it can be seen in the manipulation of the body like an object through plastic surgery, the 'customisation of the flesh', and body modification such as piercing or tattooing, all of which are becoming increasingly common. Some – like Michael Jackson, Orlan and the woman known as the Bride of Wildenstein – have gone as far as completely reinventing their original appearance to make themselves more appealing or to change their own significance. This objectifying of the body also, as Simon Penny points out, 'fulfils the industry's need for technological desire. The transference of libidinal desire onto fetish objects which offer the promise of ecstasy but never finally consummates, drives the consumer to the next purchase in an unending coitus interruptus'.[25] Dissociation could also imply seeking to suspend any illusion of immersion with strategies similar to Brecht's alienation effect, so deliberately making the experience one of the intellect rather than of the ego.

Dissociation could extend, in VR, to the experience of being someone else – potentially a healthy alternative to egotism. Ideally, the future of VR should help us to experience the 'other', as Hosea points out: 'In VR the potential is not just to don an arbitrary avatar and act out a self-absorbed fantasy. The real potential is for a new method of communication of experience, for the WASP businessman to have the simulated experience of being a Jew persecuted in wartime Nazi Berlin or an African on a slave ship.'[26] Hosea believes the challenge for VR, if it wants to develop beyond an escapist state of solipsist fairground attraction into more challenging territory, is to 'work with the specificity of the medium as well as its content. The key to this is the position of the subject within the experience. This could imply engaging with the concept of immersion and using it as a tool to experience the "other" '.[27]

But somewhere in us is a desire not for dissociation but for fusion. In contemporary science fiction, from *Neuromancer* to the Borgs in *Star Trek*, there are many images of human beings merging or twinning with technology. Hosea sees it thus:

> This can be seen as an end of millennium phenomenon, a searching or 'yearning' to define our place as human beings in the world. However, although the transcendence of the body is a prime cultural concern of the moment, we are physical beings. We hunger, we thirst, we tire, we are sexual and, indeed, much discussion of VR technology has revolved around trying to replicate the unreplicable: the infinite sensory experiences of the sexual act.[28]

There are already some ways, though, for VR to enhance awareness of the body, such as Char Davies' 'Osmose', a VR project in which an awareness of the body is central. The subject wears a stereoscopic head-mounted display and an interface vest, and since movement is controlled by breathing, the subject is constantly aware of their body as it swims through the virtual environment.

Immersion

Hosea considers immersion – the feeling of being inside the environment and surrounded by it – as the most problematic issue to define.

> Perhaps a useful starting point would be the feeling of being an actor and not a voyeur, albeit in a limited scenario that someone else has programmed, in contrast to the more passive filmic identification processes of suture. In addition, there is a spatial awareness affected by sight, hearing, inner ear balance and touch, not a static audiovisual experience. There is also a distinction to be made between first person encumbered simulation (ie physically wearing technology such as a head-mounted display) and third person unencumbered simulation utilising video technology. The difference here is experiencing self as 'I' or 'he/she'.[29]

Heim is another who feels that the psychic atmosphere produced by virtual worlds is vital:

> When the immersive feature of virtual reality creates a world where the user becomes a participant, then we can no longer rely on behavioural psychology to convey what is happening. What Suzuki describes as a 'psychosphere', 'psychic atmosphere', or 'inner field of consciousness' is what I mean by a psychic framework. We should not think of psychic framework as 'consciousness' if by consciousness we mean a private subjective state that peers from within to confront a separate world of alien objects. A psychic framework sets the tone that a field of awareness has when it seamlessly flows with a set of furnishings, tools and physical movements. The 'empirical' originally refers to the sensations we receive in experience. The way we move through information space, as architects well know, affects our feelings about being in that space.[30]

Healthy whole-body interface with computers

Exteroception gives us perception of our environment, while proprioception gives us cues about our own body: acceleration, position and orientation of limbs and so on. Heim is a leading proponent of the whole-body experience rather than the neck-up experience. Using theories and elements of Eastern thought, particularly t'ai chi mind/body awareness, Heim believes Western thinking has until recently underestimated the role of the human body in our cognitive understanding of the world, that there is a fundamental participation of bodily awareness that belongs to human knowledge. He sees the study of virtual reality as beginning to correct this Western ignorance as we increasingly learn to visualise abstract data on the computer and use all the bodily senses at the interface. Sound, sight, tactile feedback and even physical orientation become ways to interact.

Heim warns that since 'repeated and undisciplined forays into VR can threaten the integrity of human experience', it is essential to have a balance of body in reality and body in cyberspace, such as provided by the example of t'ai chi. He even goes as far as proposing that time in cyberspace should start with a t'ai chi 'workout' from a virtual master:

> A virtual t'ai chi expert invites you into the CAVE as you release your focus from HMD (Head-Mounted Display) applications. The

t'ai chi expert is a computer-generated composite that models the movements and postures of actual t'ai chi masters. The computer-generated master not only teaches a series of movements, but also adjusts meridian circulation, tests body structure, balance and earth-energy strength. You play pushing hands, and even spar with the expert. An hour in the VR decompression chamber is a complete workout, and now you link smoothly to the primary world after reclaiming the integrity of conscious life in a biological body. The procedure offsets the disintegrating aspects of reality lags and Alternate World Syndrome. The VR experience becomes health-enhancing rather than health-compromising.[31]

Info Ecology

Info Ecology is a phrase Heim uses for the 'grafting of information systems onto planetary health'.[32] He adapts environmentalist Svend Larsen's work to show the potential harmony between machine and ecosystem. Larsen's suggested six features of the natural world are:

- Infinite
- Inaccessible
- Overwhelming in power
- Fearsome
- Wild
- Primal.

Heim recommends we do not dismiss these important dimensions through 'technology sickness' – spending long periods of time with the lower halves of our bodies immobile while our upper nervous systems work overtime. He recommends a combined VR experience, containing both HMD technology and projection-room immersion. The former offers greater information intensity, the latter enables collaborative group viewing and has the advantage of no cumbersome headgear, low viewer fatigue and user mobility.

Heim illustrates his idea of balance by citing two musicians occupying opposite extremes – Jim Morrison, the epitome of the physical, Glenn Gould, the disembodied intellectual – as 'two sides of future interactivity. The rebellious body protests its exile by seeking participation; the mind's inner ear forsakes physical contact and uses technology to merge with other minds'.[33] Balanced virtual worlds should avoid the excesses of these two geniuses, and effect a union of mind and body, so that any definition of a 'world' is what he calls a 'functional whole'.

VR as art

Heim, like many theorists of VR, considers the medium too important to be left in the hands of the entertainment industry. The VR 'world' depends on how it is created, designed and implemented. 'More than just technological know-how is required: structural design is only the beginning of world building. Software architecture must become interactive. The human interaction side of world design is art.'[34]

Heim believes the art of virtual reality shatters our whole modern aesthetic, where we sit back as passive spectators or jaded listeners or bored manipulators. It can become 'transhuman' and approximate to something that shamans, mystics, magicians and alchemists sought to communicate. It can break through well-worn perceptions in artistic or psychological ways. This breaking of moulds is at the heart of P-creativity and close to the idea of H-creativity. He gives the example of 'surfing' in VR, in which the 'rider', wearing a head-mounted stereoscopic display, stands on a swivel platform, which, like a surfboard, responds to his or her movements, so that 'the rider experiences a vivid sense of motion and the ability to surf a surreal ocean of geometry'.[35]

Heim has created 'a metaphysical laboratory' since 1997 with a team of art students at the Art Center College of Design in Pasadena, California, building 3-D virtual worlds on the Internet that use avatars to achieve human telepresence. These avatar worlds are 3-D chat environments that have become a place for thinkers and media theorists to gather in avatar and exchange ideas about virtual reality. Such 'virtual conferences' are increasingly featured on the Internet. In the spring of 2000, a series of eight meetings took place called 'CyberForum@ArtCenter' and future series of Internet events are planned that will create a more international telepresence in avatar worlds. Heim's work helps to reinforce and extend the presence of art in the evolution of VR, and he is not alone in bringing the sensitivity and vision of the artist to the medium.

Joanna Buick argues that VR may also borrow the idea of minimalism from art: 'only minimal cues may be required, since – as when we read a book – the imagination of the user will do much of the work'. She points out that the history of art is one of working within material constraints and transcending them, and that in VR it should be possible to leave the maximum control possible in the hands of the user. In the other direction art may borrow ideas and images from advancing technology, such as in the work of Paul Laffoley, whose paintings are 'interactive' collages of sci-fi imagery and look like a mixture of Dali and scientific blueprints.

Heim sees art's openness and willingness to use the image experimentally as the way forward:

> Perhaps the essence of VR ultimately lies not in technology but in art, perhaps art of the highest order. Rather than control or escape or entertain or communicate, the ultimate promise of VR may be to transform, to redeem our awareness of reality – something that the highest art has attempted to do and something hinted at in the very label 'virtual reality', a label that has stuck, despite all objections, and that sums up a century of technological innovation.[36]

TEN

The Net

The origins of the Internet go back to the telegraph system of the mid-19th century. When the Atlantic cable was laid in 1866 it allowed binary communication – the dot dash of Morse code – between continents. This was a portent for the binary code of computing – the on/off electrical state or the zero and one of binary digits. It was also an economic portent of globalisation. No longer was the place the important factor in a market economy – the price of commodities now became the crucial determinant, and businesses reorganised themselves to exploit this new worldwide trading opportunity. The final thing the telegraph did was allow instant communication between countries, replacing communication by ship, which could take three weeks to cross the Atlantic. The 'virtual' nature of such communication was puzzling at the start (one woman tried to send a plate of sauerkraut to her son) and there were widespread fears that electricity would make whole cities glow. With the development of new technology there had arrived the simultaneous development of techno fear.

Just over a hundred years later we have the Net – again originally a transatlantic co-operation. The 'World Wide Web' – the www. in domain names – is a communications tool invented by a British scientist working for a Swiss-based research lab working on the Internet – a communications network originally designed for use by the US Defence Department. The US origin of the Net has given the USA a head start in Internet technology. Of the estimated $110 billion processed through the Net in 2000, 75 per cent was through internal transactions in the USA. Even European shoppers presently buy more from US Web sites than their own. This situation is, however, predicted to last only a short time – no more than a third of Internet users will be American by the year 2002, according to the Computer Industry Almanac.

Meanwhile, global Net use grows steadily, from 2.6 million in 1990 to 385 million in 2000. In Britain half of all adults are expected to be online by 2002. The 15 million present users spend four hours a week online, and two thirds said that it had become part of their everyday lives. More men than women use the Net, and while three quarters of professional and managerial professions use it, only a quarter of manual workers do. The main usage is both for sending e-mails to family and friends and for more serious information-finding among the many Net sites. Not far behind come entertainment and work use. This may well change as convergence introduces a variety of streaming media onto the Net. At present a third of people regard the Net as a necessity, while three quarters see it as a luxury. Again, this may change with convergence if entertainment becomes cheaper, more varied or more accessible via the Net. The Net is still a young person's activity – only 18 per cent of the over-55s use a computer and only 10 per cent are online.[1] Partly this is due to resistance to new technology in the more elderly.

Computer phobia

The phenomenon of 'computer phobia' describes people who resist using computers despite having the opportunity. Such people resist talking and thinking about computers, and show both fearful and anxious responses and hostile and aggressive thoughts about them. The typical computerphobe resists interaction with a personal computer, while more severe cases resist anything automated such as hole-in-the-wall cash machines. A study from the eighties estimated that on average, between one quarter and one third of all people were computer phobic to some degree.[2] Five per cent were considered severely phobic, showing dizziness and nausea. Another study concluded that nearly a third of American college students and corporate managers were computer phobic.[3] Studies from China show broadly similar results, suggesting the phenomenon may have universal validity.

Fear of computing has some basis in reality, like radiation fears, but most anxiety is considered 'irrational', whether it is about the consequences of computer use in general, or more personal fears such as being replaced in one's job by a machine. Anxiety needs to be distinguished from resistance to computers resulting from negative attitudes to IT, which may be perfectly rational, and it is further possible for people to simultaneously have a range of pro-computer and anti-computer attitudes based on different aspects of their use. Some anxiety is about being thought slow or stupid by peers while learning to use computers. The latter may decrease as children learn to use computers from an early age. However, computer anxiety is found to be related to general maths and number anxiety, which clearly predates computer training in schools, and also to low general self-esteem.

One result of computer anxiety is less use of computers, and consequently lower achievement levels in computing. For those with severe computer phobia, increased use of computers even leads to more anxiety rather than less, though with slightly anxious novices experience tended to lower anxiety after a year or more of experience.[4]

During the seventies female participation in computer science education peaked at 25 per cent, since when it has gone down severely (7 per cent in UCCA, 1991), so there continues to be a gender difference. Many studies show that males have a greater preference for computing, and know significantly more about computers than females, though females who do computing courses actually perform as well as males. Factors proposed for the difference include:

- boys in schoolrooms tend to aggressively monopolise the available computers
- boys have better spatial ability
- boys are more rationalising and less emotional
- in co-ed schools computing was considered 'male', while in single sex girls' schools this attitude was much less prevalent, and it was easier for girls to show 'masculine psychological gender' interests than in co-ed schools where the culture associated such interests with males themselves.

Females who used computers also liked working with them less than their male counterparts did. They showed both more anxiety and more negative attitudes to computer use, and this held true right across the age range from child to adult.

If we look at cutting-edge data from UCLA freshers in 2000 we find that use of computers has equalled, but confidence has not. First-year college women and men reported almost equal computer use, with 77.8 per cent of women reporting frequent computer use, compared to 79.5

per cent of men. But female freshmen were only half as likely as men to rate their computer skills highly. Only 23.2 per cent of women, compared with 46.4 per cent of men, rated their computer skills as 'above average' or 'within the top 10 per cent' of people their age. What is interesting is that females are favourable to certain computer uses, and in terms of online shopping may even show more usage than men, so in future hardware and software may be more tailored to positive female interest.

Reducing female anxiety for future use of computers seems to require both a more positive attitude and more actual hands-on experience, and so far increased experience seems to correlate to a more positive attitude in females. The way computing is taught plays a role in negative reactions, and received wisdom suggests starting with practice not concepts, and possibly teaching high-anxiety students in separate groups. The important factor for women is decreasing the prevalent attitude that computing is a male subject, so that they have more opportunity to develop skills that are potentially equal to their male counterparts.[5]

Phobia towards new technology is not confined to computers. The same is seen for cars, video recorders, washing machines – even the telephone. One explanation is the difference between passive and active technology. TV sets and radios are purely passive technologies that work when they are switched on and the channels are adjusted. Computers and other machines are active technology – when you press buttons they do things. The secret nightmare may be cars with a mind of their own, washing machines spewing out soapy water, videotape looping out of control, printers whirring for no reason and text being gobbled up into word processors.

Young people who have grown up with active technology are not afraid of these things because their fundamental approach is one of mastery over machines, as Douglas Rushkoff points out:

> The more new media technology with which we come in contact, the less mysterious and more natural it all seems. A VCR lets us tape the news and watch it later in our own time. A camcorder lets us make our own television. The computer and modem let us upload the images we record for anyone else to see. When technology is more something we do than it is something done to us, it is no longer threatening. It is an extension of who we are, and what we want to be. For new media to promote humanity and the nature that drives us, it must never be seen as acting 'on' us but rather as acting 'for' us. We must refuse to be intimidated into believing that someone else knows better than we how it should be used.[6]

The use of technology may be rationed or age-related in some educational theories. For instance, in Steiner (Waldorf) Schools virtual technology is only introduced at appropriate stages and times in a child's development and TV itself is strictly rationed. Not only does this keep children in the real world for longer, but it may counteract the kind of impatience, intolerance and 'click culture' generated in children by over-frequent use of the handheld game remote, the TV remote and the mouse. Children with more time on their hands and no escape button may develop more patience for linear arguments and more tolerance for the quieter parts of life, or those aspects of life that generate anxieties that can be transcended rather than simply escaped from.

Part of the resistance is ecological, as in protests against non-renewable energy forms in technology and the huge number of chemical by-products of the manufacturing process. Whether 'Luddites' can resist for ever is doubtful – it is significant that the Amish now have several Web sites offering their goods online. One obvious effect is that elderly people will be increasingly disadvantaged, as anyone with 80-year-old grandparents begging for help with programming their video recorders will know all too well. Technological progress increasingly favours younger generations.

The N-Generation

In *Growing Up Digital: The Rise of the Net Generation*, Don Tapscott documents the new 'Net Generation' of techno kids. Based on some 300 interviews with today's gadget-conscious children – an enormously influential population of 2- to 22-year-olds totalling around 88 million in North America alone in the year 2000 – he sees this 'tsunami' as a force changing communications, retailing, branding, advertising, education – even the way we build communities.

What makes this generation different from all of its ancestors is not just its demographic muscle but that it is the first to grow up surrounded by digital media. Computers can be found in the home, school, factory and office and digital technologies such as cameras, video games and CD-ROMs are commonplace. Increasingly these new media are connected by the Internet, an expanding web of networks that is attracting a million new users monthly. Today's kids are so bathed in bits that they think it's all part of the natural landscape. To them the digital technology is no more intimidating than a VCR or toaster. For the first time in history children are more comfortable, knowledgeable and literate than their parents about an innovation central to society. And it is through the use of the digital media that the N–Generation will develop and superimpose its culture on the rest of society.[7]

This N–Generation is so familiar with technology that older generations feel threatened by it and find it hard to understand its values – acceptance of diversity, because the Net doesn't distinguish between racial or gender identities, curiosity about exploring and discovering new worlds over the Internet, and assertiveness and self-reliance, resulting from the kids' realisation that they know more about technology than the adults around them. Tapscott argues that

few parents even know what their children are doing in cyberspace. School officials are grappling with the reality of students often being far smarter on cyber-issues and new ways of learning than the teachers. Corporations are wondering what these kids will be like as employees since they are accustomed to very different ways of working, collaborating and creating and they reject many basic assumptions of today's companies.

Governments are lagging behind in thinking about the implications of this new generation on policies ranging from cyber porn and the delivery of social services to the implications of the N-Gen on the nature of governance and democracy. Marketers have little comprehension of how this wave will shop and influence purchases of goods and services. I believe… that there is no issue more important to parents, teachers, policy makers, marketers, business leaders and social activists than understanding what this younger generation intends to do with its digital expertise… we can learn much about a whole generation which is in the process of embracing the new media from the children who are most advanced in their adoption of this technology.[8]

Internet addiction

The indicators of Internet addiction are, according to Bezilla and Keliner, the following:

- Logging on an unnecessarily large number of times per day
- Excessive irritation when the system is inaccessible
- Preference for composing thoughts online
- Preference towards conducting relationships online
- Logging on 'just one more time' before stopping work.[9]

Since the early years of identifying Net addiction, further studies have shown that increasing numbers are being drawn onto the Web. Net users overall spend about 10 hours per week on the Net in the USA and five in Europe, but while usage in the USA is increasing by about 5 per cent per year, in Europe the increase is over 10 per cent. Self-reported 'addiction' is surprisingly high – in a sample of 445 users 46 per cent claimed to be 'addicts' averaging 60 hours per week online, as opposed to non-addicts averaging 28 hours.[10] Of the self-defined addicts, 51 per cent were women, suggesting that the phenomenon really is not just a male one. The average age of the study was 28, and younger respondents showed more Net enthusiasm than older ones.

A crucial finding of the survey was that higher levels of Internet use could be related to higher levels of introversion, depression (measured on Eysenck and Beck scales) and withdrawal from social contact. This is a potentially worrying finding regarding prolonged Net use. Nie and Erbring carried out a survey of over 4,000 adults for the Stanford Institute for the Quantitative Study of Society (SIQSS). A key finding of the study is that 'the more hours people use the Internet, the less time they spend in contact with real human beings. This is an early trend that, as a society, we really need to monitor carefully'. Other findings were:

- Up to a quarter of the respondents who use the Internet regularly (more than five hours a week) feel that it has reduced their time (in person or on the phone) with friends and family or attending events outside the home.
- A quarter of regular Internet users who are employed say the Internet has increased the time they spend working at home without cutting back at the office.
- 60% of regular Internet users say the Internet has reduced their TV viewing, and one third say they spend less time reading newspapers.
- The largest changes are reported by those who spend more than 10 hours a week on the Net – individuals who currently account for only 15% of all Internet users but are likely to be a much larger fraction in the future.

'As of today, heavy Internet users are still a small fraction of the total population,' Nie said, 'but that fraction is steadily growing.'

But Douglas Rushkoff has a wholly different explanation for dissatisfaction among Net users, which is that the Net provides quality experiences in the virtual domain which make us bemoan their lack in real life:

> Why would the addition of electronic relationships into our lives make us more depressed than we were to begin with? Is it just because of the time that online interaction takes away from the rest of our lives, reducing our opportunity to interact with family and friends? If so, why would online interaction be so compelling? Might it offer something that the real world, right now, does not? Maybe online community simply whets our appetite for the kind of community that so-called 'real life' has been denying us for too long. We have marketed and mediated ourselves into extreme isolation relative to what human beings experienced for the past few centuries. Might our experiences online be revealing to us some of what we've left behind? I have a nagging suspicion that our online interactions might tell us more about what happened to us 'before' the Internet's invention than anything it's done to us since it came into existence. In newsgroups, we learn about the true and appalling nature of local and global politics, and in chat rooms we confront the desperation with which so many people are struggling simply to be heard and understood by someone who cares. On the Internet, we learn a lot more about the real world than we do from, say, the television shows we have created to distract us from the depressing realities of modern life. In fact, the whole of the entertainment culture might be a form of anaesthesia – electronic Prozac that keeps us from experiencing the full weight of our market-driven, highly divided global society. Like the musicians on the deck of the Titanic, our entertainments keep us calm and distracted as the boat sinks into the ocean. If the Internet gives us a temporary glimpse at what's really going on, we might best take a look – even if it turns out to be depressing.[11]

Techno self-help

How much do Net users need self-help material to deal with their Net habits? A recent study by Dr Alvin Cooper suggests that if 'compulsivity' is the criterion, then users of sex sites are only 3 per cent more at risk than the general population.[12] How this may change with the advent of virtual reality sex experiences offering much greater immersion than simple two-dimensional pictures or streamed video material remains to be seen.

Given the large quantities of self-help material and practitioners in circulation, it would be surprising if the counselling industry did not start to stake out territory on the Internet, and such is increasingly the case. *The Therapeutic Super Highway* by Kathleen M. Douglas[13] provides a guide for online psychotherapy in the near future, taking advantage of broadband technology, and we can expect this to be an ever-increasing option for those who want to talk immediately or exactly when they feel the impulse – the equivalent of 'therapy on demand'.

Self-help literature on the new technology is already proliferating. One typical text is *Virtual Survival: Staying Healthy on the Internet* by Walter I. Zeichner, whose mission is to guide the techno ingénue towards health, sanity and self-awareness in the new techno culture, using multiple formats like essay, personal story, workbook and talking points.

We start by examining some of the attraction to being online, and some of the effects. We continue by exploring the basic human emotions of fear, joy, sadness, anger and love. The need for connection with the physical and spiritual is greater than ever, we must affirm connection with our bodies, our emotions and our spirituality as we extend our collective consciousness, disembodied, into cyberspace. Cyber is dangerous but it is also immensely wonderful and has the potential to bring people together in unprecedented ways. The alternative is to go dangerously off balance, with possible ramifications like neglect of health, extreme isolation from other people and ultimately destruction of the natural environment due to neglect and ignorance.

Virtual reality will soon be providing complete fantasies for people – sexual, violent, sensual; all designed by programmers to fit a commercial paradigm. The realm of the imagination for VR users will be controlled by programmers and not by the user's own native creativity. The potential is for brainwashing, heretofore unimagined dulling of individuality and identity, all potentially leading to a kind of techno totalitarianism. Millions of people have conversations online every day. People have cyber marriages, live in cyber communities, go to school, work, visit with friends, have sex, all in cyberspace.[14]

Literature on the Net

The SIQSS study already shows regular Net users reading fewer newspapers, and even books are now available online and as downloadable files. But is the Net the right medium for reading? Will people read online or will they simply carry on their tradition with the printed word through 'print-on-demand'? Proponents of real-life books and the printed word have their doubts:

> In terms of new serious literature, the Web has not been very hospitable. It tends to be a noisy, restless, opportunistic, superficial, e-commerce-driven, chaotic realm, dominated by hacks, pitchmen and pretenders, in which the quiet voice of literature cannot easily be heard or, if heard by chance, attended to for more than a moment or two. Literature is meditative and the Net is riven by ceaseless hype and chatter. Literature is traditionally slow and low-tech and thoughtful, the Net is fast and high-tech and actional. As for hyperfiction, the old Golden Age webworks of text have largely vanished, and hypertext is now used more to access hypermedia as enhancements for more or less linear narratives – when it's not launching the reader out into the mazy outer space of the World Wide Web, never to be seen again. In a sense, it's back to the movies again, that most passive and imperious of forms. And even the word, the very stuff of literature, and indeed of all human thought, is under assault, giving ground daily to image-surfing, hypermedia, the linked icon. Indeed, the word itself is increasingly reduced to icon or caption. Some speak hopefully of the binding of word and image, many, perhaps also hopefully, of the displacement of word by image. There is a genuine fear – or hope – that our old language of the intellect, systematic discourse and poetic metaphor may very soon be as foreign and esoteric as ancient Sumerian cuneiform tablets.[15]

In terms of news, the wind seems to blow either way – first towards Net sites, and then back to print. News Corporation closed News Digital Media in January 2001, at the same time as the *New York Times* cut back 69 people in its digital division – 17 per cent of its workforce – and further Net site cuts are a wave flowing through the industry. Since most revenue for newspapers and news sites comes from advertising this whole area is one subject to fluctuating market forces.

The sociology of the Net

The Net can be broken down into a complex range of activities all carried out over the Internet – exchanging electronic mail, photographs, video and sound clips; e-commerce and shopping offering everything from books and CDs to cars; real-time audio and video conferencing; chat rooms and newsgroups. Soon to come are the telephone, broadcasting and real-time streaming of films. A huge network of virtual links and physical optical and electronic networks, running through portals and ISPs, joins together not only computers but people. One analogy for the way people are joined up is 'swarming' around 'hives' like Plastic, Slashdot, Amihotornot, Amazon's 'People Who Bought', Napster's peer-to-peer music archives and Google's relevancy rankings.

Some of the communication on the Net is random, as people meet in chat rooms and discuss everything from car mechanics to art. Some is territorial and indeed hierarchical, as newsgroup contributors form 'inner circles' according to longevity, expertise, wit and persuasive muscle and maintain a friendly but somewhat superior attitude to newer 'lurkers'. As new users or 'newbies' increasingly join in they have to run the gauntlet of the old guard, and they are tested on relevance to the discussion, interest of postings and above all integrity – spam and you are *persona non grata*. Respect the group and you are made welcome. When pressed, such elite members can easily deny hierarchical 'intent', though clumsy newbies are quick to attribute it. In a recent thread on rec.music.classical.recordings a small number of posters congratulated the 'authorities' in the group for their erudition. This sparked a heated democratic debate on the concept of 'authority', which in this case was replaced by common consent with the word 'expert' so as not to imply the use of power. Experts on newsgroups, or 'Electric Minds' as Howard Rheingold put it, nevertheless enjoy considerable respect and recognition – 'wizard' status – in keeping with the level of their expertise, intelligence, wit and encyclopaedic knowledge, and become household names for Net communities. They add stability to groups and can shape their direction.

The content of groups is determined by their audience, which can be large, but the flavour and popularity of groups depends on chance elements like the happy convergence of like-minded spirits with something to say. The names of newsgroups can be quite misleading – the best jazz group is not rec.music.jazz but rec.music.bluenote, the best classical one not rec.music.classical but rec.music.classical.recordings. Promisingly titled psychology groups are empty; unpromisingly titled ones are lively.

While the Internet has changed many aspects of our lives, from the way we work, to the way we shop, to the way we socialise, the Internet is still a fairly new subject for social scientists to grapple with. *Doing Internet Research: Critical Issues and Methods for Examining the Net*, edited by Steve Jones, offers some explorative strategies for doing social research on the Internet.[16] Contributors are from communication studies, computer science, sociology and also English departments.

Online sex

Inevitably, one of the hot potatoes of the Internet is sex. The study by Dr Alvin Cooper mentioned earlier, based on replies from over 13,500 Net users, gives interesting insights into online sex. It found that most people – 92 per cent of the survey – are mild users of sex sites (defined as less than 11 hours per week) and have no obvious negative effects from visiting sexually oriented sites. They appear to use such sexual material as a source of entertainment more than for sexual release and reported that online experiences were satisfying but not particularly arousing.

Those spending 11 hours or more per week visiting online sex sites are, however, more prone to psychological difficulties such as sexual compulsivity. This group admitted psychological distress and reported that their behaviour interfered with some areas of their lives. The study identified 'online sexual compulsivity' as a relatively rare condition, though 8 per cent of the survey respondents were found to be at risk compared to an estimated 5 per cent of the general population. While time spent online for sexual pursuits may partly point to pre-existing problems, the findings did indicate the possibility of online sex creating further dependence.

Specific findings were:

- Men are the largest consumers of sexually explicit material on the Internet. Male respondents (86%) outnumbered female respondents (14%) by a ratio of six to one.
- Women favour the use of chat rooms, which offer more interaction and the development of relationships (49% females to 23% males).
- Men favour visual erotica (50% males to 23% females).
- Most individuals (64%) were either married (47%) or in a committed relationship (17%).
- Of the single individuals (36%), half were dating and half were not.

Visiting sex sites remains a somewhat covert activity – three quarters of respondents said they were secretive about the time they spend online, although 87 per cent did say that they felt no guilt or shame about doing so. Use of such sex sites may, at this early stage in Internet history, be purely experimental for many people. Such experimenters may choose to reveal little of themselves, or alternatively take the opportunity – under the cloak of anonymity in an Internet café – to express repressed anger or sexual urges. They may also experiment with identity. The study reveals the extent of 'acting' on the Net – 61 per cent said they occasionally 'pretended' about their age while on the Net and 38 per cent admitted presenting themselves as a different race from their own.

There are many choices facing Net users – how much to reveal, how much to invent, how much to lie. Allucquere Rosanne Stone suggests that reinventing oneself has both positive and potentially destructive implications, as people can fragment into multiple personalities.[17] She finds sex on the Net both exciting and potentially dangerous, as does another female author, Cleo Odzer. Odzer, an anthropologist with a speciality in human sexuality issues and an unabashed enthusiasm for cybersex, provides a fairly uncensored look at how real people sexually interact in fantasy environments and how though the physical interaction is fictional, the psychological and emotional interactions are totally real. The virtual environments range from simple chat areas to complex MOOs and palaces.

Odzer explores how cybersex can interact with the 'face to face' world, providing a role in both healthy and unhealthy sexuality, and how ethical issues of sexuality – from gender discrimination to pornography – apply both online and off.

Many people feel guilty or confused by their virtual love affairs. They don't understand why they are so obsessed with someone they've never met, sometimes someone whose appearance, age, or even gender they can't verify. They are certainly not alone in their urges, and their feelings of love and lust are not 'weird' but normal. Cybersex will be incorporated in the lives of many of the computer-age generation. It is not an oddity. It's a growing part of our global culture. A good cybersex encounter is totally absorbing. Your mind and body are completely focused on your virtual reality. You're plugged right into the fantasy part of your brain, but now someone else is interacting with it. The vagaries of real life – a doorbell, a news story breaking on CNN, a real-life party going on elsewhere – cannot compete with the compelling nature of this phenomenon. It's all consuming. Your brain is alive and engaged with another cyber citizen, one equally committed to the cyber way of life. We who live there – cyber citizens – live in the virtual reality (VR) world. We participate in real life (RL) too, of course. But our First World exists in the computer. The political economists of the 19th century would laugh if they knew what we've done to their term First World. To us it no longer represents Capitalism. It's the main world to which we belong, the cyber world. Cyber citizenship exists; I know it because I live it. My home is in cyberspace.[18]

Odzer thus makes a startling declaration – it is possible to feel you exist more in a virtual world than a real one, to be an orphan in RL and have an adoptive home in VR. Is this delusion, is it addiction to cyberspace, or is it simply that cyberspace can be a whole world you can fashion exactly to your requirements in a kind of ultimate existential makeover? These are new questions raised by new technology. Odzer goes on to tell us more about this new environment and how it feels:

This new world mirrors the old world in various ways. The passions, jealousies, obsessions, needs are no less strong than their real-life counterparts because they trigger the same internal emotional states. A cybersex scene can be as arousing as a real one. There is no physical touch among lovers and no pain in cyber masochism; yet cyber love affairs call out feelings no less intense than real ones. Cybersex is identical to real sex in many ways and is different in others. It's a thing in its own right and a phenomenon of its time. It is on the Net that our innermost secrets are revealed in all their agonising beauty. Part of all relationships exists only in our minds, and that is what is undeniable in cyber passion – when we don't know what our love object looks like, have never heard his or her voice, can't be sure of age or even gender; then we realise that the emotions come from within ourselves.[19]

The expanding Net – convergence and new media

As more and more people log on to the Net it expands in throughput. With the convergence of digital entertainment on the Net, the snarl-ups already caused by people downloading pop songs from Napster will expand exponentially as films and other streaming media become downloadable in real time and broadcasters and telephone companies start to use the Net.

Welcome to 'broadband' – the transmission of high-density information on the Net. We may, it is estimated, need to cope with traffic a thousand times greater than we have at present on the 'backbones' or main arteries of the network. The key to this expansion is optical technology, or 'fibre optics' – long fibre tubes carrying not electrical signals but light. Optical technology can handle considerably greater bandwidth than satellites or microwave transmitters, so it remains the hope for the future.

One thing that holds up the effectiveness of an optical network is that the transmission of data by light along cables is substantially faster than the electronics used to process it; the conversion process itself from one medium to the other further slows throughput. So the future of high-speed communication is 'photonics', optical technology that will manipulate data by combining, amplifying, transmitting and switching it. At present speed increases in optical technology are over double those of Moore's law – the rule-of-thumb observation that the density of transistors on computer chips, and hence the cheapness of processing the same amount of information electronically, doubles every 18 months. If all goes well, networks may become all-optical to the extent that there will be more capacity than demand. This raises the same issue as the laser – that of an invention waiting for uses. Possible data-intensive future uses include online virtual reality, 3-D holography, telepresence and metacomputing – joining up multiple sites on the Web to do huge calculations. Metacomputing can be done in hardware to perform data-intensive calculations, or by analogy it can be used in software to form 'hives' or super-sources of information that are greater than the sum of the constituent parts.

The convergence of D-entertainment

Information superhighway, entertainment superhighway – the Internet is on its way to becoming both. In autumn 2000 Microsoft announced its new multimedia plans, centred on the Media Player bundled with its new Windows Millennium operating system. The keyword to online entertainment is 'streaming' – transmitting or downloading 'content' such as audiovisual material in real time, exactly as TV and radio provides real-time programmes. The content is transmitted as digital information, of course, but then radio (DAB – Digital Audio Broadcasting) and TV are starting to go digital already and storage is moving from video recorders to the forthcoming digital DVD (Digital Versatile Disk) recorders.

So the new future of broadcasting is on the Net, as broadcasting organisations – now referred to as 'content providers' – transfer to Net technology and make more and more services available to computer users. Besides convergence of content, there will also be convergence of platforms, as the computer takes on the functions of the TV and the TV starts to incorporate Internet access, computers download and play music, record CDs and are hooked up to home theatre installations, games machines access the Net and computers play the very same games. And finally there will be convergence of distribution, how the content gets to your platform, between broadcast and wireless, disk, Internet, satellite and cable. These three convergences form between them the 'Big Convergence' of D-entertainment and information, with feedback systems to support human interactivity.

Speed of transmission is critical for the future of these convergences. Transmitting films is currently even more painful than downloading MP3 (20 minutes for a 4MB file) – the average movie downloading on a 56k dial-up modem takes 833 hours. Broadband networks will soon cut this to 53 seconds in Europe, a massive difference and the start of genuine video on demand. Microsoft, Compaq and Telesystems Inc. (owners of the largest fibre-optic backbone in Europe) are currently working on a European streaming service that will eventually serve up to 1 million concurrent streams. Other high-speed backbone networks like Servecast.com will add to this and use Windows Media. As far as content goes, Sony, Yacast and Pathe (via its European subsidiary Netcine) are all signed up with Windows Media and ready to go. Netcine is releasing 1,000 titles from Pathe's extensive film library, offering full video on demand.

The first offerings are jerky, blocky and constantly rebuffered but are presently available from BBC Online and Servecast.com. Clearly the technology is set to improve dramatically, and when content is downloadable on demand there will be less need for present recordable storage systems like CD-R and DVD-R. This is already a growing trend in the MP3 world, and broadband will extend this technology to content, with larger storage requirements such as film and multi-channel media. Wider access to broadband is scheduled for 2002 in the UK, and this will mean considerable changes in 'convenience viewing'. Just as video recorders liberated viewers from timetables, so video on demand will make it possible to watch whatever you want when you want – missing programmes will be a thing of the past. Not far behind will be viewing where you want, via new generations of laptops and mobile phones, and even wristwatches and dashboard displays (Delphi Automotive in the USA is already taking advance orders). Predictions for the general use of broadband to replace all existing media like TV and radio – even newspapers, magazines and books – estimate somewhere around the year 2020.

Another major shift in the sociology of viewing could come with 'personal video recorders', available from TiVo and RelayTV, which allow users to pause and replay live TV, skip through commercials and store and replay programmes. Indexing systems will increasingly direct choice towards the favourite viewing material of users, creating 'user profiles' of benefit to both user and content provider. Such machines would either compete with derivatives of games machines like PlayStation 2 (PS3 etc) or even merge with them. Which way the market goes may depend on the plans, and range of subsidiary companies, of huge multinationals like Sony, who have interests in both content and hardware. Future marriages will have important strategic effects, such as that of Time Warner and America Online. And if it becomes possible to scroll through commercials, how will this change programme finance – would content providers install some sort of 'watermark' to counteract scrolling or would advertisers change the way in which they advertise?

The big 'if' in all this is how robust and stable the technology will be. Microsoft software, for instance, is still based on DOS, and commercial imperatives mean that in real-world terms new products are released onto the market when they work rather than when they are theoretically perfect, hence the continual downloadable updates and upgrades. It is possible to design virtually bug-free software, and where this is needed – as in NASA's space programme, where the cost of mistakes in human lives and lost investment would be unacceptable – it is done. But such software has complex problem analysis routines built into it and may triple-check functions for security, all of which means large teams of specialised developers and high-speed computers with large storage. NASA's operating system is another generation ahead, and there are no indications yet as to when ordinary users will get to use such a sophisticated operating system. The reality in the near future will be the familiar bugs, system crashes and network logjams. For now, this leaves old bug-free technology like books and CDs still very much in the running.

The broadcasting companies are investing heavily in the Net – whether the Net is added to TV or vice versa – and hope to make greater profits through convergence. For a start, the Net is interactive and has, as Douglas Rushkoff points out, 'a buy button':

> By reducing the opportunity for interaction online down to the single decision of whether or not to make a purchase, the Web's commercial developers successfully channelled the widespread desire for a more responsive media towards a very particular end: selling more stuff. And now they hope to do the same to television. Convergence, the Holy Grail of Internet developers, television executives and the investors fuelling their war chests, is the term being used to describe the next generation of interactive devices: television sets with high-speed Internet connections. Although no one has developed any real content for these devices, the idea is to create 'interactive programming' through which viewers might choose to follow their own storylines, or, better yet, click on the objects used or clothes worn by actors during TV shows in order to buy them. By adding the functionality of the Internet to television, marketers hope to enhance their ability to create entertainment and environments that induce more spending.[20]

But Rushkoff warns that Internet people are used to total concentration and control of their medium and may simply not tolerate commercial breaks, something that may force content providers to play by 'Internet rules':

> They won't tolerate commercial interruptions – or they'll move to environments that don't have them. Competition for 'viewers' will dictate the format of this newly fluid medium. Everything else be damned. That's why the most likely scenario I see for the future of convergence media is the disappearance of commercials altogether, replaced by what could be called 'sponsored media'. Just as early television consisted of programmes sponsored entirely by one company who put its name over the title, companies will pay to have their names associated with an interactive environment that people enjoy inhabiting – and that the sponsors feel enhances the value of their brands. It's a compromise I'm willing to make – and one to which marketers may just have to submit. Commercial forces invaded our interactive mediaspace and turned it into a marketplace. Let's see what we can do when we have the keys to their city.[21]

Computer users as content creators

As far as content goes, the next stage is being able to create it on home computers and distribute it. This is made very much easier by the new digital camera technology. The savings compared to film are colossal. One hour of 35 millimetre film, developed and edited in a suitable studio, can typically cost around £3,000. The same hour's digital tape, edited on something like iMovie 2 software on a home computer, can be done for as little as £20 once you have the hardware, and that is now available for a few thousands.

The proliferation of content will mean dealing with a range of new legal and technological issues, and it remains to be seen how much the big corporate players will react to a variety of individual content providers coming into the marketplace. Certainly films could be made for a fraction of their present cost, so this may force economies. A key question would then be that of distribution – whether individuals distribute from their own Web sites, or use larger-scale distribution outlets, or some mix of both.

The implications of ordinary people as content creators go far beyond merely providing content. In an interactive medium like the Internet, people expect to participate, send e-mails, chat in chat rooms and own their own Web sites, which already act as their window on the world and on which they can put images, music and words, allowing them to be seen and heard. So when mass media converges onto the Internet – the territory already staked out by the common man in the techno gold rush for domain names, and peopled and run by the 'ordinary Joe' – then one should expect the mass media to converge with the spirit of the Net. If they don't meet the culture of the so-called 'new media' they may not meet the typical Net punter. And this is what is happening in the cutting-edge ad agencies. The latest Calvin Klein ads feature not sultry unapproachable models on their pedestals of anonymity but ordinary faces with e-mail addresses. The message is, 'when in Rome, do as the Romans do' – when on the Net, do as real Net people do.

In the convergence of everything on the Net, the big becomes little and the little becomes big. Web sites can now even overturn viewing habits – Yahoo is already more popular than *The X-Files, Ally McBeal* or *NYPD Blue*. And at the same time the huge proliferation of entertainment options is humbling the old bastions of broadcasting:

In these days of cable, satellite and the beginnings of digital TV, it's *all* niche programming now. A show that gets 10 million households – 10 ratings points – is a Top 10 hit, and a show that gets a million has gone from unproduceable to solid performer. The miracle of *Seinfeld* was that any show could reach a quarter of the country in the face of this proliferation of choices. *E.R.*, the post-*Seinfeld* heavyweight, only reaches 20 per cent of the country, and no show that has launched this season has broken 15 per cent. The hand-wringing about the end of *Seinfeld* was occasioned in part by the recognition that a show that reached even a quarter of the country at once was the last of a dying breed. *Sic transit nihilum mundi.* Both the Web and TV are being divided into three tiers: a handful of huge properties (Yahoo; the Superbowl), a small group of large properties (AltaVista; *Dharma and Greg*) and an enormous group of small properties (EarAllergy.com; *Dr Quinn*). The TV curve will always be flatter than the Web's, of course – the difference between a hit TV show and an average one could be a factor of 100 (10 per cent of the audience to 0.1 per cent), while the difference between a Web mega-site and someone's collection of wedding pictures easily exceeds a million-fold, but the trends are similar. As advertisers, content creators and users get used to this changed landscape, the advantage may move from simply being the biggest to being the best loved – a world where it is better to be loved by 50 thousand than to be liked by 5 million.[22]

Another crucial dimension to survival may be the ability of new content providers to experiment with what Douglas Rushkoff calls the way 'content' is used as a medium. He cynically observes that the 'social currency' of most social interaction is about jaded common denominators mostly deriving from the media world itself, and suggests that innovation may come in unexpected ways, such as when sports cards given away in cereal packets as 'content' became collectible in their own right, were sold by themselves without the cereal and became a 'medium' for card collectors to socially interact.

We think of a medium as the thing that delivers content. But the delivered content is a medium in itself. Content is just a medium for interaction between people. The Internet allows people to post their own content or make their own Web sites. But what do most people really do with this opportunity? They share the social currency they have collected through their lives, in the form of Britney Spears fan sites or collections of illegally gathered MP3s of popular songs. The myth of the Internet – and one I believed for a long time – is that most people really want to share the stories of their own lives. The fact that 'content is king' proves that they don't. They need images, stories, ideas and sounds through which they can relate to one another. The only difference between the Internet and its media predecessors is that the user can collect and share social currency in the same environment. Those of you who think you are creating online content, take note: your success will be directly dependent on your ability to create excuses for people to talk to one another. For the real measure of content's quality is its ability to serve as a medium.[23]

ELEVEN

Into the Future – The knotty problems of cyberspace

'The future's not ours to see,
Whatever will be will be.'

'Que Sera, Sera' (popular song)

The fact that we can't see into the future has not stopped people trying. Here we are in Arthur C. Clarke's 2001. What we have this year is the forecast for 2015, from the CIA. Apparently – if you are an American – the future looks like this:

- The future threat to the USA will be from cyber-attack and from terrorists – political, ethnic, ideological and religious – rather than from larger countries like Iraq or Russia. This will be made worse by the widespread availability of cheap weapons, and only partly offset by America's Missile Defence Shield.
- Globalisation will continue as the main driver of future culture. 'Unrestricted flows of information, ideas and capital' will lead to ever greater riches for Europe and North America. Not far behind will be Latin America and Asia – particularly the fast developing economies of India and China. Those further behind will experience 'deepening economic stagnation, political instability and cultural alienation'.
- Poor countries like Africa will be the big losers, beset by malnutrition, internal wars and diseases like AIDS.
- Non-governmental groups – anti-globalisation demonstrators, private corporations, drug-trafficking gangs – will become as important as governments.

- Unless new or existing global epidemics significantly affect the population, it will rise by around a billion, with widespread migration to overcrowded cities, which will grow and grow until they include nearly half the world's population.
- Technology remains our hope for the future – new medicines, advances in science, new materials and more sophisticated computers.
- Global warming will increase, one consequence being water shortages and even wars.

The gurus of new technology broadly agree on the areas of interest and concern, and most are listed above. But their predictions, reactions and attitudes vary. So do the attitudes of theorists on the whole question of how much impact the present 'information age' will have on the evolution of mankind.

How many 'ages' have there been in man's evolution? Hobart and Schiffman propose three ages of man, each of which started with the following key developments:

- the invention of writing: the 'classical' era of information;
- the development of the printing press: the 'modern' era of information; and
- the information age: the 'contemporary' age of computers and cyberspace.[1]

They make the controversial claim that the present information revolution, while creating much faster change than the other two, will actually have less impact on human thought and culture than its predecessors, and will fall short of the predicted world 'Renaissance'. They consider the invention of writing to be the most dramatic shift in our use of information, since it created knowledge that could be stored outside the memory of individual humans. The printing press was then responsible for bringing information to the masses, and fostered the growth of numeracy and finance. The 'contemporary' age of computers and cyberspace develops this, but they see it as less of a paradigm shift in terms of the actual nature of knowledge itself.

Utopia or dystopia?

More than any time in history, mankind faces a crossroads. One path leads to despair and utter hopelessness. The other, to total extinction. Let us pray we have the wisdom to choose correctly.

Woody Allen, *Side Effects*, 1981

Just as we argue about the impact of new technology, we argue about whether its effects will be good or bad – a 'utopia' or a 'dystopia'. Theorists have taken both positions. The utopian position is well expressed – with a touch of irony – by Donald Fagan in the song 'I.G.Y.' (International Geophysical Year) from the album 'The Nightfly':

> What a beautiful world this'll be
> What a glorious time to be free
> On that train all graphite and glitter
> Undersea by rail
> Ninety minutes from New York to Paris
> More leisure for artists everywhere
> A just machine to make big decisions
> Programmed by fellows with compassion and vision
> We'll be clean when their work is done
> We'll be eternally free, yes, and eternally young.

The dystopian view – cynicism at our acceptance of a technotopia – is expressed by authors like Theodore Roszak.[2] Why do we idolise 'intelligent' machines, he asks, when far from being a panacea, they have created as many new problems as they have solved old ones. Roszak blames most of all:

- the omnipresent persuasiveness of multinationals through advertising and PR;
- the espousal of new technology by all parts of our society, public and private;
- governments' desire to control information;
- last and above all the credulity of a techno-hungry gullible public that has not paused to consider the role of technology in their lives.

The downsides cited by Roszak include 'data glut', the confusion of knowledge with data, the dumbing down of 'edutainment' software, the education of children by machines and the misplaced belief that a scientific broom can sweep away our messy problems. He warns of the unreality of carrying out so many transactions in cyberspace, and beyond this he sees a threat to human-based values like justice and life purpose, as the rise of a digital power base displaces existing social structures.

Politically Roszak warns of increasing invasion of privacy, over-reliance on polling in politics and the creation of a new military decision-making technocracy. He does see some potential advantages: immediate online knowledge and democratic communication via the Net. But he warns that we should go into such potentially huge social changes with our eyes open rather than surrender ourselves blindly to the complex ecology of the techno age.

Another dystopian view, that of Nick Fulford, sees escapism running out of control in a materialistic world. He regards our age as increasingly escapist, with the escapism being constantly fuelled by multinationals who try to persuade an affluent society that it is dissatisfied and has constant need for formalised products and activities that can be packaged and sold worldwide:

Escapism abounds in our age. Whether one looks at television – the 'glass teat' of Harlan Ellison – or the tremendous draw of video games or the future of 'virtual' realities, escapism is the mantra of Western society. Whether marketing gurus created it or just learned how to exploit it is a subject all on its own. The fact is we live in a society where most people spend most of their unallocated time engaged with various forms of escapist activities. Mass entertainment promotes disengagement with people and society, and seduces a person into spending time and money experiencing 'virtual' things – video games, soap operas, game shows. Escapism – at its worst a means of building addictive behaviours for the creation of profit – is strenuously encouraged within our society. It and dissatisfaction, from which desire can be built, are the key components for the materialist paradigm to work.

Dissatisfaction can be with anything that is deemed as insufficient or lacking, or it can be with oneself or one's relationship with others. Provided basic needs are maintained at a level that does not endanger health and safety, and drives such as the sex drive are met, then dissatisfaction is largely contrived. It is generated to promote consumption, since when people are satisfied there is no impetus for change. There can be a positive creative side of dissatisfaction, and where there is extreme dissatisfaction, often in the form of a threat to individuals or a community, there is strong impetus to create, invent or change things for the better. But who is to say that creativity will not be used to generate increased profit for the person, institution or group which owns or controls the means of escapism?[3]

Francis Fukuyama takes a more right-wing dystopian view, concentrating on the social order. In *The Great Disruption: Human Nature and the Reconstitution of Social Order*, he argues that civilization is in the midst of a revolution on a par with hunter-gatherers learning how to farm, or with agricultural societies turning industrial. Whatever the benefits of advances in our culturally developed, information-based economy, 'certain bad things also happened to our social and moral life'.[4]

Individualism, for Fukuyama, has had the benefit of fuelling innovation and prosperity, but has also corroded virtually all forms of authority and weakened the bonds holding families, neighbourhoods and nations together. He sees the 1960s as something of a watershed in terms of social evolution, but believes we are outgrowing that decade's social innovations, and that the transition from an industrial to an information economy is largely complete. He therefore sees the need, now, for a coming era of vital social re-ordering. 'Social order, once disrupted, tends to get remade again because humans are built for life in a civil society governed by moral rules. We are social animals and it is in our nature to reconstitute society into viable and functional forms. We're on the tail end of the great disruption.'[5]

Fukuyama argues that the dawn of the post-industrial era, roughly since the 1960s, has been accompanied by dramatic increases in crime, family break-up and public distrust. He cites traditional reasons for the break-up of family and social order – the greatly increased number of women in the workforce in a post-industrial intellectual economy, naturally disruptive teenagers having fewer family checks on their actions, the increase in juvenile crime, the promiscuity of young people following the introduction of the pill and legalised abortion. He argues that the family is not 'socially constructed' but originates from informal norms that create social order. Stable families, he argues, mean socialised kids, low crime and trust-based capitalism.

Criticised for his essentially conservative views, he uses plentiful data and graphs to support his arguments on crime, marriage, fertility and public opinion about values. He views the new basis of economic life in information and knowledge as 'just as monumental as the Industrial Revolution, and just as disruptive'. He believes that there are concrete signs that the old order has broken apart and a new social order is already taking shape, suggesting the 'Great Disruption' of the 1960s and 1970s may be giving way to a 'Great Reconstruction', as Western society weaves a new fabric of social and moral values appropriate to the changed realities of the post-industrial world. Whether this is more than a conservative viewpoint remains to be seen.

Perhaps one of the most frightening forecasts comes from Bill Joy, chief scientist at Sun Microsystems: 'With each technology (genetic engineering, nanotechnology and robotics) a sequence of small, individually sensible advances leads to an accumulation of great power, and concommitantly, great danger. Accidents and abuses are widely within the reach of individuals or small groups... This destructiveness will be hugely amplified by the process of self-replication.'[6] Nanotechnology, for instance, could at worst saddle us with rapidly reproducing viruses that could endanger the whole of human life. And what if robots start to self-replicate?

Social relationships in virtual communities

> Technology is evolving a thousand times faster than our ability to change our social institutions.
>
> Bill Joy

What will be the nature of social relationships in the future? Pierre Levy sees us as moving past an information economy into an economy based on human interactions; a 'social economy' where the quality of social interactions will become a greater concern than real-world economies.[7] 'Our humanity', Levy writes, 'is the most precious thing we have', and predicts that we will take greater control of this humanity as we group ourselves in cyberspace into what he calls 'Living Cities'. Levy sees us in a social paradigm shift of the magnitude of the Renaissance, where physical location is less important than the interactions of people and the lack of territorialities will challenge present methods of government. He rejects free market dogmas in favour of the emergence of a 'Collective Intelligence' derived from French intellectual traditions.

For some of the utopians the prospect seems so exciting that you see the phrase 'virtual communities' mentioned next to McLuhan's 'global village' or Teilhard's 'Omega Point'. Pierre Teilhard de Chardin, the French Jesuit palaeontologist, envisioned the convergence of humans in a single massive 'noosphere' or 'mind sphere' (in Ionian Greek, 'noos' = mind). This giant mental network would surround earth to control the planet's resources and shepherd a world unified by love. For Teilhard, the mental sphere held out the meaning of history, the omega or end point of time, much as the Christian rapture at the Final Coming of Jesus.

Take out universal love and you have the more realistic view expressed by Douglas Rushkoff – the idea of an increasingly 'global' psyche as the Internet and its future forms knit together fundamental attitudes of far-flung communities:

> Although it will certainly occur more subtly than in a science fiction movie or new age novel, I do believe we are in the midst of a transition – intimated by the Internet – towards a more collective thinking, where the individual psyche becomes a component of a larger group mind. This doesn't mean we stop existing as individuals, but it could mean we become more fully aware of every other living being, much in the way a coral reef's individual organisms respond to one another as if they were part of the same, single body. We already know that women moving into a house together will synchronise their menstrual cycles. Why shouldn't people communicating for the first time on a global level experience analogous sympathetic reactions?[8]

Others are less impressed. Michael Heim is sceptical of the idea of virtual communities. On present evidence he sees them as merely enhancing the isolation and alienation humans already experience in their houses, cars and offices. What if, in this brave new world, shopping, learning, business and socialising can be done through computer networks? Where is the guarantee of happiness?

> I know people in rural communities who hear wishful thinking in the phrase 'virtual community'. It sticks in their craw. For many, real community means a difficult, never-resolved struggle. It's a sharing that cannot be virtual because its reality arises from the public places that people share – not the artificial lots you choose but the spaces that fate allots, complete with local weather and a mixed bag of family, neighbours and neighbourhoods. For many, the 'as-if community' lacks the rough interdependence of life shared.[9]

Ironically, many have seen the Internet as just the kind of virtual 'civic space' Heim alludes to – a 'virtual public park' in contrast to the advertisement-saturated commercialism of TV.

Technology meets nature on the path to utopia

Where does nature figure in an increasingly technological society? Modern science has tended to stand to one side of nature and has even treated it as an antagonist, an object for human exploitation or modification, as Douglas Rushkoff points out:

> We didn't invent technology to promote nature – at least not consciously. We invented it to conquer nature's inconvenient and sometimes frightening rhythms. We use electric lights to break the tyranny of day and night. We use heating and air conditioning to thwart the cycle of the seasons. We invented airplanes to travel through 10 time zones in as many hours, melatonin pills to fall asleep when we get to our destination, and dexedrine to wake up the next morning. Our technology has separated us from the natural rhythms of our world.[10]

Many recent books have criticised modern science and technology for creating the distance between humans and nature that has led to the crisis of planetary ecology. The ecological movement began, after all, as a protest against the misuse of technology.

As our technological worlds become more and more invasive, how do we preserve a respect for nature? Nature seems, on the face of it, excluded from cyberspace, so how can we preserve a respect for the natural world when we inhabit computer space? Although the materials of technology – metal and plastic – lack the sensuality of nature and its atmosphere lacks the balmy freshness of a spring day, we have invested too much money and culture in technology not to look for some solution. Michael Heim's solution is what he calls 'virtual realism'. Heim is neither a naïve realist nor a techno–utopian like Alvin Toffler and the 'digerati' of *Wired* magazine. Typically concerned with balance in order to survive well, he writes:

> Social and technological changes stir debate about the future. On one side are network idealists who promote virtual communities and global information flow. On the other side are naïve realists who blame electronic culture for criminal violence and unemployment. Between them runs the narrow path of virtual realism. We must balance the idealist's enthusiasm for computerised life with the need to ground ourselves more deeply in the felt earth

affirmed by the realist as our primary reality. This uneasy balance I call 'virtual realism'.[11]

Heim sees this balance as existing on all levels, from resisting the constant urge to upgrade computers and their software down to the elementary matter of how to sit in front of a computer for long periods of time:

> I see myself involved in a continuous struggle every time I pull my body away from its tendency to collapse and slump in front of a computer monitor, every time I rest my eyes from their intense fixation on the screen, every time I pull myself from virtual worlds to go outdoors where I feel my physical dimensions shrink under the stars and moon of the night sky. Loosening the organism from its fixations after long hours of computer work belongs to the daily practice of virtual realism. Walking the path likewise means continually moderating those moments when our cultural trajectory jolts us with ever-changing upgrades of hardware and software.[12]

Given that the path to healthy use of new technology is a narrow one, Heim nevertheless allows himself some degree of utopianism:

> In coming decades, we will build virtual realities in cyberspace. Real telepresence requires a deep harmony of the active viewer and the virtual abode. No cheap tricks can achieve such harmony. Only long experiments by artists, who patiently apply wise traditions, can bring about the still point of presence. Perhaps, the still point of presence, enhanced by electronics, may one day become omnipresence. Then the Zen of the garden and the virtual worlds we inhabit will cease to be two different things. Then, all space and time will fold into a harmonious play of perception, and cyberspace will be our rock garden.[13]

Virtual workplaces and teleworking

One way of reconciling nature and work in the future is teleworking – something that holds out the prospect of people being able to live in close communion with the natural world while still linking up to their previous office environments. 'Hard day at the office, darling?' is an expression that may gradually vanish into the recent past if we see an acceleration in the trend for people to work from more domestic locations.

'Telecommuting' is by now a familiar expression. Teleworking can be carried out from home, satellite offices, telecentres with sophisticated network links and the new European term 'telecottages' – a rural version of the latter. Suggested gains are in independence, time freedom and reduced commuting and traffic congestion. Potentially it can offer a more agreeable work environment, or at least one that may more suit partner, childcare or family needs. It also favours people excluded through various disabilities. So what are the indications so far as to its effectiveness?

One large-scale European survey of teleworking was carried out by PATRA in 1994.[14] This showed a third of teleworkers spending no time at all in a central office. Another third spent less than half their time in a central office, and the balance spent over half their time there. Pay and work status varied greatly, including hourly freelance work as well as part-time and salaried employment. Much of the work was data handling or word processing. Training was scant – 84 per cent stated they received no initial training. Most received no ongoing in-post training, and two thirds received no health and safety advice about working on the Net. So in its initial stages in Europe teleworking appears to be very much a cheap convenience rather than a considered option.

The reaction to this new kind of out-of-office experience was mixed. Managers showed the most negative responses, feeling that their control and the 'people management' part of their role was eroded when they couldn't actually see and talk to their workers. They feared that increased teleworking would reduce their role to a task-oriented one of monitoring data rather than managing people. Not surprisingly, task-focused managers were more accepting of teleworking than people-focused ones.

Both managers and workers nevertheless opted in favour of keeping a hierarchical management system with clearly set objectives – a win–win situation reinforcing the formal position that managers like to manage and workers – particularly when at a distance – like to feel properly managed. This included having managers listen to workers' ideas, support their demands and needs, and represent their interests to higher management. In other words, a proper organisational culture is just as necessary for effective teleworking as it is for a formal office setting. Equally important is the thread that holds the various independent parts of the organisation together – the actual organisational structure and culture. The culture favourable to teleworking should optimally be people-centred, task-focused and participative, with an open but goal-setting style of management.

Communication is another paramount issue, and worker satisfaction increased with the frequency of e-mails. Obviously, satisfying the need for personal support in the case of both managers and workers is going to be one of the main challenges of teleworking, and this was one of the main recommendations of the PATRA report – a reward-based and open style of communication, with easy informal access. (This style is certainly borne out by other flourishing fields of teleworking like the Open University, which has just such an approach to its students.)

In terms of job satisfaction, the highest was seen in city-based workers who spent the least time in the office – no doubt this relieved them of the frustration of wasted hours travelling and unnecessary social interaction in the office. Rural workers, on the contrary, liked to spend some time in the office, no doubt to counteract solitude and because commuting in their case was more pleasant. More time in the office was also found helpful when the work involved was more cognitively demanding, like discussion of strategy and feedback on results.

Where teleworking is tailored to the needs of the work and the workforce, teleworkers can be as happy as part-time office workers.[15] Research in the USA, where terminology encompasses 'frontline workplace' and 'cyberlink workplace', confirms this. Teleworking consultants like Crandall and Wallace have found the challenge for managers to be similar – how to manage workflow (assigning, monitoring and measuring work), how to guarantee job satisfaction, and creating reward systems in a virtual environment where employees may be given simply a cell phone and a laptop.[16] The authors are upbeat about the future effectiveness of 'virtual work', and like the Europeans, suggest that there are a variety of key procedures that help to implement change effectively, and that certain industries are more suitable than others.

What happens, however, when we extend teleworking beyond national borders? We already have the 'cyber-nomads' – the high culture of technology's new hired guns, moving from country to country to get the best deals or the best living conditions. Demand is so high that they can name their price from Bangalore to Baltimore. No casual unskilled workers, they are increasingly aware of their global marketability. As Beerud Sheth – co-founder of California-based job site eLance.com – points out, 'The first big wave on the Net was content. Then you had commerce. We realised that the next big wave would be services.'[17] The computer services market may become, like the film industry, a project-based world where a cast is assembled and disassembled ready for the next call. Web site freelance.com is already a showcase for the talents of the best freelancers in the business.

And those that don't want to move can secure contracts for virtual work via the Internet. They can even, crucially, undercut the services of those living in rich economies. Eliminate the overheads and you have a global workforce at your fingertips. Calling... calling... Bulgaria, Bucharest, Bangladesh, Bukina Faso...

Cultural impacts of new technology

In a new world of teleworking and 'virtual communities', what of those old elements 'time' and 'money'? Time on the Internet is, in fact, rather different from our terrestrial time. It is a little-known fact, but in Internet time the 24-hour clock is divided into 1,000 units or beats. The present 'Directors of Time' (see page 252) in various countries, not surprisingly, don't appreciate these competing units of time.

As for money on the Net, the financial market has been initially confused by 'dot com' companies. After a flourish of optimism and venture capital the situation has now settled into a 'wait-and-see' scenario: markets are waiting to see, somewhat cynically, how much money there actually is in e-commerce. One factor that has to be taken into account is the lopsided global economy. At present, the top 20 per cent of the earth's population consumes 86 per cent of the world's wealth. The bottom 20 per cent consumes 1 per cent. In terms of Internet use, 20 per cent of the population represents 92 per cent of its traffic.

This is the world of rich and poor predicted by the CIA, where whole populations are in the grip of multinationals. Can the 'global village' and its shared global information subvert the power of multinationals? Or will society be more and more influenced by the mass multinational economy, especially those that have the muscle to win in the law courts? Multinationals have exploited the third world to expand their product base. They form cartels, they influence and shape trade organisations, they lobby governments. There is a feeble 'best practice' influence on multinationals, but this is largely toothless. Litigation takes time, as shown in the endless ongoing litigation involving Microsoft, so breaches are not corrected instantly and trading malpractices may continue.

Children know more brand names than plants these days – not a good sign. Uniformity of image and brands destroys creativity and innovation and also the healthiness of difference. Global problems need global solutions, such as those proposed by Friends of the Earth, Greenpeace and similar organisations with mottos like 'think global, act local'. NGOs have found that they are only taken seriously when they have global influence, thereby enabling them to bring pressure to bear on a variety of local issues. The Global Anti-Cartel Network, made up of law firms in most countries, is currently claiming back money for CD users and Microsoft customers. Their target is price fixing, and their current concerns include pharmaceuticals and vitamins. Pig feed and vitamin cartels in the USA have so far paid out over $1 billion, though nothing has happened yet in Europe. Capitalist gurus like Milton Friedman warn against the Network, maintaining that old adage that competition between enterprises protects the consumer. He would, for instance, eliminate the US Sherman Act, which passed anti-trust legislation.

Protests by the public show that they reject this and are increasingly against multinationals alleged to be anti-environment, such as GAP for its supposed involvement in logging in California. More and more multinationals are selling their factories and getting out of actual production, because of public criticism of sweatshop labour. Instead they buy through middlemen, and concentrate on their 'cultural image'– creating a lifestyle image for their brand names. Protestors believe that the multinationals' only real fear is consumer revolt, and that they are more likely to put money into 'reputation management' than into correcting global imbalances in health, education and lifestyle.

Consumer groups are, at least, getting progressively cleverer. They buy shares in companies like Shell in order to lobby the board meetings from within. The backbone of the revolt is the belief that life is not about freedom of choice but about equality of opportunity – society should therefore take on the job of controlling these multinationals. If not – so the theory goes – poor countries or even whole continents like Africa will descend into anarchy and we will be left with a violent world where people hardly dare to venture outside their homes, their lives fed by home shopping and online movies. This will be made worse by the problem of 'information poverty' in poorer societies, one illustration being the substitution of entertainment for information at the lowest cultural levels. This is pretty close to the CIA prediction, in fact.

Privacy and surveillance

Multinationals try to control economies. They and other bodies are also trying to control information. One way that this is done is through surveillance, which is becoming very big business. The age of Big Brother is already upon us – cameras are everywhere and social control through surveillance is a growing trend. The idea of surveillance as a means of guaranteeing compliance with rules is not new, and has been explored by philosophers such as Michel Foucault and earlier still Jeremy Bentham in his 'panopticon', a circular prison where warders at the centre could see everything, and which induced the observed to internalise the rules set by the observer.

Modern surveillance technology derives largely from Second World War military intelligence, and has mushroomed into all the electronic data surveillance of the information revolution, where satellites in space can theoretically see everything at a certain scale. Surveillance at a local level is used for a variety of uses both good and bad. It exposes ordinary people to taped scrutiny while they are in the course of their everyday lives – at work, at school, on the Net, shopping, enjoying themselves. The question is where the information goes. It can be used later for public, private, or purely prurient interests. It goes into the files and statistics of information brokers who feed the commercial world with information. It adds to information about credit status, tax, jobs and health. It records private conversations and a variety of things including vast amounts of detailed and seemingly useless trivia. The whole thing constitutes a vast network of 'Little Brother' databases, data companies and a pool of virtually unaccountable information.

Reg Whitaker warns in *The End of Privacy: How Total Surveillance Is Becoming a Reality* that current technology goes far beyond questions about the security of e-mails and could theoretically allow employers to monitor workers' every move throughout the workday, and the US Treasury to track every detail of personal and business finances.[18] The vulnerability of consumers is implicit in the use of bar coding, credit and debit cards, credit data banks and the growing use of 'smart cards' that encode personal details like medical and criminal records. When surveillance is carried out at DNA level, traces of our movements can be retrieved from years back in history. Such DNA can be used together with other information to create 'profiles' of people for the purpose of inclusion or exclusion and making probability predictions of people's future behaviour.

One question Whitaker asks is: Who watches the watchers? Another is why we are so acquiescent to this intrusive power – do we simply accept it as the cost of being a consumer? Do we have progressively less power and autonomy than we think we have, and are we in reality members of a 'disciplinary society' such as that envisioned by Foucault? If we are subconsciously aware of some degree of surveillance, such as the possibility of having our e-mails monitored by secret services, do we then internalise certain 'correct' behaviours and obey, without external coercion, simply so as not to get into trouble? Why do we not rebel against intrusion into our health and personal finance details – does the threat of compromising our whole access to credit and insurance and the rest of our familiar social structure outweigh our inherent dislike of being subjected to increased scrutiny? Or do we recognise the benefits of surveillance, for instance in the fight against crime?

David Brin takes a similar line to Whitaker, seeing the growth of surveillance in public places as inevitable. Brin, however, proposes that however important privacy is, freedom should be our primary concern and goal. It is more important for the public, in a democracy, to control how information is used and who has access to it:

> History shows that only one tool has enabled people to maintain liberty. That tool is accountability – the power to make sure the mighty (whether governments, aristocrats or any other elite) must answer questions and reveal their schemes. In other words, we have one answer to Juvenal's old question: 'Who will watch the watchers?' The answer must be… us. This topic is just beginning. Let's argue like a free people, and don't fall for easy assumptions. In the long run, light will protect us better than secrecy or masks.[19]

Brin thus argues that people will have nothing to fear from the watchers because everyone will be watching each other. The cameras would become a public resource to assure us that no mugger is hiding around the corner, that our children are playing safely in the park and that the police will not abuse their power.

One of the wackier forms of the backlash against surveillance is seen in the 'Surveillance Camera Players', performance artists who enact various kinds of 'silent movie' scenes in front of cameras in public places, with boards indicating Act 1, Act 2, etc and their various protest messages. The 'counterspy' movement urges everyone to start showing opposition to the proliferation of surveillance devices and processes.

They warn that Big Brother is not a fictional creation but a real process happening now.

A Forrester Research survey found that 67 per cent of people are 'extremely concerned' about the way personal data is handled online. For a population already concerned, a bridge too far – if the technology were to become more widespread – is the kind of electronic surveillance used for tracking prisoners released into society. The Web site www.gurl.com carried out a poll of a thousand subjects on this topic, with these results:

Q: If the government required everyone to get a microchip implanted into their heads, would you:

Option	Percentage
a) Protest in the streets	49%
b) Run as far as possible	42%
c) Accept it, because they have good reason	9%

Interestingly, after all that Europe went through in the 20th century, there is always somebody that thinks a government has a good reason to do anything.

Ironically, part of the alternative street scene in New York actually promotes surveillance. This happens both in the covert form of 'spy TV', a kind of urban voyeurism using night vision cameras to film nightlife and clubbers, and in the overt form of 'public access TV', where individuals with cheap mobile digital cameras film themselves and the various kinds of street life they get involved with.

Security and cyber crime

> What disturbs me is the people making viruses. That's the only thing I'm in favour of the death penalty for.
>
> Arthur C. Clarke

Surveillance goes hand in hand with security, and the threat to the latter is hackers. We already have a lengthening history of cyber crime, and some of its perpetrators are surprisingly young and surprisingly close to home. In the Solar Sunrise threat to NASA during the Gulf War the culprits were not, in fact, the Iraqis but two 16-year-olds from California, though these were mentored by foreign interests. Chameleon was another teenage hacker who was paid to use his skills to get information. Moonlight Maze was an additional sophisticated hacking, targeting US naval codes and missile guidance systems. The perpetrator this time was in Moscow, and remains anonymous. Countries like the Philippines, which originated the Love Bug, have not yet developed adequate resources to deal with the growing problem, and some countries are likely to stay outside the law to some extent.

The ultimate risk is that someone can bring down entire systems, with possibly fatal results for human victims of computer errors. To counter these threats much money is being spent in a frantic race to stay one step ahead of the hackers. Japan's defence forces are going to spend US $13 million of the 2001 budget on anti-hacking measures. Ex-hackers have some degree of cult status, like the many and various outlaws of legend, and are now used in the war against hackers in the USA and elsewhere.

A cyberculture underground?

Hackers are featured in *Cyberpunk*[20], an exposé of three of the most notorious – Kevin Mitnick, who penetrated top secret networks, Pengo, a West Berliner working with the Soviets, and Robert Morris, who alerted us to the capabilities of viruses. Yet more of the denizens of the punk underground are described by Mark Dery in *Escape Velocity: Cyberculture at the End of the Century*[21], where he argues for the existence of such an underground inhabited by cyberpunk authors and musicians, cyberhippies, would-be cyborgs, high-tech performance artists and cybersexers inhabiting a technosex dream-park.

Dery asks whether this underground society can attain sufficient 'escape velocity' to free itself from the gravitational pull of history and tradition. The Internet may be a medium uniquely suited to techno 'outlaws' or indeed content providers of subculture material. The courage to inhabit new frontiers – in artistic or social terms – has always perplexed and disturbed the establishment, but because of the sophistication of a lot of computer technology and research, much of the cutting-edge development is happening in establishment arenas like universities, multinationals and the military, which may remain one step further into the future by dint of their sheer financial and technical muscle.

This is alternately a black vision of denizens of a Ballard-like sci-fi world where 'the cyber-crazies are already circling around us and we should keep them in our sights' and a new world where the freedom of our ideas is guaranteed by real-life cyberpunks pursuing the bright promise of new technologies on the digital fringe. Both trends are possible. The 'third way' is that the establishment will simply buy up the best maverick thinkers with alternative visions, as happened with the development of VR and is increasingly happening with hacking – some of the most celebrated hackers are now part of computer security research. This can only be a partial solution since it assumes that renegades can be bought, and that compulsive, thrill-seeking computer addicts with an arrogant belief in their own intelligence are employable.

Individualism and the Net

So what will be the place of the individual in this new society? This is a question asked by Andrew L. Shapiro, 'one of our brightest young cyberwriters seeking to bring a more realistic dialogue to the topic of technology', according to *Newsweek*. His book *The Control Revolution: How The Internet is Putting Individuals in Charge and Changing the World We Know* led to him being dubbed a co-founder of 'technorealism'.

He sees the Microsoft advertising slogan 'Where do you want to go today?' as symbolising a central dilemma of our times – what to do with freedom of choice. But freedom is responsibility, and as the Net allows individuals to take power from institutions the result will be the re-evaluation of hierarchies in politics, commerce and social life. So how will governments and businesses respond to these threats to their power? We may even find ourselves limited by increasingly narrow choices. Alarmed by the prospect of the Net becoming a new version of 'network television', Shapiro suggests solutions like limiting certain intellectual property rights to free the market for new operating systems, and creating incentives for virtual 'public squares', and warns that we must achieve a new balance of power for the digital age, a conception of self-governance that takes into account the shifting of control from institutions to individuals.

After five years of study, I have come to believe that new technology is enabling fundamental changes, particularly regarding the status of the individual in society. The Net is giving each of us the ability to control aspects of life that were previously controlled by our most powerful institutions: government, corporations and the news media.

We can decide for ourselves what information we're exposed to; how we learn and work; whom we socialise with; and even how goods are distributed and political outcomes are reached. This development deserves to be seen as revolutionary. But it's not a revolution we can yet celebrate for it has all the tenuous attributes of any political upheaval. There is resistance from institutions struggling to maintain their authority. And there is a grave danger that we will push the revolution too far, blinding ourselves to the need for balance between personal indulgence and commitment to something more. Technology bestows great privileges upon us. The question is whether we will shoulder the responsibilities that accompany them.[22]

The Internet and the law

The Internet has a reputation as a kind of Wild West where lawlessness abides and it is difficult to bring villains to justice. But one crucial responsibility citizens have is living within the law, and for any censorship or other control to take place, there must be laws governing the Net. There are, in fact, more laws in operation on the Net than one might imagine. Cyberspace is not exactly lawless space, and it is well defended by the usual terrestrial vested interests.

The whole Napster story has highlighted the question of copyright protection, and this will be as nothing compared with the wars around film copyright, with its substantially higher artistic investment. Despite the perception that the Net is 'free', copyright law still protects the creations of authors, artists and film-makers. So how can copyright be protected in practice? Watermarking is one controversial way to manage serial copying. It inserts some modification to the material, which is in theory undetectable by the user. First impressions of the proposed Verance waveform modification system in DVD-A are, however, inconclusive, since demonstrations of it to the hi-fi press have been extremely cautious. There could easily be multiple watermark systems for different material or zones, just as there are different zone standards in existing software. The fly in the ointment, as usual, is hackers. Since hackers have shown themselves adept at reconstructing the codes behind watermarks, SDMI (The Secure Digital Music Initiative) can at best only hope to stay a few steps ahead of the code crackers.

Further laws concern what one says on the Net – in chat rooms (slander) or on Web sites (libel) – and this is as subject to laws as what one says in the street or in a printed publication. Pornographic sites and their users and abusers are regularly raided under existing laws, and copyright and fraud are also regulated. Customers of Web sites are protected by several measures, including a new seven-day returns policy designed specifically for the Net. Since some issues are peculiar to the Net, like the regulation of domain names with its attendant trademark and copyright angles, we can expect to see further laws in the future.

In the UK, at present, there are – in addition to the Defamation Act of 1996 – the following pieces of legislation:

Regulation of Investigatory Powers Act 2000
This applies to the interception of communications, and the area of debate is how much right governments and their secret services should have to eavesdrop on the Net. At present, for instance, the police can demand encryption codes on pain of penalties, and employers are able to read internal e-mails, however much this offends human rights groups. This has the potential to become a hot potato in employment – one large insurance company recently sacked 90 employees for using the Net for non-business reasons, such as sending humorous e-mails – one example being indecent versions of *The Simpsons* cartoons. One interesting piece of data is that 70% of hits on porn sites are carried out during office hours. The grey area here is that surveillance by bosses may bring to light anything – from time wasting to actual content of correspondence – and there is good reason to consider this a bridge too far in the use of 'Big Brother' technology.

Electronic Communications Act 2000
This ongoing legislation applies to encryption, digital signatures, telecoms licensing and similar matters, and is likely to be used more in the future.

Data Protection Act 1998
The DPA already regulates the storage of information about individuals, and this is extended to the Net, requiring certain procedures to be met, including privacy of information. Personal use of data is exempt, but businesses are required to register, though at present control is lax.

Computer Misuse Act 1990
The law that prohibits hacking – simple and effective up to a point.

Copyright, Designs and Patents Act 1988
Not updated in the last 13 years, this is the law that protects the creations of authors and artists of various kinds.

In the wings for 2001 or 2002 is the Cyber Crime Directive of the European Union, and more EU directives such as those in the Data Protection Act and the Consumer Rights Act, which the UK is obliged to implement.

One general problem is finding the person to prosecute. It is easy to write anonymously on the Net, as any victim of spam will be painfully aware. Companies, however, are required to have a registered office, and Web sites are registered with Internet Solutions and with their hosts. There are still loopholes, such as Web sites that are legal in their country of registration but provide content or services that are illegal in other countries. This is the tip of a huge cultural iceberg – for instance, offence may be caused to particular groups, like Muslims, by material they consider blasphemous, as already anticipated by the Salman Rushdie case. Material legal in one kind of regime might be unacceptable in another. Other areas of different values could be age, race and sex.

The ISPs themselves, though willing and able to pass on complaints to the police, Customs and Excise or Inland Revenue, have limited numbers of staff for the purpose. The complaints office of AOL Europe, for instance, has a staff of 30 at the time of writing. They do, however, cut off offending accounts, and can require Web content to be modified under threat of terminating the account.

Censorship of the new mass media

The imminent convergence of entertainment on the Internet is going to mean the availability of considerably more material that can be accessed and downloaded into people's homes. Those already concerned about the need for censorship of TV, film and video are going to have to deal with increased levels of concern regarding the Internet. Censorship is a means of protection, so that potentially harmful material is not conveyed to the public via the media. In post-millennium Britain, for instance, the regulators of programme material and the areas they cover are numerous. In 1998 they spent £29 million. The present bodies include the following:

- the Department of Trade and Industry;
- the Department for Culture, Media and Sport;
- OFTEL (the Office of Telecommunications – telephone, cable, mobiles);

- ICSTIS (premium rate lines and services);
- the Radio Authority;
- the Independent Television Commission;
- the Broadcasting Standards Commission;
- the British Board of Film Control;
- the governors of the BBC;
- the Office of Fair Trading.

In the face of the worldwide phenomenon of media convergence, Britain is to introduce greater convergence of regulation. Not surprisingly the proposal to create a super-regulator – OFCOM – has met with resistance from existing bodies unwilling to volunteer their demise. The BBC claims that it can regulate itself, and defends itself from the accusation that it has become as commercial as any other content provider by pleading that it is only a medium player on the world scale, albeit a large one in European terms. OFCOM seems inevitable in the light of Internet streaming of programmes and hugely increased consumer content choice, but it calls upon two types of regulation – that of content itself and that of fair trading and deciding between differing commercial interests. OFCOM will certainly be a committee, but it remains to be seen who it will include. Concerns clearly include the fear that a supercommittee will have superpowers.

Protecting children

Whenever censorship is discussed one factor that practically everyone agrees on – rare in this volatile area – is the protection of children. Concerns have been raised over evidence of nightmares following exposure to certain horror films, and evidence that there are recurrent traumatic images that children find hard to get out of their minds.[23] In the UK anxiety escalated following the James Bulger murder, when violent videos were blamed for influencing the toddler's two 10-year-old killers. Following the Bulger case, Elizabeth Newson outlined the following concerns regarding violence in 'entertainment':

- The viewer receives the implicit message that 'this is all good fun' and a suitable leisure activity.
- A child viewer receives distorted images of emotions it has not experienced fully and so must accept as portrayed – particularly dangerous where love, sex and violence are equated.

- The ingenuity with which violence is portrayed tends to escalate as the entertainment industry seeks more and more shock value.
- So as not to disturb the 'entertainment', victims must be seen as subhuman in some way, so they need not be pitied. At worst they are portrayed as actually deserving in some way of violent treatment, so the perpetrator of the violence may reason, 'I had to do it' and be implicitly socially rewarded for such violence.
- Children exposed again and again to violence, eg graphic descriptions of victims' suffering – may become desensitised to it, so changing their behaviour patterns. It is particularly difficult to study this area, since it would be unethical to subject children to a controlled experiment.
- In current films, viewers usually identify with the perpetrators of violence, as opposed to traditional fairy tales where they identify with the victims of gruesome goings-on.
- Violence may be more persuasive when seen in familiar or realistic circumstances.[24]

Research in the nineties, collating various long-term studies and looking at various sources of evidence, was convincing enough for some to find a significant causal factor. S. M. Bailey found that a sample of 40 adolescent murderers and 200 young sex offenders showed 'repeated viewing of violent and pornographic videos was a significant causal factor, a potent source of immediate arousal for the subsequent act' and that acts included mimicry of the violent images witnessed.[25] Others, however, find fault with such research or fail to produce significant links.

Yet other psychologists feel there is insufficient study into the particular reactions of younger viewers as determined by their age and intellectual maturity. Children under eight, for example, are generally more visually dependent, and so are frightened by scary-looking images of monsters and creatures such as the Incredible Hulk. Over-eights, on the other hand, are more conceptual, and more likely to be scared by the undercurrents in the plot – suggestions of danger lurking out of sight and something about to happen, as in the film *Poltergeist*.

One suggestion is that classification by 'overt violence' may not sufficiently cater for these kind of underlying tensions in the plot, though objectors do admit that censorship boards are sensitive to the context of material. Another objection is that one brief shocking moment (eg slicing the eyeball in *Un Chien Andalou*) may have more effect than several scenes of less shock value. B. J. Wilson has studied the harmful effects of broadcasting and suggests a new age divide at eight to cater for differences in child development, combined with ratings for content similar to those already in existence.

Research in the USA shows that parents do try to control their children's viewing habits, and find that age classification is easier to understand than content ratings. The difficulty is that other research shows that even with parental goodwill control is often ineffective in practice, and that a number of parents are either uninterested in control or lax and ineffective about putting it into effect. If this is already the case in homes with televisions, it can be assumed that controls will be no better when computers – or even games machines – are used to access material.

One interesting though not surprising piece of research concerns the viewing preferences of boys and girls. When left to their own devices, boys are more rebellious and want to view more adult material than that which is recommended for their age group. This is referred to as the 'forbidden fruit' effect. Interestingly, while subjects chose 'unsuitable' material for their own viewing they believed that 'others' should abide by the proper recommendations – a clear double standard. The personality types that were most prone to 'forbidden fruit' choices were those already showing a higher intolerance to having their freedom restricted.

Girls are more influenced by age recommendations and tend to abide by them more.[26] This is what is called the 'tainted fruit' effect – labelling contents harmful, such as tobacco, so as to put people off. It is now accepted that age restrictions enhance the appeal of films in pre-adolescent boys, and even that film-makers manipulate their material to fit into the most desirable category to drum up their expected audience – the 'forbidden fruit' effect again. Clearly labelling content as unsuitable repels some and attracts others. One suggestion for a way forward in the light of such research is more sophisticated labelling to allow for the various psychological effects. For instance, the repellent tendency is stronger when linked to a high authority like the surgeon general.[27, 28]

Classification or cuts? This is a long-running debate, and both have been used. A larger number of entertainment producers and professionals prefer classification, since they believe cuts can spoil the product. This does, though, increase the possibility of the forbidden fruit effect. In the USA, the MPAA has two age divides for classification – 13 and 17. In the UK, the BBFC uses the ages of 12, 15 and 18. These are supplemented by 'advisory' categories. Enforcement of these measures is initially provided by the law, and there are various other means of control like watersheds for more adult material at 8, 9 or 10 pm, and chips in TVs that can be programmed to block certain categories of material.

In more general terms what does and does not get on screen is the result not so much of censorship but of those 'committees in dark rooms' that govern acquisition and distribution of products. In theory such people can wipe out, say, the entire African film industry by not buying or distributing any of it. They can also heavily favour material from powerful multinationals. One potential advantage of streaming film content from the Internet and the proliferation of multichannel and digital TV may be to restore minority interests and provide more varied and inclusive programme content. It may not be too much longer before any number of smaller Web sites can provide programme content. But then we come back full circle to the problems of censorship, and on an even wider scale.

Censorship of future games and virtual reality

Cartoons are notoriously violent. They don't affect us because the 'reality effect' of them is very limited. But cartoons evolve, and there is currently a more interesting genre of semi-adult cartoons – sometimes called 'kidult' because they appeal to all ages – like *The Simpsons* and *South Park*. While *The Simpsons* is an example of adult wit and ingenuity in a child's format, *South Park* is closer to the edge in its use of adult language and violence. Interestingly, to offset this the cartoons are considerably rougher and less realistic than *The Simpsons*.

But where do we go from there in terms of censorship? Games figures started off as cartoons, but figures like Lara Croft have become more photo realistic as rendering gets more sophisticated and data storage in games consoles increases to realistic proportions. So as content continues to be violent and images become lifelike we are starting to approach the kind of censorship criteria now used for film. Present censorship of violence in film and broadcasting takes into account the degree of realism the viewer experiences, and the same principle must surely apply to animation when it becomes truly photo realistic.

The big difference is that games are interactive, and there is as yet neither the psychology nor the censorship structure to deal with truly realistic interactive media like VR. This is a whole conceptual leap when we consider 3-D capability and increasing degrees of immersion, including physical movement through bodysuits, gloves and sophisticated headgear. No doubt games are going to be one of the chief commercial spin-offs of VR, and if they are to be as violent as they are at present, then the realism might be frightening.

There are other possible harmful effects of VR besides exposure to violence. There is already evidence, for instance, that exposure to immersive VR can cause nausea, dizziness and visual disturbances.[29] This may be partly a result of the inevitable delay that occurs between participant-initiated movement and the consequent updating of the screen display, creating visual-vestibular asynchrony. The delay, during which time the screen display is redrawn and re-rendered, is usually small and varies with the complexity of the scene represented. Not all users suffer from this, and those that do often get used to the effect, but this is still a potential health and safety and indeed ethical concern. The use of VR may consequently be limited in the case of psychiatric patients, who may be more vulnerable to such effects.

There is as yet no evidence that VR is addictive, in contrast to games and the Net. But this may be simply a case of not having enough data available – VR is in its infancy compared to what it may develop into. If censorship is complex at present, it is as nothing compared with what it will need to be to cope in the near future.

What will be the effects of future technology on people?

How will a world of increasing simulation affect us psychologically? Will we become more introverted in our 'primary' worlds but more communicative on the Web or in virtual reality, as is shown already in organisations where employees use e-mail rather than talk? Can we tolerate – psychologically, physically or in other ways – this new virtual environment? How much synthetic reality can we take – MPG3, digital as a type of sound, music without real instruments, synthetic environments?

One obvious effect of emerging technology is simply that machines, computers, chips and most other things go faster. As they go faster they seem to urge us all to follow them. The brilliantly titled *Faster: The Acceleration of Just About Everything* by James Gleick describes how civilized life over the course of the manic 20th century – from microchips and the media to economics – has accelerated the pace of everyday experience to the point where 'never in the history of the human race have so many had so much to do in so little time'.[30] He gives many examples: the door close button on lifts routinely pushed by Type A people (who are driven, stressed, goal-orientated and more at risk of heart attacks), the New York Philharmonic's 'rush-hour concerts', the wristwatch displacing the pocket watch, telephone redial buttons, multi-tasking on computers and the remote control devices that have led to a frenzy of channel surfing. Everything runs faster − sex lives, prayers, computers.

New technology means that we even have to redefine time itself, 'real time' being something we didn't need a word for before the computer made it necessary. The accuracy of atomic clocks, paradoxically, has led to an even more scientific study of time. In the USA there actually is a 'Director of the Directorate of Time' − the official US government bureau that keeps track of the time and oversees the scientists and engineers who manage, calibrate and interpret the atomic clocks.

Everything speeds up, as we 'bump against the speed limit'. So when do we reach the end stop? Gleick says:

Who knows? There must be a limit to how fast a human being can run 100 metres or 22 miles, but somehow the records keep getting broken. They get broken by tinier and tinier intervals, but that's OK, because we have better and better technology to deploy at the finish lines − another example of how finicky we've gotten about tiny intervals of time. But there must be a limit to how quickly we can process information. How many different frames can we handle in the 30-second television commercial? We certainly feel as though we're pressing against a limit. But then a new season comes around, and the music videos are faster, and the news cycles are shorter, and stock trading and instant foods and TV game shows all seem to have sped up yet again.[31]

Paradoxically, the more we fill our lives with time-saving devices and time-saving strategies, the more rushed we feel. Queues and waiting rooms stir up our impatience, air-traffic control centres redefine time pressure, film production studios test the high-speed limits of our perception. The incessant hurry seems to obey the old law of 'more haste, less speed'. Gleick cites several common time-consuming irritants, such as tollbooths, queues at unemployment and passport offices and telephones that put you on hold or present you with a complex array of options.

The downside of an increasingly fast-paced existence is, according to Gleick:

> We get rushed, we lose control, we act hastily, we think superficially, we feel stressed. The mythical 'saved time' goes nowhere. When we press the Fast Playback button on the telephone-answering machine, or use a laser printer to accomplish in one minute what formerly took typists a day, we imagine that we're saving time for some mythical thing called leisure, which presumably involves doing nothing at all. Somehow it doesn't work that way. The more time we save, the more we do. Even leisure has become a very busy, fast-paced business.[32]

'Hurry sickness' is typical type A behaviour. Some of Gleick's examples of this time obsession are illuminating:

> Occasionally I would catch this guy about to heat up his lunch in the microwave oven, punching 8-8 instead of 9-0 to save the millisecond it would have taken him to move his finger from one button to the next. Then I would catch the same guy looking for something to read, or calculating the roundtrip time to the bathroom, so he wouldn't feel the pain of actually wasting 88 seconds standing and doing nothing.[33]

Michael Heim agrees:

> Online communication accelerates the tempo of life. The faster our interpersonal communications, the faster will be all our other social interactions. As the cliché affirms, the very rate of change continues to change. Just look at someone browsing the World Wide Web, and see how the screens flash past. The television remote control has become the daily mode of reading. Reading is no longer contemplative but has become thoroughly dynamic. The world we feel is undergoing an ontological shift, a reconfiguration of the cultural tectonic plates that support all our other activities. Change the way we organise and access knowledge, and you eventually change the world. The world that is emerging from hypertext appears to be a 'hyper' world in the sense that psychiatrists and healthcare workers use the term: agitated, upset, pathologically nervous.[34]

All this destroys what Wordsworth called 'that inward eye which is the bliss of solitude'. If the young increasingly grow up in speedy times, how do they benefit? It does seem clear that the younger we are, the more comfortable we tend to be with a multi-tasking, channel-flipping, quick-reflexed existence. Then again, the younger we are, the less comfortable we seem to be with long periods alone with our thoughts. Have we lost our capacity for deep concentration, or have we gained a capacity for fast and flexible visualisation? Gleick is philosophic about time itself: 'Recognise that neither technology nor efficiency can acquire more time for you, because time is not a thing you have lost… It is what you live in. You can drift or you can swim, and it will carry you along either way.'[35]

Information overload

'Information overload' is a simple phrase for a complex phenomenon: the overwhelming sense that modern media technologies churn out more words and images than our culture can usefully absorb. David Shenk, broadcaster and contributor to *The New York Times* and the *Washington Post*, maintains in *The End of Patience: Cautionary Notes on the Information Revolution* that we have come no further in the search for meaning in the new info-tech 'progress' than when he wrote *Data Smog*. The title refers to the expression he coined for Internet spam, junk mail and multiple TV channels filled with very little substance. Shenk voices the now common cynicism about misguided or perplexing applications of technology, including the corporatisation of scientific research, the ethical dilemmas of biotechnology, the proliferation of Web sites and above all the human consequences of nations of 'info-hungry, data-dizzy button smackers, risking quality of our life and culture for the doubtful thrill of instant knowledge'.[36]

Shenk proposes replacing the plethora of quasi-information with true information, a 'World Wide Library', which could be filtered so as to contain information that would remain indefinitely useful. He compares radio, which forces people to think more, to television, which substitutes rapidly moving images and visual entertainment. His message is the importance of content rather than delivery in a world crazy about the image. Shenk is already aware, in a statement made in 1998, that delivery is everything: 'attaching microchips to squishy stuff is likely to make a lot of people very, very rich', and asks 'where is the human in all of this?' In March 1998, he co-wrote and published a document called *Technorealism*, along with 11 other prominent technology writers, advocating a more balanced approach to technology.

Sensory overload and Alternate World Syndrome

With information can come sensory overload, as we become bombarded with images. Even among film-makers – the sultans of the image – we see great caution about the dynamism of future media. In his film *Until the End of the World*, director Wim Wenders shows a population plagued by video disease. Eyes, minds and hearts have become weary with continual exposure to powerful images that tap into and stimulate every aspect of the human psyche. Worn down by the pace of flickering images, the video-crazed protagonist of Wenders's film becomes literally blind. He seeks healing for his video disease by travelling to Japan and undergoing a Zen therapy treatment not unlike the tea ceremony.

To Michael Heim this is reminiscent of what Taoists call 'the sealing of the five senses':

> The Taoists believed that overuse of the senses, especially the eyes (the most yang-powered organs in the energy, or chi, body), depletes the powers of vision. The internal energies need occasional 'sealing off' or closure by turning within to heal the senses and restore their power. Higher stages of meditation require that the senses be sealed so that the spirit (shen) can draw on the energy drained out of the senses by their daily use. I see the Wenders film as a parable about interface design in the age of virtual reality: We need the tea ceremony to heal the Western split between the body and the mind, between the overused, electronically stimulated sensibility and the earth-centred, serene poise of our natural good health. The tea ceremony can inspire, I think, such a crucial balance.[37]

Speed, quantity and quality of information are crucial dimensions in the new 'information society' and as we have seen all are beset by problems as well as benefits. In an increasingly virtual world there is another source of potential stress, and that is the whole divide between the real and the artificial, a pathology that Heim calls 'Alternate World Syndrome'.

AWS, according to Heim, is a problem emerging with the use of VR and one that can break the harmony between the biological body and the 'cyberbody'. Experiences in the virtual world bring the body out of sync with the ecology of planetary experiences. Alternate World Syndrome represents an illness of lifestyle, which Heim became aware of while researching the simulator sickness that appears in many virtual reality systems. The military have done extensive research on simulator sickness, and much of that research points to serious problems ahead for a culture that frequently uses virtual reality:

> The high-speed dynamics and aggressive tempo of cyberspace brings with it a disharmony between the earth-rooted biological self and the digitally trained mind. The person is split between personal experience based on computer life and personal experience based on felt bodily awareness. The more we move into virtual worlds, the thinner becomes the umbilical cord that ties us to the earth.[38]

Man, meet man...

Heim also hypothesises a connection between VR and alien worlds, with their visitations and abductions. He coined the term 'Relativity Sickness' to describe the state 'that comes from switching back and forth between the primary and virtual worlds'. He suggests, also, that we are afraid of our own technological alter egos, and that we project onto them the idea of 'aliens' in our real world.

Symbolically, we could be 'abducted' by our own technological creations. 'We experience our full technological selves as alien visitors, as threatening beings who are mutants of ourselves and who are immersed and transformed by technology to a higher degree than we think comfortable and who are about to operate, we sense, on the innards of our present-day selves. The visitors from outer space descend from our own future.'[39]

The future facing all of us is how to live in a world that is part actual, part virtual. In the history of our life on earth we are somewhere in between creation and destruction, as our little planet depends on a sun that must one day burn up. We have so many dualities in our existence already – day and night, man and woman, life and death – that man and machine is simply one more. But it is a crucial duality since it might lead to our creating, as Heim suggests, our own 'aliens' – sophisticated new versions of the products of Frankenstein and his laboratory.

There is a saying in Norwegian, 'to meet oneself coming in the door'. It is a way of saying that one day we will meet ourselves and have to account for all that we have been and done. As we live in our future utopia or dystopia – some kind of evolved intelligent system served by our humanoid robots – we may one day turn on our computers and meet a whole new being. This being that we might meet in virtuality – some new avatar with artificial intelligence – may be none other than a strange version of ourselves. Not us 'in fact' maybe, but us 'in essence'.

References

Introduction
[1] Dawkins, Richard (1976) *The Selfish Gene*, Oxford University Press, Oxford

Chapter 1
Perception and Representation
[1] Gregory, R (1986) *Odd Perceptions*, Routledge, London
[2] Simons, D J and Levin, D T (1998) Failure to detect changes to people during real-world interaction, *Psychonomic Bulletin and Review*, **4**, 18 November
[3] Halligan, P and Oakley, D (2000) Greatest myth of all, *New Scientist*, 18 November
[4] See Reference 1
[5] Jastrow, J (1900) *Fact and Fable in Psychology*, Riverside Press, Cambridge, MA
[6] Hodgson, R and Davey, S J (1887) The possibilities of mal-observation and lapse of memory from a practical point of view, *Proceedings of the Society for Psychical Research*, **4**, pp 381–495
[7] Blackmore, S and Hart-Davis, A (1995) *Test Your Psychic Powers*, Thorsons, London
[8] Colman, A M (1987) *Facts, Fallacies and Frauds in Psychology*, Hutchinson, London
[9] See Reference 1
[10] Morris, R L (1996) A pentalogue on parapsychology, *The Psychologist*, August

[11] Randi, J (1983) The Project Alpha Experiment, *The Skeptical Enquirer*, Summer/Fall editions
[12] Tuan, Yi-Fu (1998) *Escapism*, John Hopkins, London
[13] McLuhan, M and Fiore, Q (1967) *The Medium is the Massage*, Penguin, Harmondsworth
[14] Evans, A and Wilson, G (1999) *Fame: The Psychology of Stardom*, Vision Paperbacks, London
[15] Ibid.
[16] Rushkoff, D 'Social Currency', www.rushkoff.com

Chapter 2
Reality, Deception and Spin

[1] Reber, A S (1952) *The Penguin Dictionary of Psychology*, Penguin, Harmondsworth
[2] Green, J (1984) *The Cynic's Lexicon*, St Martin's Press, New York, NY
[3] Heaton, J A (1995) *Tuning In Trouble*, Jossey-Bass, New York, NY
[4] BBC, *Panorama*, 12 November 2000
[5] Wiseman, R (1996) Towards a psychology of deception, *The Psychologist*, February
[6] Lewis, M and Saarni, C (eds) (1993) *Lying and Deception in Everyday Life*, Guildford Press, New York, NY
[7] De Paulo, B M *et al* (1980) Humans as lie detectors, *Journal of Communication*, **30**
[8] Lewin, R (1987) Do animals read minds, tell lies?, *Science*, **238**
[9] Leigh-Kile, D (1999) *Sex Symbols*, Vision Paperbacks, London
[10] Ibid.
[11] Hobday, P (2000) *Managing the Message*, London House, London
[12] Ibid.
[13] Posted on Internet newsgroup rec.music.classical.recordings

Chapter 3
What is Escapism?

[1] Evans, A (1994) *The Secrets of Musical Confidence*, HarperCollins, London
[2] Internet survey carried out in 2000, Andrew Evans. For details visit http://www.artsandmedia.com
[3] Maltz, M (1960) *Cybernetics*, Prentice-Hall, New Jersey
[4] Hosea, B (1998) *In Effect, Though Not in Fact – Virtual Reality and Art*, London Guildhall University, London
[5] Quoted in *Virtual Worlds*, B Woolley (1993) Penguin, Harmondsworth

6   Kroker, A and Kroker, M (1997) *Digital Delirium*, New World Perspectives

7   Berlioz, H *Almanach des Lettres Françaises* (no other information available)

8   Berne, E (1970) *Games People Play*, Penguin, Harmondsworth

Chapter 4
Healthy and Unhealthy Escapism

1   Tuan, Yi-Fu (1998) *Escapism*, John Hopkins, London

2   Storr, A (1989) *Solitude*, Fontana, London

3   Ibid.

4   Ibid.

5   Jones, E (1953–57) *The Life and Works of Sigmund Freud* (three vols), Hogarth Press, London

6   Freud, S (1958) *Formulations on the Two Principles of Mental Functioning*, Standard Edition vol XII, London

7   Ibid.

8   Berne, E (1974) *What Do You Say After You Say Hello?*, Andre Deutsch, London

9   Fulford, N (2000) Posted on the Internet

10   Ibid.

11   Ibid.

12   Jay, M (2000) *Emperors of Dreams: Drugs in the Nineteenth Century*, Dedalus

13   Wills, G and Cooper, C (1988) *Pressure Sensitive*, Sage, London

14   See Reference 9

15   Name withheld

16   Name withheld

17   Carter, J (2000) Posted on the Internet

18   Muensterberger, W (1994) *Collecting: An Unruly Passion*, Princeton University Press, Princeton, NJ

19   Belk, R W (1995) *Collecting in a Consumer Society*, Routledge, London

20   Danet, B and Katriel (mid 1980s) University of Haifa, Israel

21   Benjamin, W (1999) *Illuminations*, Pimlico

22   Forrester, J (1994) *The Cultures of Collecting*, Harvard University Press, Harvard, MA

23   See Reference 18

24   Posted on Internet newsgroup rec.music.classical.recordings

Chapter 5
What Defines the Escapist?

1. Tuan, Yi-Fu (1998) *Escapism in Literature*, John Hopkins, London
2. Stapledon, W (1939) *Scrutiny*, ed F R Leavis
3. Storr, A (1989) *Solitude*, Fontana, London
4. Evans, A (1994) International Conference on the Performing Arts, Institute of Psychiatry, London
5. University of Southampton ageing project
6. R D Laing, in conversation with Andrew Evans, Paris, 1984
7. Quoted in *Acid: The Secret History of LSD* (1998) David Black, Vision Paperbacks, London
8. Kohlberg, L (1973) Implications of developmental psychology for education: examples from moral development, *Educational Psychologist*, **10**, pp 2–14
9. de Bono, E (1967) *The Uses of Lateral Thinking*, Penguin, Harmondsworth
10. Evans, A (1994) *The Secrets of Musical Confidence*, HarperCollins, London
11. Quoted in *Pressure Sensitive* (1988) G Wills and C Cooper, Sage, London
12. Brown, G W *et al* (1990) Self-esteem and depression, *Social Psychiatry and Psychiatric Epidemiology*, **25**
13. Conley, J J (1994) The hierarchy of consistency, *Personality and Individual Differences*, **5**, pp 11–25
14. Myers, I B and McCaulley, M H (1985) *Manual For Use of the MBTI*, Consulting Psychologists Press

Chapter 6
Escapism in the Arts and the Media

1. Arieti, S (1976) *Creativity – The Magic Synthesis*, Basic Books, New York, NY
2. Getzels, J W and Jackson, P W (1962) *Creativity and Intelligence: Explorations with Gifted Students*, John Wiley, New York, NY
3. Stapledon, W (1939) *Scrutiny*, ed F R Leavis
4. Ormsby, J (1997) *Don Quixote* (Introduction) Project Gutenberg
5. Ibid.
6. Ibid.
7. McFarlane, J (1989) *Peer Gynt* (Introduction), Oxford University Press, Oxford
8. Gide, A (1961) *Les Caves du Vatican*, ed F J Jones, University of London Press, London

⁹   See Reference 3

Chapter 7
Simulation and Creativity in Human Evolution
¹   Storr, A (1989) *Solitude*, Fontana, London
²   Ibid.
³   Ibid.
⁴   Freud, S (1959) *Creative Writers and Day-dreaming*, Standard Edition 9, pp 141–53
⁵   See Reference 1
⁶   Ibid.
⁷   Ibid.
⁸   Gernsback, H (1926) editorial, *Amazing Stories*
⁹   Pesce, M www.feedmag.com
¹⁰ Casti, J L (1998) *Would-be Worlds: How Simulation is Changing the Frontiers of Science*, John Wiley, Chichester
¹¹ Casti, J L (1993) *Searching for Certainty*, Abacus
¹² Casti, J L *Balance of Power* (no other information available)
¹³ Hofstadter, D R (1995) *Concepts and Creative Analogies*, Basic Books, New York, NY
¹⁴ Offill, J (2000) 'Simple Minds', www.feedmag.com
¹⁵ Boden, M (2000) Computer models of creativity, *The Psychologist*, February
¹⁶ Gregory, R (1986) *Odd Perceptions*, Routledge, London

Chapter 8
Games
¹   Bateson, G (1972) *Steps to an Ecology of Mind*, Ballantine Books, New York, NY
²   Ross, D R *et al* (1982) Space invaders obsession, *Journal of the American Medical Association*, **248**, 1117
³   Berne, E (1961) *TA in Psychotherapy*, Grove Press, New York, NY
⁴   Griffiths, M (1993) Are computer games bad for children?, *The Psychologist*, September
⁵   Skirrow, G (1986) Hellivision, in *High Theory, Low Culture*, ed Colin McCabe, St Martin's Press, New York, NY
⁶   Hosea, B (1998) *Virtual Reality and Art*, Guildhall University, London
⁷   Wober, J M and Fazal, S (1994) Age and involvement with computers and their games, *The Psychologist*, December
⁸   See *The Psychologist*, September 1993 and September 1997 for details

of the studies
[9] Duncan, T (no other information available)
[10] Soper, W B and Miller, M J (1983) Junk-time junkies, *School Counsellor*, **31**
[11] Shotton, M (1989) *Computer Addiction?*, Taylor and Francis, London
[12] Rushkoff, D www.rushkoff.com
[13] Rushkoff, D 'Hollywood lays an egg the myth of the content provider', www.rushkoff.com
[14] Dauphin, G www.feedmag.com
[15] Miyamoto, S www.feedmag.com
[16] See Reference 14
[17] Pesce, M (2000) 'The Trigger Principle', www.feedmag.com
[18] Ibid.
[19] Meier, S www.feedmag.com
[20] Kushner, D (2000) 'Playing God', www.feedmag.com

Chapter 9
From Cartoon to Virtual Reality

[1] Storr, A (1989) *Solitude*, Fontana, London
[2] Bazin, G (1989) in *Solitude*, ed A Storr, Fontana, London
[3] Freud, S (1959) *Creative Writers and Day-dreaming*, Standard Edition 9, pp 141–53
[4] See Reference 1
[5] Anders, P (1998) *Envisioning Information in Cyberspace*, McGraw-Hill
[6] Forte, M and Siliotti, A (1997) *Re-creating Ancient Worlds*, Harry N Abrams
[7] Heim, M (1999) 'Transmogrification', Conference paper, Graz University: www.mheim.com
[8] Wilcox, S K (1998) *Guide to 3-D Avatars*, John Wiley, Chichester
[9] Damer, B (1998) *Avatars! Exploring and Building Virtual Worlds on the Internet*, Peachpit Press
[10] See Reference 7
[11] Ibid.
[12] Ibid.
[13] www.outerworlds.com/worldcon/
[14] Moody, F (1999) *The Visionary Position*, Times Books
[15] Moody F (1996) *I Sing the Body Electric*, Penguin, New York, NY
[16] Leary, T (1990) *Unlimited Virtual Realities For Everyone!*, Art Futura
[17] Quoted in *Virtual Worlds*, B Woolley (1993) Penguin, Harmondsworth
[18] Rose, D and Forman, N (1999) Virtual reality, *The Psychologist*,

November
19 Weiss, A E (1996) *Virtual Reality, A Door to Cyberspace*, 21st Century Books
20 Druckry, T (1991) Revenge of the Nerds, An Interview with Jaron Lanier, *Afterimage*, May
21 Hosea, B (1998) *In Effect, Though Not in Fact – Virtual Reality and Art*, London Guildhall University, London
22 Aukstakalnis, S and Blatner, D (1992) *Silicon Mirage: The Art and Science of Virtual Reality*, Peachpit Press
23 Heim, M (1997) *Virtual Realism*, Oxford University Press, Oxford
24 Penny, S (1992) *VR: The Fragmented Body and the Conquering Eye*, March, unpublished
25 Ibid.
26 See Reference 20
27 Ibid.
28 Ibid.
29 Ibid.
30 Heim, M 'Virtual Reality and the Tea Ceremony', www.mheim.com
31 Heim, M (1993) *The Metaphysics of Virtual Reality*, Oxford University Press, Oxford
32 See Reference 23
33 Ibid.
34 Ibid.
35 Ibid.
36 See Reference 31

Chapter 10
The Net

1 Information from a Gallup Poll, December 2000
2 Wienberg, S B and Furst, M (1984) *Computerphobia*, Banbury Books, Wayne, PA
3 Weinberg, S B (1982) Coping with computerphobia, *Mademoiselle*, 12 August
4 See *The Psychologist*, February 1994
5 See Brosnan, M J and Davidson, M J (1994) *The Psychologist*, February
6 Rushkoff, D 'Man-made Materials', www.rushkoff.com
7 Tapscott, D (1999) *Growing Up Digital: The Rise of the Net Generation*, McGraw-Hill
8 Ibid.
9 Bezilla, R and Keliner, A 'Electronic network addiction', Paper

presented at National Computer Conference, California, 1980
[10] Petrie, H (1998) BPS London conference paper
[11] Rushkoff, D 'Depress this', www.rushkoff.com
[12] Cooper, A *Professional Psychology: Research and Practice*
[13] Douglas, K M (1999) *The Therapeutic Super Highway*, Four Seasons Publishing
[14] Zeichner, W I (1997) *Virtual Survival: Staying Healthy on the Internet*, Crystal Point Publishing
[15] Coover, R www.feedmag.com
[16] Jones, S (ed) (1998) *Doing Internet Research: Critical Issues and Methods for Examining the Net*, Sage
[17] Stone, A R (1996) *The War of Desire and Technology at the Close of the Mechanical Age*, MIT Press, Boston, MA
[18] Odzer, C (1997) *Virtual Spaces: Sex and the Cyber Citizen*, Berkley Publishing Group
[19] Ibid.
[20] Rushkoff, D 'Convergence: Our last, best hope for peace', www.rushkoff.com
[21] Ibid.
[22] Shirky, C www.feedmag.com
[23] Rushkoff, D 'Social Currency', www.rushkoff.com

Chapter 11
Into the Future – The knotty problems of cyberspace

[1] Hobart, M and Schiffman, Z (2000) *Information Ages: Literacy, Numeracy and the Computer Revolution*, Johns Hopkins University Press, Baltimore, MD
[2] Roszak, T (1994) *The Cult of Information: A Neo-Luddite Treatise on High Tech, Artificial Intelligence and the True Art of Thinking*, University of California Press
[3] Fulford, N (2000) Posted on the Internet
[4] Fukuyama, F (2000) *The Great Disruption: Human Nature and the Reconstitution of Social Order*, Touchstone Books
[5] Ibid.
[6] in 'The Future Doesn't Need Us', Bill Joy
[7] Levy, P (2000) *Collective Intelligence: Mankind's Emerging World in Cyberspace*, Perseus Press
[8] Rushkoff, D 'The Future of Psychology', www.rushkoff.com
[9] Heim, M (1995) 'The Nerd in the Noosphere', www.mheim.com
[10] Rushkoff, D 'Man-made Materials', www.rushkoff.com

11 Heim, M (1997) *Virtual Realism*, Oxford University Press, Oxford
12 Heim, M (1999) 'The Narrow Path', www.mheim.com
13 Heim, M 'Virtual Reality and the Tea Ceremony', www.mheim.com
14 Psychological Aspects of Teleworking in Rural Areas (PATRA) (1994) European Commission
15 Dooley, B (1996) 'At work away from work', *The Psychologist*, April
16 Crandall, N and Wallace, M J (1998) *Work & Rewards in the Virtual Workplace: A 'New Deal' for Organizations & Employees*, AMACOM
17 The Cyber Nomads, *Newsweek*, December 2000–February 2001
18 Whitaker, R (2000) *The End of Privacy: How Total Surveillance Is Becoming a Reality*, New Press
19 Brin, D (1996) Privacy is History – Get Over It, interview in *Wired* magazine, February
20 Hafner, K and Markoff, J (1991) *Cyberpunk: Outlaws and Hackers on the Computer Frontier*, Fourth Estate, London
21 Dery, M (1997) *Escape Velocity: Cyberculture at the End of the Century*, Grove Press
22 Shapiro, A L (2000) *The Control Revolution: How The Internet is Putting Individuals in Charge and Changing the World We Know*, Public Affairs
23 The Bulletin of the Royal College of Psychiatrists (1985)
24 Newson, E (1994) Video violence and the protection of children, *The Psychologist*, June
25 Bailey, S M (1993) *Criminal Justice Matters*, pp 6–7
26 Cantor, J *et al* (1996, 1998) *Ratings and Advisories for Television Programming – National Television Violence Study*, Sage, Newbury Park, CA
27 Bushman, B J and Stack, A D (1996) Forbidden fruit versus tainted fruit, *Journal of Experimental Psychology: Applied*, **2**, pp 207–26
28 Gunter, B (2000) Classifying TV programmes, *The Psychologist*, April
29 Rizzo, A A (1998) in *Virtual Environments in Clinical Psychology*, ed Riva *et al*, IOS Press, Amsterdam
30 Gleick, J (2000) *Faster: The Acceleration of Just About Everything*, Vintage Books, London
31 Ibid.
32 Ibid.
33 Ibid.
34 Heim, M 'Virtual Reality and the Tea Ceremony', www.mheim.com
35 See Reference 30
36 Shenk, D (1999) *The End of Patience: Cautionary Notes on the Information Revolution*, Indiana University Press

[37] Heim, M 'Virtual Reality and the Tea Ceremony', www.mheim.com
[38] Ibid.
[39] Heim, M (1997) *Virtual Realism*, Oxford University Press, Oxford

Web sites and general search engines

http://about.com – good reference site

http://eldred.ne.mediaone.net/iag/oblomov.htm – text of *Oblomov* on the Net

http://www.artsandmedia.com – author Andrew Evans' Web site; papers on arts and media psychology and many links, including e-mails to him and details of his other books

http://www.ask.com – Ask Jeeves reference site

http://www.feedmag.com – magazine of Futurist theory and digital technology; authors include Mike Pesce

http://www.flickphilosopher.com – film reviews

http://www.gurl.com – forward-looking feminist site

http://www.imdb.com – International Movie Database

http://www.mheim.com – Michael Heim and ActiveWorlds Web site; writings and VR worlds

http://www.performanceandmedia.com – Andrew Evans' Web site; includes articles on creativity and media psychology

http://www.rushkoff.com – Douglas Rushkoff's Web site; includes his *New York Times* columns

http://www.salon.com – hard and soft news; big site with varied content

http://www.wired.com/ – hard news with techno-futurist leaning

http://www.xrefer.com – good guide to dictionary definitions and topics

Index

About the Author

Born and brought up in South Wales, Andy Evans graduated in modern languages at Oxford University, followed by a postgraduate diploma in journalism studies from Cardiff University. After a brief career as a journalist, a performer's certificate in double bass and composition from the Royal Academy of Music led him to a professional career as a freelance jazz musician, both in England and abroad.

In his mid-thirties Andy studied psychology in Oslo, Paris and London, with the specific aim of working with performers, creatives and media people. After graduating he founded Arts Psychology Consultants in 1988, and this remains the leading arts and media psychology consultancy in the UK.

Having worked for over 12 years with more than 500 performers, Andy has increasingly become the pioneer of new methods and strategies for performance psychology and overcoming stage fright, as described in his book *The Secrets of Musical Confidence* (Performance and Media Publications).

Andy is a contributor on media issues to a number of newspapers and magazines, and also broadcasts frequently on subjects connected with the arts and media, notably fame and the effects of celebrity. This media work led to his previous book for Vision Paperbacks, *Fame: The Psychology of Stardom* (with Glenn D. Wilson, 1999) and now *This Virtual Life*.

He is single with one son, lives in Kensington and enjoys competitive sport, building audio equipment and creative writing. He can be contacted at andy@artsandmedia.com or through his Web site: http://www.artsandmedia.com.